CIMA

Strategic

E3

Strategic Management

Course Book

For exams from
4 November 2019
to January 2021

BPP
LEARNING
MEDIA

Second edition 2019

ISBN 9781 5097 3185 5

eISBN 9781 5097 3190 9

ISBN (for internal use) 9781 5097 2775 9

British Library Cataloguing-in-Publication Data

A catalogue record for this book is available from the British Library

Published by

BPP Learning Media Ltd

BPP House, Aldine Place

London W12 8AA

learningmedia.bpp.com

Printed in the United Kingdom

Your learning materials, published by BPP Learning Media Ltd, are printed on paper sourced from sustainable, managed forests.

The contents of this book are intended as a guide and not professional advice. Although every effort has been made to ensure that the contents of this book are correct at the time of going to press, BPP Learning Media makes no warranty that the information in this book is accurate or complete and accept no liability for any loss or damage suffered by any person acting or refraining from acting as a result of the material in this book.

We are grateful to the Chartered Institute of Management Accountants for allowing us to reproduce extracts from the CIMA exam blueprint. An up-to-date version of the full blueprint is available at www.cimaglobal.com/examblueprints.

A note about copyright

Contents

Essential Reading

Description of the paper

Strategy lies at the heart of what organisations do, how they do it, and why they do it. This exam looks into the processes that lie behind how an organisation sets out to achieve its stated aims and goals. In doing so these organisations must take account of their internal resource constraints, the threats and opportunities that lie within their environment, and the need to satisfy the needs of a wide range of stakeholders. In the digital world the nature of competition and collaboration is changing, as so-called 'ecosystems' emerge, with collaboration perhaps being the key to competitive success. To that end, harnessing digital technologies and aligning these with more traditional operational and strategic tools will be essential.

Syllabus

E3 examination blueprint

The syllabus outcomes each detail what you need to **know**, and each syllabus outcome has a number of associated representative task statements which make clear what you need to be able to **do** with that knowledge, eg do you need to simply be able to identify and understand a theory or do you need to use that theory to perform calculations? You will also see these critical representative task statements clearly referenced at the beginning of each chapter as well as throughout the chapters, giving you confidence that you are learning exactly what you need for success in your CIMA exam.

BPP worked closely with CIMA to help create these vital exam blueprints, so you can trust our learning materials to give you all the information you need to pass your exam.

Areas and weightings

Content area	Weighting
A. The strategy process	15%
B. Analysing the organisational ecosystem	20%
C. Generating strategic options	15%
D. Making strategic choices	15%
E. Strategic control	20%
F. Digital strategy	15%
	100%

(CIMA exam blueprint, 2019)

Blueprint

* Key: RU = Remembering and understanding; AP = Application; AN = Analysis; EV = Evaluate

E3A: The strategy process		Skill level				Representative task statement
Lead outcome	Component outcome	RU	AP	AN	EV	
1. The purpose of strategy	a. Strategy			✔		Analyse the advantages and disadvantages of strategy development.
	b. The purpose of strategy			✔		Analyse the essential features and characteristics of strategy including the long-term time horizon, considering the organisation as a whole, stakeholder analysis, gaining sustainable competitive advantage, and environmental analyses.

E3A: The strategy process		Skill level					Representative task statement
Lead outcome	Component outcome	RU	AP	AN	EV		
2. The types and levels of strategy	a. Types of strategy			✔			Analyse the different approaches to strategy development including the traditional top-down approach, emergent strategies, incrementalism and freewheeling opportunism.
	b. Levels of strategy			✔			Analyse the levels of strategy including corporate, business, and functional and the impact of strategic lenses on those levels.
3. The strategy process	a. The rational and emergent processes of arriving at strategy			✔			As part of the strategy process, analyse the organisational ecosystem, strategic options or choice, and strategic implementation and control. As part of the strategy process, analyse the organisational ecosystem, strategic options or choice, and strategic implementation and control.

E3B: The organisational ecosystem		Skill level					Representative task statement
Lead outcome	Component outcome	RU	AP	AN	EV		
1. The elements of the ecosystem	a. Markets and competition			✔			Perform or review a SWOT (strengths, weaknesses, opportunities and threats) analysis to analyse an organisation's internal and external options related to overall strategy.
				✔			Perform or review a Mendelow's Matrix analysis to analyse an organisation's stakeholders related to their level of interest and power.
				✔			Prepare, or review, a Porter's Five Forces analysis to analyse an organisation's competition.
				✔			Prepare or review a Porter's Diamond analysis to analyse an organisation's position related to national competitive advantage.

E3B: The organisational ecosystem		Skill level				Representative task statement
Lead outcome	**Component outcome**	**R U**	**A P**	**A N**	**EV**	
	b. Society and regulation			✔		Perform a PESTEL (Political, Economic, Social, Technology, Legal and Environment) analysis to analyse the impact of society on an organisation.
2. The drivers of change in ecosystem	a-e. Institutional/ systemic, social, market, technology, and sustainability			✔		Analyse the drivers of change in an ecosystem including globalisation, geopolitical impact, demographics, customer empowerment, digital technology, automation and sustainability.
3. The impact of the ecosystem on organisational strategy	a. The impact of strategic networks and platforms on organisational strategy			✔		Analyse what an organisation can do to create value in an ecosystem and how that organisation can capture the value they helped to create.
	b. Stakeholder analysis in networks			✔		Analyse the participants and interactions in networks and platforms and their associated roles, reach, capabilities, rules, connections and courses.
				✔		Analyse how technologies such as cloud computing, social media, mobile and analytics impact ecosystems.
				✔		Analyse how technologies that create a more open, connected and complex business environment impact corporate social responsibility.

E3C: Strategic options		Skill level				Representative task statement
Lead outcome	**Component outcome**	**R U**	**A P**	**A N**	**EV**	
1. The context of generating strategic options	a. The role of governance and ethics in the strategy process			✔		Analyse the role of governance and business ethics in the context of generating strategic options.

E3C: Strategic options		Skill level				Representative task statement
Lead outcome	Component outcome	RU	AP	AN	EV	
	b. Purpose, vision, and values of organisation and their impact on strategy			✔		Analyse the linkage between purpose, vision, and values to each other and to generating strategic options.
2. Option generation	a-b. Key strategic questions and an organisation's starting position			✔		Prepare or review Porter's generic strategies, Ansoff's matrix, and method of growth for establishing a choice of possible future strategies.
	c. Potential organisational operation ecosystem			✔		Use trend analysis and system modelling to forecast potential organisational operating ecosystems.
	d. Frameworks to generate options			✔		Use scenario planning and long-range planning as tools in strategic decision-making.
				✔		Analyse value drivers (tangible and intangible) and the data needed to describe and measure them.
				✔		Analyse game theory approaches in strategic planning and decision-making (complex numerical questions will not be tested).
				✔		Analyse Real Options as a tool for strategic analysis (complex numerical questions will not be tested).

E3D: Strategic choices		Skill level				Representative task statement
Lead outcome	Component outcome	RU	AP	AN	EV	
1. Options	a. Criteria for evaluation			✔		Analyse strategic options and criteria for evaluation including the application of the suitability, acceptability and feasibility framework.
	b. Options against criteria			✔		Analyse options against criteria for strategic options.

E3D: Strategic choices		Skill level				Representative task statement
Lead outcome	Component outcome	R U	AP	A N	EV	
	c. Recommend appropriate options				✔	Recommend appropriate action for strategic options.
2. Choices into coherent strategy	a. Value analysis			✔		Prepare or review a Porter's value chain analysis to assess whether an organisation has a sustainable competitive advantage.
	b. Portfolio analysis				✔	Recommend how to manage the product portfolio of an organisation to support the organisation's strategic goals.

E3E: Strategic control		Skill level				Representative task statement
Lead outcome	Component outcome	R U	AP	A N	EV	
1. Strategic performance management system	a. Detailed action plans			✔		Set appropriate strategic targets through the use of non-financial measures of strategic performance and their interaction with financial ones.
	b. Action plan communication				✔	Evaluation of strategic targets through the development of critical success factors (CSFs).
	c. Implementation			✔		Link CSFs to Key Performance Indicators and corporate strategy and their use as a basis for defining an organisation's information needs.
	d. Incentives to performance			✔		Effective communication of strategic performance targets, including the need to drive strategic performance through stretch targets and promotion of exceptional performance
2. Resource allocation to support strategy implementation	a. Resource availability			✔		Perform an analysis of key resources and capabilities needed for strategy implementation.
	b. Resource allocation to strategic choices			✔		Perform an analysis of forecasts, trend analysis, system modelling, and in-depth consultation with experts to aid resource allocation.

E3E: Strategic control		Skill level				Representative task statement
Lead outcome	Component outcome	R U	AP	A N	EV	
3. Change management techniques and methodologies	a. Impact of strategy on organisation	✔				Understand the importance of managing critical periods of adaptive, evolutionary, reconstructive, and revolutionary change.
	b. Change management strategies			✔		Analyse the impact of change on organisational culture (including the cultural web and McKinsey's 7s model).
	c. The role of the leader in managing change				✔	Evaluate the role of leadership in managing the change process and building and managing effective teams.
					✔	Evaluate the approaches and styles of change management and managing the resistance to change.

E3F: Digital strategy		Skill level				Representative task statement
Lead outcome	Component outcome	R U	AP	A N	EV	
1. The governance of digital transformation	a. The roles and responsibilities of the board and executive leadership in digital strategy			✔		Analyse the board's and senior leadership's role in an organisation's digital strategy including defining value and charting, articulating, and overseeing the execution of digital strategy and transformation.
2. Digital transformation	a. Digital technologies			✔		Analyse an organisation's use, or potential use of, digital technologies including cloud computing, big data analytics, process automation, AI, data visualisation, blockchain, internet of things, mobile and 3-D printing.
	b. Digital enterprise				✔	Advise management how to survive digital disruption and thrive in a digital age by rethinking their traditional business model and incorporating digital business and operating models.

E3F: Digital strategy		Skill level				Representative task statement
Lead outcome	Component outcome	R U	AP	A N	EV	
3. Elements of digital strategies	Economics of digitalisation				✔	Advise management on how digital transformations and the creation of vast, interconnected ecosystems driven by business to business can disrupt and reshape industries.
	Digital ecosystems				✔	Advise management on how the participants in an ecosystem impact an organisation's strategy, including the participant's role within the environment, reach through the environment and capability or key value proposition.
	Digital consumption				✔	Advise management on how technology and experience with new platform technologies and business models have transformed customer expectations to integrated and customized experiences.
	Data and metrics			✔		Analyse digital traction metrics including scale, active usage, and engagement to assist management in measuring the success of a digital business.
	Leadership and culture				✔	Advise management on leadership's role in building a digital workforce including attracting and retaining talent, becoming an employer of choice, creating a workforce with digital skills, brining leadership to the digital age and fostering a digital culture.

(CIMA exam blueprint, 2019)

Examination structure

The Objective Test exam

Pass mark	70%
Format	Computer-based assessment
Duration	90 minutes
Number of questions	60
Marking	No partial marking – each question marked correct or incorrect All questions carry the same weighting (ie same marks)
Weighting	As per syllabus areas All representative task statements from the examination blueprint will be covered
Question Types	Multiple choice Multiple response Drag and drop Gap fill Hot spot
Booking availability	On demand
Results	Immediate

What the examiner means

The table below has been prepared by CIMA to further help you interpret the syllabus and learning outcomes and the meaning of questions.

You will see that there are five skills levels you may be expected to demonstrate, ranging from Remembering and Understanding to Evaluation. CIMA Certificate subjects only use levels 1 to 3, but in CIMA's Professional qualification the entire hierarchy will be used.

Skills		Verbs used	Definition
Level 5	Evaluation *The examination or assessment of problems, and use of judgment to draw conclusions*	Advise	Counsel, inform or notify
		Assess	Evaluate or estimate the nature, ability or quality of
		Evaluate	Appraise or assess the value of
		Recommend	Propose a course of action
		Review	Assess and evaluate in order, to change if necessary
		Select	Choose an option or course of action after consideration of the alternatives

Skills		Verbs used	Definition
Level 4	**Analysis** *The examination and study of the interrelationship of separate areas in order to identify causes and find evidence to support inferences*	Align	Arrange in an orderly way
		Analyse	Examine in detail the structure of
		Communicate	Share or exchange information
		Compare and contrast	Show the similarities and/or differences between
		Develop	Grow and expand a concept
		Discuss	Examine in detail by argument
		Examine	Inspect thoroughly
		Monitor	Observe and check the progress of
		Prioritise	Place in order of priority or sequence for action
		Produce	Create or bring into existence

Skills		Verbs used	Definition
Level 3	**Application** *The use or demonstration of knowledge, concepts or techniques*	Apply	Put to practical use
		Calculate	Ascertain or reckon mathematically
		Conduct	Organise and carry out
		Demonstrate	Prove with certainty or exhibit by practical means
		Determine	Ascertain or establish exactly by research or calculation
		Perform	Carry out, accomplish, or fulfil
		Prepare	Make or get ready for use
		Reconcile	Make or prove consistent/compatible
		Record	Keep a permanent account of facts, events or transactions
		Use	Apply a technique or concept

Skills		Verbs used	Definition
Level 1/2	**Remembering and understanding** *The perception and comprehension of the significance of an area utilising knowledge gained*	Define	Give the exact meaning of
		Describe	Communicate the key features of
		Distinguish	Highlight the differences between
		Explain	Make clear or intelligible/state the meaning or purpose of
		Identify	Recognise, establish or select after consideration
		Illustrate	Use an example to describe or explain something
		List	Make a list of
		Recognise	Identify/recall
		State	Express, fully or clearly, the details/facts of
		Outline	Give a summary of
		Understand	Comprehend ideas, concepts and techniques

(CIMA exam blueprint, 2019)

How to pass

Effective study

Study the whole syllabus

You need to be comfortable with all areas of the syllabus, as questions in the Objective Test exam will cover all syllabus areas. Wider reading will help you understand the main risks businesses face, which will be particularly useful in the Case Study exam.

Lots of question practice

You can develop application skills by attempting the Test Your Learning questions at the end of each chapter. While these might not be in the format that you will experience in your exam, doing the full question will enable you to answer the exam questions. These have been designed to test as much breadth and depth of your knowledge as possible – they don't follow the exam format but will leave you well prepared to tackle any exam question on the topic. For example, you will only be able to answer a question on an element of an interest rate swap calculation if you know how to do the full calculation. When preparing for your exam you should practice exam standard questions, which you will find in the BPP Exam Practice Kit, your recommended accompanying study support to this Course Book.

Good exam technique

The best approach to the computer-based assessment (CBA)

You're not likely to have a great deal of spare time during the CBA itself, so you must make sure you don't waste a single minute.

You should:

(a) Click 'Next' for any that have long scenarios or are very complex and return to these later

(b) When you reach the 60th question, use the Review Screen to return to any questions you skipped past or any you flagged for review

Here's how the tools in the exam will help you to do this in a controlled and efficient way.

The 'Next' button

What does it do? This will move you on to the next question whether or not you have completed the one you are on.

When should I use it? Use this to move through the exam on your first pass through if you encounter a question that you suspect is going to take you a long time to answer. The Review Screen (see below) will help you to return to these questions later in the exam.

The 'Flag for Review' button

What does it do? This button will turn the icon yellow and when you reach the end of the exam questions you will be told that you have flagged specific questions for review. If the exam time runs out before you have reviewed any flagged questions, they will be submitted as they are.

When should I use it? Use this when you've answered a question but you're not completely comfortable with your answer. If there is time left at the end, you can quickly come back via the Review Screen (see below), but if time runs out at least it will submit your current answer. Do not use the Flag for Review button too often or you will end up with too long a list to review at the end. Important note – studies have shown that you are usually best to stick with your first instincts!

The Review Screen

What does it do? This screen appears after you click 'Next' on the 60th question. It shows you any incomplete questions and any you have flagged for review. It allows you to jump back to specific questions or work through all your incomplete questions or work through all your flagged for review questions.

When should I use it? As soon as you've completed your first run through the exam and reached the 60th question. The very first thing to do is to work through all your incomplete questions as they will all be marked as incorrect if you don't submit an answer for these in the remaining time. Importantly, this will also help to pick up any questions you thought you'd completed but didn't

BPP
LEARNING
MEDIA

answer properly (eg you only picked two answer options in a multi-response question that required three answers to be selected). After you've submitted answers for all your incomplete questions you should use the Review Screen to work through all the questions you flagged for review.

The different Objective Test question types

Passing your CBA is all about demonstrating your understanding of the technical syllabus content. You will find this easier to do if you are comfortable with the different types of Objective Test questions that you will encounter in the CBA, especially if you have a practised approach to each one.

You will find yourself continuously practising these styles of questions throughout your Objective Test programme. This way you will check and reinforce your technical knowledge at the same time as becoming more and more comfortable with your approach to each style of question.

Multiple choice

Standard multiple choice items provide four options. One option is correct and the other three are incorrect. Incorrect options will be plausible, so you should expect to have to use detailed, syllabus-specific knowledge to identify the correct answer rather than relying on common sense.

Multiple response

A multiple response item is the same as a multiple choice question, except **more than one** response is required. You will normally (but not always) be told how many options you need to select.

Drag and drop

Drag and drop questions require you to drag a 'token' onto a pre-defined area. These tokens can be images or text. This type of question is effective at testing the order of events, labelling a diagram or linking events to outcomes.

Gap fill

Gap fill (or 'fill in the blank') questions require you to type a short numerical response. You should carefully follow the instructions in the question in terms of how to type your answer – eg the correct number of decimal places.

Hot spot

These questions require you to identify an area or location on an image by clicking on it. This is commonly used to identify a specific point on a graph or diagram.

A final word on time management

Time does funny things in an exam!

Scientific studies have shown that humans have great difficulty in judging how much time has passed if they are concentrating fully on a challenging task (which your CBA should be!).

You can try this for yourself. Have a go at, say, five questions for your paper, and notice what time you start at. As soon as you finish the last question try to estimate how long it took you and then compare to your watch. The majority of us tend to underestimate how quickly time passes and this can cost you dearly in a full exam if you don't take steps to keep track of time.

So, the key thing here is to set yourself sensible milestones, and then get into the habit of regularly checking how you are doing against them:

- You need to develop an internal warning system – 'I've now spent more than three minutes on this one calculation – this is too long and I need to move on!' (less for a narrative question!)
- Keep your milestones in mind (eg approximately 30 questions done after 45 mins). If you are a distance from where you should be then adjust your pace accordingly. This usually means speeding up but can mean slowing down a bit if needs be, as you may be rushing when you don't need to and increasing the risk of making silly mistakes.

A full exam will be a mix of questions you find harder and those you find easier, and in the real CBA the order is randomised, so you could get a string of difficult questions right at the beginning of your exam. Do not be put off by this – they should be balanced later by a series of questions you find easier.

The Case Study exam and links with E3

Upon passing all of the exams at the Strategic level, you will be eligible to sit the relevant Case Study exam. As an example, you will need to have passed E3, F3 and P3 to sit the Strategic Level Case Study exam. CIMA will release a pre-seen document, providing comprehensive operational, strategic and financial details about a fictional company that you will be working for in your Case Study exam. There are four exam sittings a year (February, May, August and November) and at each sitting there are five exam variants; your exam will be selected from these five at random.

The format of the Case Study exam is a three-hour CBE, comprising three or four scenario-based questions, with each scenario having three or four associated requirements. These requirements will feature a mix of narrative and calculation questions, and the provision of the pre-seen and exam scenarios will necessitate a high degree of application. Therefore, what you study in this Course Book will provide you with part of the core knowledge required to answer the technical content of the Case Study exam.

For example the Strategic Level Case Study exam has 19 assessment outcomes, and each of these can be mapped back to knowledge you will have gained studying for the Strategic Level exams:

- I can evaluate strategic options (digital and otherwise).
- I can recommend strategic decisions (digital and otherwise).
- I can evaluate potential acquisitions and divestment opportunities.
- I can recommend responses to opportunities and threats arising from digital technologies.
- I can select and apply suitable strategic analytical tools.
- I can conduct an analysis of stakeholder needs and recommend appropriate responses.
- I can recommend appropriate responses to changes in the business ecosystem.
- I can recommend KPIs that encourage sound strategic management.
- I can recommend responses to economic, political and currency risks.
- I can recommend suitable sources of finance.
- I can recommend dividend policy.
- I can recommend and apply business valuation models.
- I can evaluate risks and recommend responses and can maintain the corporate risk register.
- I can identify ethical dilemmas and recommend suitable responses.
- I can evaluate and mitigate cyber risks.
- I can recommend internal controls.
- I can apply internal audit resources.
- I can recommend appropriate controls and evaluate the implications of compliance failures.
- I can recommend responses to the threats arising from poor governance.

When you commence your Case Study exam studies, we recommend you attend a BPP course or purchase BPP's Case Study Workbook, which will provide you with essential question practice and exam guidance on how to use the knowledge gained from this Course Book and apply it to the format of the Case Study exam.

Features in this Course Book

Key term
A key definition which is important to be aware of for the assessment

Formula to learn
A formula you will need to learn as it will not be provided in the assessment

Formula provided
A formula which is provided within the assessment and generally available as a pop-up on screen

Activity
An example which allows you to apply your knowledge to the technique covered in the Course Book. The solution is provided at the end of the chapter.

Illustration
A worked example which can be used to review and see how an assessment question could be answered

Assessment focus point
A high priority point for the assessment

Real life examples
A practical real life scenario

The strategy process

Syllabus learning outcomes

Having studied this chapter you will be able to work through the following syllabus outcomes:

Exam context

In the exam, you will be expected to demonstrate competence in the following representative task statements:

- Analyse the advantages and disadvantages of strategy development
- Analyse the essential features and characteristics of strategy including the long-term time horizon, considering the organisation as a whole, stakeholder analysis, gaining sustainable competitive advantage, and environmental analyses
- Analyse the different approaches to strategy development including the traditional top-down approach, emergent strategies, incrementalism, and freewheeling opportunism
- Analyse the different levels of strategy including corporate, business, and functional and the impact of strategic lenses on those levels
- As part of the strategy process, analyse the organisational ecosystem, strategic options or choice, and strategic implementation and control

Chapter overview

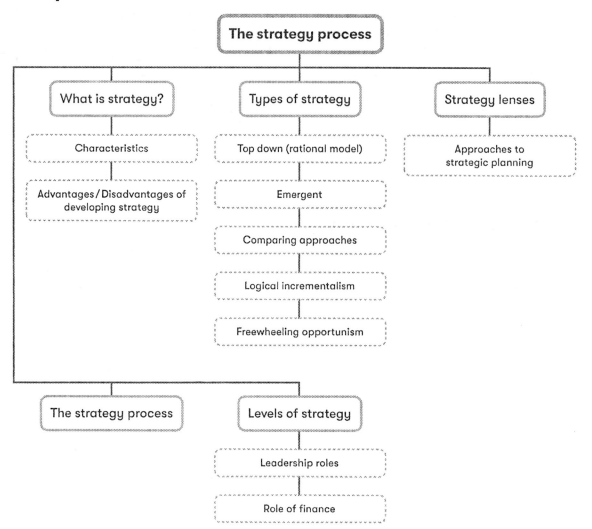

The strategy process

What is strategy?
- Characteristics
- Advantages/Disadvantages of developing strategy

Types of strategy
- Top down (rational model)
- Emergent
- Comparing approaches
- Logical incrementalism
- Freewheeling opportunism

Strategy lenses
- Approaches to strategic planning

The strategy process

Levels of strategy
- Leadership roles
- Role of finance

1 Introduction

This chapter introduces the rest of the E3 syllabus. It begins by looking at the essential characteristics of strategy, before moving on to look at different types and levels of strategy, and the leaders who have responsibility for them.

The chapter highlights the contrast between rational and emergent models of strategy.

In subsequent chapters, we will follow the broad structure of the rational model (analysis, choice, implementation and control) to look at the way strategy is carried out by the directors and senior management of an organisation.

- Different definitions of strategy
- Essential features and characteristics of strategy
- Intended and emergent strategy
- Corporate, business and functional strategies
- Analysis of organisation ecosystems – see also Chapter 3
- Generating options – see also Chapter 5
- Strategic choice – see also Chapter 7
- Strategic control – see also Chapter 9

2 What is strategy?

2.1 The purpose of strategy

Strategy acts a planning tool, helping organisations set goals and objectives for long-term growth and development.

Strategic planning requires management to understand the current position of their organisation so that they can make choices for the future, about how to create value and how to achieve competitive success.

In order to develop a strategy, an organisation needs to understand:

- Its fundamental **goals** (mission, vision or objectives) and its key **stakeholders** (and what they expect of the organisation)
- The **environment** and **ecosystem** in which it operates (eg markets, political, economic, social, technology ('PEST' issues); customers, competitors, suppliers, partners)
- Its **resources** or **capabilities** (which will enable it to achieve its goals and objectives)

The organisation can then decide how it aims to achieve a sustainable competitive advantage in the markets it operates in.

Real life example – Tesla

Tesla have entered the automotive manufacturing with a very different strategy to their mainstream rivals; they have focused entirely on fully electric vehicles rather than fossil fuel or hybrid driven cars. The unique aspects of their corporate strategy have included:

(a) Initially producing an expensive car, with no mass market appeal. Tesla's original Roadster had a limited production run and was expensive to purchase. Quite simply Tesla did not have the infrastructure to mass produce electric cars. Importantly, this vehicle was designed and marketed to be iconic, therefore establishing the brand.

(b) The next stage was to develop a mass market product, the Model 3, but within this there were three key strands to its strategy:

    (i) Direct sales – unlike other manufacturers, Tesla's vehicles can only be purchased directly from the company itself, with the company moving away from dealerships and into internet only sales.

    (ii) Service centres – all sales showrooms are built with service centres where cars can be charged and receive maintenance.

(iii) Supercharger network – to overcome the lack of infrastructure, Tesla has created its own network of fast charging points where vehicles can be full charged, free of charge, in 30 minutes.

2.2 Definitions of strategy

Strategy is essentially the way an organisation seeks to achieve its goals and objectives. However, there are many different definitions of strategy. We'll begin by looking at just a few of these:

> **Strategy:** 'A course of action, including the specification of resources required, to achieve a specific objective' (*CIMA, 2005, CIMA official terminology*).
>
> 'The long-term direction of an organisation' (*Johnson et al, 2017*).
>
> 'The direction and scope of an organisation over the long term which achieves advantage in a changing environment, through its configuration of resources and competences with the aim of fulfilling stakeholder expectations.' (*Johnson, Scholes and Whittington, 2007, p3*).

2.3 Characteristics of strategy

We can take the highlighted phrases out of Johnson, Scholes and Whittington's (2007) definition, to highlight the key elements of strategy:

Direction and scope – organisations generally have objectives, and then organise themselves to meet those objectives. Setting direction and scope provides something to aim at.

The **long term**: this will typically mean a number of years, which can be thought of as 'three horizons' (Johnson et al, 2017); and managers need to consider all three horizons in formulating strategy:

- Horizon 1 means defending and extending the current business.
- Horizon 2 businesses are emerging activities that should provide new sources of profit.
- Horizon 3 ventures are new and risky, and might provide returns in several years' time.

Achieving advantage – how the organisation will achieve a sustainable competitive advantage.

Changing environment – consideration of the current and future environment; how the organisation can respond to changes in the environment.

Configuration of resources and competences – where these will be used to help achieve competitive advantage.

Stakeholder expectations – how these will be fulfilled. Organisations typically contain stakeholders with differing views and interests, which are relevant in setting strategy (eg employees; suppliers; partners; customers; investors; regulators). Organisations need to consider their stakeholders and boundaries – what to include in, or exclude from, their activities.

2.3.1 Characteristics of strategic decisions

Having identified what strategic decisions are about, Johnson, Scholes and Whittington (2007) also describe some important **characteristics of strategic decisions**:

- Decisions about strategy are likely to be **complex**
- There is likely to be a high degree of **uncertainty** surrounding the decision
- Strategic decisions have extensive impact on **operationaldecision-making**
- Strategic decisions affect the **organisation as a whole** and thus will require an **integrated approach**
- Strategic decisions are likely to lead to **change,** and may have an impact on the **organisational culture**

2.4 Advantages and disadvantages of strategy development

There is often no single 'right' or 'wrong' strategy to use in any given situation, and there are different approaches an organisation can take to developing its strategy. The formal approach to strategy formulation (eg rational model) has been both praised and criticised. We can therefore suggest that it will be better suited to some circumstances, and organisations, than others.

Activity 1: Formal strategic planning

Required

Using the picklist note whether each comment describes an advantage or disadvantage of formal strategic planning approaches:

Identifies risks [▼]

Enforces consistency at all levels [▼]

Trying to predict the future [▼]

Impact of external factors [▼]

Imposes rigidity [▼]

Forces decision making [▼]

Assumptions required [▼]

Clarifies aims and objectives [▼]

Better control [▼]

Cost and effort [▼]

Picklist:

Advantage

Disadvantage

Solution

2.5 Suitability of different approaches to strategy development

The circumstances in which **formal approaches** to strategic planning are likely to be appropriate:

- Industries which are relatively stable
- Where significant external finance is required and investors need a business plan

The circumstances in which **less formal approaches** are likely to be appropriate:

- Dynamic, rapidly-changing industries or environments
- When organisations have experienced, innovative managers who can identify opportunities or threats quickly, and respond to them effectively

> ### Assessment focus point
>
> The syllabus requires you to be able to analyse the advantages and disadvantages of strategy development.
>
> This analysis might often include an evaluation of the advantages and disadvantages of formal strategic planning (rational model), but it is also important that you are aware of the advantages and disadvantages of the other approach to strategy that we will discuss later in the chapter.

3 Types of strategy

The following approaches to strategy development can be used by businesses to achieve their goals.

3.1 Rational planning

This involves detailed, advance planning, analysis and strategy formulation in order to achieve the organisation's stated goals.

Rational planning is a **top-down approach**: an organisation's senior leadership team determine objectives and strategy, and the business then has to work towards achieving them.

The rational planning approach to strategy consists of the following elements:

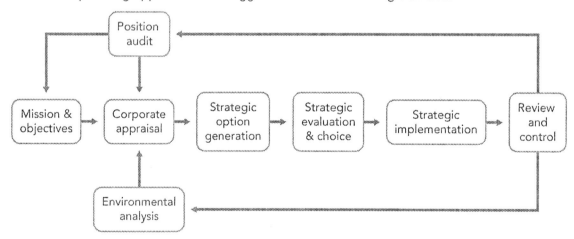

3.1.1 Position, choice and implementation

The rational (top-down) approach to strategy can be summarised into three main elements:

- Analysis – analysis of current strategic position, including objective setting, understanding internal strengths and weaknesses, and external opportunities and threats.
- Choice – generating and evaluating strategic options, before choosing an agreed strategy.
- Implementation and control – converting the overall strategic plan into detailed plans and targets for operating units (implementation); monitoring how effectively the organisation is progressing towards its strategic objectives (control).

3.2 Emergent strategy

The rational model assumes a formal, top-down sequence of strategic planning and decision making, in which strategies are imposed by senior management and then implemented across the organisation. As such, the model assumes organisations follow an intended strategy which has been mapped out for them, with a view to achieving pre-defined objectives.

Mintzberg (1987) argues that strategy is better viewed as an emergent process.

> **Emergent strategy:** Strategy that emerges on the basis of a series of decisions which form a pattern that becomes clear over time (*Johnson et al, 2017*).

Real life example – Pfizer

In the 1990s, Pfizer's research teams in England were researching the use of the synthesised compound UK-92,480 as a blood pressure and angina treatment. During clinical trials it was noted that the drug, called Sildenafil at that time, had unintended side-effects on male patients. Pfizer was quick to recognise the potential of these side-effects, and repositioned the drug as an erectile dysfunction treatment, filing for a patent under the tradename 'Viagra'.

Emergent strategy involves the formulation of a plan but includes the ability to flex the plan by **crafting in** to existing operations newly emerging opportunities, which were not identified at the planning stage, and **crafting out** intentions which have become redundant.

There can be a high degree of experimentation in emergent strategy as an organisation tries to find the most productive way to respond to new opportunities or threats.

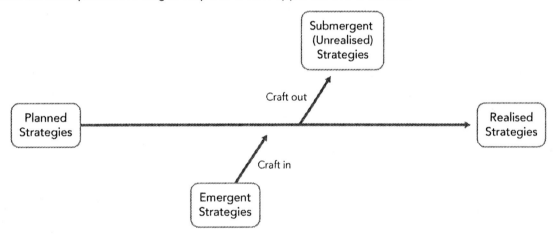

3.3 Crafting strategy

Mintzberg (1987) mentions the following essential activities in strategic management.

- **Manage stability.** Managing 'business as usual' during the period of change.
- **Detect discontinuity.** Environments do not change regularly, nor are they always turbulent. Some changes are more important than others.
- **Know the business.** This has to include an awareness and understanding of operations.
- **Manage patterns.** Detect emerging patterns and help them take shape if appropriate.
- **Reconcile change and continuity.** Avoid concentrating on one or the other.

3.4 Unrealised strategy

Mintzberg (1987) tells us that some aspects of a planned strategy will not be realised; for example, because the environment changes, meaning the planned strategy is no longer appropriate or workable.

Assessment focus point

The emergent approach does not necessarily mean that an organisation does not have a formal strategic plan for the future. However, the emergent approach suggests that for the organisation to be successful it needs to be flexible enough to amend this strategy for unexpected events.

3.5 Logical incrementalism

This approach suggests that strategy tends to involve small-scale ('incremental') extensions of past policy, rather than radical shifts.

Instead of being determined by autonomous strategic planning teams evaluating all the options and deciding on an optimal solution, strategies are based on past policies (which are known to have worked well previously.) This is often because decisions are taken by operational staff, rather than by senior leadership teams.

Incrementalism also reflects the idea of **bounded rationality** (*Simon, 1982*). Managers do not have time to research and evaluate all the potential opportunities available to them. Therefore, they have to choose a strategy from a restricted range of options, and on the basis of it being satisfactory rather than the optimal solution.

The danger with this approach is that small-scale adjustments may not be sufficient to move with customers and their needs, so may result in **strategic drift** (ie the organisation's strategies fail to address its strategic position, particularly in response to environmental change, leading to a deterioration in the organisation's performance).

Incrementalism is also not a suitable approach for new organisations, because they have no past policy on which to base their future strategies.

3.6 Freewheeling opportunism

The **freewheeling opportunism approach** suggests that organisations should not bother with strategic plans but should exploit opportunities as they arise.

The opportunist approach means that an organisation can **seize opportunities** quickly (rather than getting slowed down by formal planning processes), so it could be appropriate for organisations in rapidly-changing environments.

However, a potential problem with freewheeling opportunism is that the lack of planning may mean that an organisation **fails to identify possible opportunities** which might be available. It could also mean that organisations are constantly **reacting** to the environment, rather than acting purposively.

Assessment focus point

The E3 syllabus expects you to be able to analyse different types of strategy, and within this you may need to assess whether an organisation would be better served by having a formal (rational model) approach or an emergent approach, given the context provided in a case study scenario. It is important that you understand the advantages and disadvantages of each approach so that you can assess which circumstances they would be most appropriate for.

 Illustration 1: Strategic approaches

Strategy is formally conceived by senior management, in advance of implementation.

Required

Which approach to strategy is described in the following situation?

A   Emergent

B   Freewheeling opportunism

C   Logical incrementalism

D   Rational planning

Solution

The correct answer is:

Rational planning

The rational planning model is a formal, top-down process, in which strategy is planned and development by senior management before being 'imposed' on an organisation.

Activity 2: EZ Limited

EZ Limited is a fast-growing internet company, employing less than a dozen people all reporting directly to the company's founder. All strategic decisions are taken by the founder who, where appropriate, is happy to authorise strategic ideas generated by staff. Growth has been rapid, and significant future growth is envisaged.

Required

Which type of strategic generation would NOT be appropriate for EZ Limited?

A   Rational planning approach

B   Freewheeling opportunism

C   Emergent strategies

D   Logical incrementalism

Solution

3.7 Decision making and uncertainty

Johnson et al (2017) also highlight that the way organisations approach strategy development is likely to vary in different contexts:

- **Simple/static environments** – static environments favour formal planning. Historical analysis and past experience can be a valuable guide to the future, because little is changing.

- **Dynamic** – requires a more flexible/emergent approach. May need to consider the environment of the future, not just the past.

- **Complex** – strategy may need to be devolved and decentralised, as the board may lack the knowledge to create a single over-arching strategy (eg in a multinational firm).

3.8 Certainty and agreement

Two other dimensions which can influence the way in which management decisions are made are the level of **agreement** about **what the outcomes should be**, and the level of **certainty** around **how to achieve those outcomes**, as in the matrix below (Stacey, 2007).

This reinforces the point that different approaches to strategy and decision making may be needed in different circumstances.

	Certainty	
	Close to	**Far from**
Agreement — Close to	Rational	Judgemental
Agreement — Far from	Political	Complex; edge of chaos

- **Rational** – high degree of certainty underpins formal planning. There is agreement on outcomes and how to achieve them.
- **Political** – there is certainty about how to achieve outcomes, but lack of agreement on the outcomes required. Negotiation and compromise may be required to determine the outcome.
- **Judgement** – an organisation knows what it wants, but not how to achieve it. A strong vision replaces a formal plan or objectives.
- **Edge of chaos** – traditional management approaches are ineffective, so it is necessary to use innovation and creativity to break with past models and create new ways of operating.

4 Strategy lenses

Looking at strategies from different perspectives can help to identify different issues and insights. The strategy lenses (Johnson et al, 2017) provide a framework for doing this:

- Strategy as **design**: This view perceives strategy as a top-down, systematic, analytical and logical process, in which managers analyse information to establish a clear course of action. The **rational planning** model is an example of strategy as design.
- Strategy as **experience**: This view sees strategy as an adaptation and extension of what has worked in the past. Strategy will be driven by an organisation's experience, taken-for-granted assumptions and established ways of doing things. The way 'strategy as experience' builds on the past means we could view **logical incrementalism** as an illustration of this lens.
- Strategy as **variety** (or strategy as **ideas**): This lens sees strategy as emerging from within and around organisations, as new ideas develop in response to an uncertain and changing environment. (Strategy as design is perceived as being too rigid to uncover new ideas, while strategy as experience builds too much on the past.)
- Strategy as **discourse**: This lens looks at the way managers use language to frame strategic problems, present strategic options, or communicate strategic decisions. Strategy discourse becomes a way for managers to 'shape' strategic analysis in their favour, to gain influence, power and support for their proposals.

Activity 3: Strategy lenses

Required

Match the following statements to the correct strategy lens.

Strategy can be a political process as an example of [▼]

Management could view logical incrementalism as an example of [▼]

Management could view emergent strategy as an example of [▼]

The rational planning model is an example of [▼]

Picklist:

Strategy as design

Strategy as experience

Strategy as variety

Strategy as discourse

Solution

4.1 Lenses and strategic choices

Another context in which using different perspectives (lenses) could be useful is when analysing strategic position and making strategic choices.

The consultancy company, McKinsey, has suggested that companies should view strategy and strategic choices through four lenses (*Laczkowski et al, 2018*):

- **Financial** – what is required to create value for the business?
- **Market** – is the company operating in markets that will deliver growth over time?
- **Competitive advantage** – what advantages does the company have eg in terms of capabilities or product portfolio, relative to competitors?
- **Operating model** – can the organisation deliver value (eg through its capabilities and talent)?

4.2 Approaches to strategic planning

It is also important to recognise that firms can take different approaches to strategic planning, meaning that they prioritise different elements of strategic analysis.

There are three main approaches to strategic planning:

- **Accounting-led**: An organisation adopting an accounting-led approach starts by looking at its key stakeholders and their objectives (eg to increase pre-tax profits by x% per year, and earnings per share by y% per year). The organisation then develops plans which are designed to achieve those objectives. However, critics argue that such an approach to strategic planning is flawed because it doesn't take sufficient account of market conditions and the external environment.
- **Position-based approach**: An organisation adopting a position-based approach analyses its environment (eg using PEST analysis) before setting its objectives and strategy. In this way, the organisation can try to ensure its strategic plans provide a good 'fit' with its environment. Importantly, the external focus of the position-based approach should help organisations be aware of changes in their environments. Moreover, if an organisation is able to predict changes in advance of them happening, this could help the organisation plan how to deal with those changes rather than simply having to react to them. (We look in more detail at the environment and uncertainty in Chapter 3.)
- **Resource-based approach**: The approaches to strategy in Section 2 (eg rational model) are position-based ie focused on how an organisation can achieve a 'fit' with its environment. An alternate approach to deriving strategy is instead to focus on an organisation's **internal competencies and capabilities**. Critics of the position-based approach argue that the extent of the changes in the environment make it very difficult for organisations to predict the future with any certainty. Therefore, rather than trying to focus on a 'fit' with the environment, organisations should focus their strategy on their own core competences and capabilities – what they are good at. However, the potential flaw with this approach is that it is too inward-looking. For example, there would be little use in an organisation being good at something if there is no longer a market demand for it.

5 The strategy process

We mentioned earlier that the rational (top-down) approach to strategy can be summarised into three main elements: analysis, choice and implementation.

5.1 Elements of the strategy process

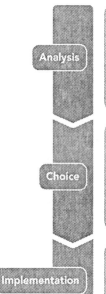

- **Stakeholder analysis**: assess power and interest of different groups, and their impact on mission and objectives
- Identify organisation's goals and objectives
- **External analysis**: opportunities and threats (PEST analysis; Porter's Five forces)
- **Internal analysis**: strengths and weaknesses (Resource audit; value chain; BCG matrix)
- **Corporate appraisal**: **SWOT** analysis (combining internal and external factors)
- Gap analysis identify difference between desired and expected position

- **Generating options** (to 'close the gap'):
- How to compete: eg Porter's generic strategies
- Where to compete: directions for growth – markets/products to be invested in (Ansoff's growth matrix)
- Method growth: organic; acquisition; joint arrangement
- **Evaluation:**
- Potential strategies need to be evaluated: suitability; acceptability; feasibility

- Formulation of detailed plans and budget
- Change management (eg changes in organisational structure required to implement plans)
- Setting targets and KPIs
- Monitoring and control

5.2 Interdependence and integration

The 'analysis – choice – implementation' model of the strategic management process can be used as an overview of many of the topics in the E3 syllabus.

However, while the rational model adopts a linear approach to strategic management, some authors (eg Johnson, Scholes and Whittington) argue strategic is not a linear process, so the three stages of 'analysis, choice and implementation' do not necessarily have to follow each other in sequence. For example, an organisation's understanding of its strategic position could be affected by its experience of implementing a strategy.

In this respect, Johnson, Scholes and Whittington (2007) stress the **interdependence** and **integration** of the three elements of analysis, choice and implementation in strategic management.

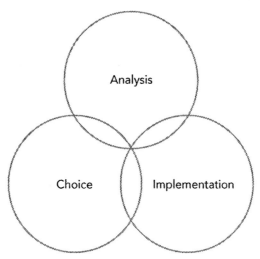

> ### Assessment focus point
>
> The syllabus requires you to be able to analyse the organisation ecosystem, strategic options/choices, and implementation/control as part of the strategy process. Although we have identified some of the key elements of each of these stages in this chapter, we will look at them in more detail in later chapters. However, as you work through the chapters in the workbook, try to think how the topics covered in them fit into the strategy process.

6 Levels of strategy

Strategy may be developed at three levels in an organisation:

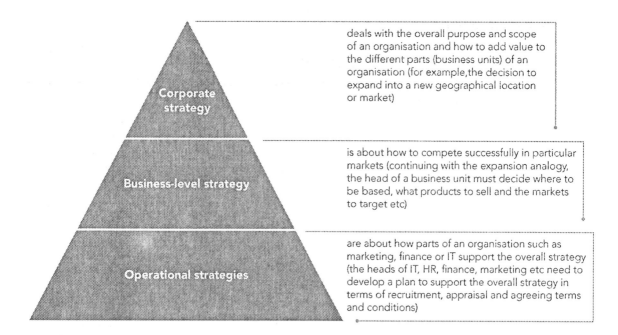

Corporate strategy — deals with the overall purpose and scope of an organisation and how to add value to the different parts (business units) of an organisation (for example, the decision to expand into a new geographical location or market)

Business-level strategy — is about how to compete successfully in particular markets (continuing with the expansion analogy, the head of a business unit must decide where to be based, what products to sell and the markets to target etc)

Operational strategies — are about how parts of an organisation such as marketing, finance or IT support the overall strategy (the heads of IT, HR, finance, marketing etc need to develop a plan to support the overall strategy in terms of recruitment, appraisal and agreeing terms and conditions)

Note. The 'corporate' level is sometimes referred to as 'strategic' in relation to planning, meaning the three levels of planning are: strategic, business and operational. Also, operational strategies can sometimes be known as **functional** strategies.

Although we can identify three different levels, it is important to remember that they are linked. A corporate or business-level strategy will ultimately only be successful if it is supported by appropriate operational (functional) strategies.

Illustration 2: Levels of strategy

Sequent is a clothing retailer, focusing on ladies' clothing. However, the company is now considering expanding and developing a new range of men's clothing products.

The list of questions below have been discussed in relation to planning for the new venture.

Required

Identify which level of planning they relate to ie corporate/strategic, business, or operational/functional.

Input	Level of planning
How do we need to change the company's mission and objectives to reflect this new venture?	▼
What geographical locations should the new stores be opened in?	▼
What IT systems need to be installed in the new stores?	▼
What pricing strategy should we adopt for the new stores (eg should we look to keep prices lower than our competitors?	▼

Picklist:

Corporate/strategic

Operational/functional

Business

Solution

The correct answer is:

Input	Level of planning
How do we need to change the company's mission and objectives to reflect this new venture?	Corporate/strategic
What geographical locations should the new stores be opened in?	Business
What IT systems need to be installed in the new stores?	Operational/functional
What pricing strategy should we adopt for the new stores (eg should we look to keep prices lower than our competitors?	Business

Assessment focus point

The syllabus requires you to be able to analyse the different levels of strategy (corporate, business and functional). An important part of this could be identifying whether strategies at different levels are properly aligned; for example, whether the way day-to-day activities are structured at functional level will help an organisation achieve its business strategy and – in turn – its corporate strategy.

6.1 Roles in the strategy process

The conventional view is that senior management is responsible for strategy. However, this is too simplistic. Senior management will focus on overall, corporate strategy, but if senior managers become too closely involved in operations and operational strategy this is likely to distract them from the issues facing an organisation as a whole.

6.1.1 Senior management

The following roles are carried out by the CEO and other senior managers:

- **Envisioning future strategy**: communicating a clear vision and strategic intent to internal and external stakeholders
- **Aligning the organisation to deliver the strategy**: building relationships of trust, ensuring that people are committed to the strategy and empowered to deliver it
- **Embodying change**: being a symbol and role model for the organisation

6.1.2 Middle management

Middle managers play a vital role in implementing top-down strategic plans, but they can also play a wider role in strategy making itself. The following are important strategy roles middle managers can play (*Johnson et al, 2017*):

- **Advisers to senior management**: middle managers are closer to day-to-day operations and may have a better understanding of competitive environments and markets than senior management.
- **'Sense making' of strategy**: middle managers play a key role in linking senior management to staff at lower levels in an organisation.
- **Reinterpretation and adjustment of strategy**: middle managers are more closely involved in implementing strategy; this may help them identify the need to adapt strategies to fit with changed circumstances.
- **Champion of ideas**: their closeness to markets and operations enables middle managers to champion new ideas that could form the basis of new strategies.

6.2 Role of finance

The **management accountant** will also have a significant role to play in the strategy-setting process. The scope of their contribution could include:

- Providing the **information and analysis** required by management and other stakeholders, to support decision making
- Compiling the **forecasts** and strategies to help deal with environmental uncertainty
- **Analysing competitorperformance** for **benchmarking** exercises
- **Analysis** of internal **cost** behaviour, linking through to pricing decisions
- Performing **investment appraisal** analysis to support investment decisions eg NPV
- Building and maintaining **performance evaluation** systems eg ROI and balanced scorecard

Perhaps the most important of these roles is the provision of information and analysis on which decisions are made. The way in which technology is impacting this process is explored in Chapter 12.

Chapter summary

The strategy process

What is strategy?

- How to achieve goals
- How to achieve sustainable competitive advantage

- How to achieve goals
- How to achieve sustainable competitive advantage

Characteristics

- Set direction and scope
- Long term
- Achieving competitive advantage
- Respond to changing environment
- Configure resources and capabilities
- Fulfil stakeholder expectations

Advantages/Disadvantages of developing strategy

Advantages:
- Identifies risks
- Clarifies aims and objectives
- Prompts decision-making

Disadvantages:
- Predicting the future?
- Assumptions required
- Leads to rigidity

Types of strategy

Top down (rational model)

Formalised process:
- Mission and objectives
- Position audit
- Environmental analysis
- Corporate appraisal
- Options generation
- Evaluation and choice
- Implementation
- Review and control

Emergent

- Strategy emerges from patterns of decisions, rather than being planned
- Bottom up rather than top down

Comparing approaches

- No single right or wrong approach
- Approach to strategy can depend on context in which organisation is operating

Logical incrementalism

- Small-scale extensions of past policies
- Reflects idea of bounded rationality
- Potential danger of strategic drift

Freewheeling opportunism

- No formal plans
- Seize opportunities as they arise
- Could be appropriate for rapidly-changing environments

Strategy lenses

- **Design:**
  top-down, systematic approach (like rational model)
- **Experience:**
  strategy as adaptation of what has worked in the past (like logical incrementalism)
- **Variety:**
  strategy emerges as new ideas develop in response to a changing environment (like emergent strategy)
- **Discourse:**
  using language to 'shape' discussions

Approaches to strategic planning

- Accounting-led
- Position-based
- Resource-based

The strategy process

- Analysis
- Choice: generate options; evaluate options
- Implementation

Levels of strategy

- Corporate
- Business-level
- Operational

Leadership roles

- Top managers:
  envisioning future strategy, aligning, embodying change
- Middle managers:
  advisers, 'sense making', reinterpretation & adjustment, champion of new ideas

Role of finance

- Insight and advice to support decision making
- Predictive as well as descriptive
- Analytics

Key terms

Strategy: 'A course of action, including the specification of resources required, to achieve a specific objective' (*CIMA, 2005, CIMA official terminology*).

'The long-term direction of an organisation' (*Johnson et al, 2017*).

'The direction and scope of an organisation over the long term which achieves advantage in a changing environment, through its configuration of resources and competences with the aim of fulfilling stakeholder expectations.' (*Johnson, Scholes and Whittington, 2007, p3*).

Emergent strategy: Strategy that emerges on the basis of a series of decisions which form a pattern that becomes clear over time (*Johnson et al, 2017*).

Activity answers

Activity 1: Formal strategic planning

The correct answer is:

Identifies risks **Advantage**

Enforces consistency at all levels **Advantage**

Trying to predict the future **Disadvantage**

Impact of external factors **Disadvantage**

Imposes rigidity **Disadvantage**

Forces decision making **Advantage**

Assumptions required **Disadvantage**

Clarifies aims and objectives **Advantage**

Better control **Advantage**

Cost and effort **Disadvantage**

Advantages	Comments
Identifies risks	Businesses operate in a context of risk and uncertainty. Strategic planning helps in managing these risks.
Enforces consistency at all levels	Long-term, medium-term and short-term objectives, plans and controls can be made consistent with one another.
Forces decision making	Companies cannot remain static – they have to cope with changes in the environment and react accordingly.
Clarifies aims and objectives	Organisations have aims and objectives, but it may be necessary to change these (eg due to changes in the environment).
Better control	Planning requires an organisation to identify its objectives, and targets can then be set in relation to those objectives.

Disadvantages	Comments
Trying to predict the future	Plans are made in order to try to guide and control future developments, but their ability to do this is restricted by the difficulty of predicting the future with accuracy.
Assumptions required	Plans require assumptions to be made about the future, but making assumptions is always fraught with the risk of error.
Impact of external factors	Plans can often be disrupted by unforeseen changes in the environment.
Imposes rigidity	Once a plan is in place, people may feel they have to stick to it, stifling innovation.

Disadvantages	Comments
Cost and effort	A formal, strategic-planning process can be a very costly and time-consuming process.

Activity 2: EZ Limited

The correct answer is:

Rational planning approach

The rational planning approach would be too bureaucratic and resource intensive for such a young and fast-growing small business.

Activity 3: Strategy lenses

The correct answer is:

Strategy can be a political process as an example of **Strategy as discourse**

Management could view logical incrementalism as an example of **Strategy as experience**

Management could view emergent strategy as an example of **Strategy as variety**

The rational planning model is an example of **Strategy as design**

Test your learning

1 **Required**

Which one of the following best describes the purpose of formulating strategies?

A   To understand the organisation's environment

B   To control the behaviour of employees

C   To achieve the organisation's objectives

D   To assess the internal resources available to the organisation

2 **Required**

In a formal (rational model) approach to strategy, what are the three main stages of the strategy process?

3 **Required**

Is the following statement true or false?

A top-down strategy develops out of the patterns of behaviour in an organisation.

A   True

B   False

4 Hesta plc uses the rational model to guide its strategic-planning process. Hesta's management team are currently assessing the political, economic, social and technological ('PEST') factors in the environment in which it operates.

Required

Which stage of the planning process has Hesta reached?

A   Choice

B   Generating options

C   Position

D   Implementation

5 **Required**

Which one of the following statements about emergent strategy is NOT true?

A   Final objectives are unclear at the beginning of the strategy process.

B   Emergent strategies are imposed on an organisation by senior management.

C   Elements of the strategy are developed as the strategy proceeds.

D   Emergent strategies typically take longer to develop than top-down strategies.

6 **Required**

Which three of the following are elements of the rational model?

A   Change management

B   Review and control

C   Corporate appraisal

D   Strategic planning

E   Mission and objectives

F   Strategic management

Stakeholders, governance and ethics

Syllabus learning outcomes

Having studied this chapter you will be able to work through the following syllabus outcomes:

Syllabus Area C: Strategic options

1	The context of generating strategic options
a-b	The role of governance and ethics in the strategy process and Purpose, vision, and values of organisation and their impact on strategy

Syllabus Area B: The organisational ecosystem

1	The elements of the ecosystem
a	Markets and competition

Exam context

In the exam, you will be expected to demonstrate competence in the following representative task statements:

- Analyse the role of governance and business ethics in the context of generating strategic options
- Analyse the linkage between purpose, vision and values to each other and to generating strategic options
- Perform or review a Mendelow's Matrix analysis to analyse an organisation's stakeholders related to their level of interest and power.

Chapter overview

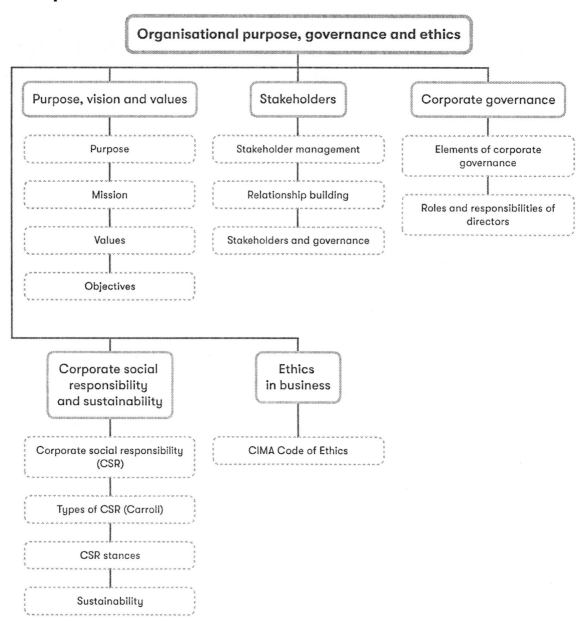

1 Introduction

In Chapter 1, we discussed what strategy is, but now we will move on to start looking at the context of developing strategy. Key questions to understand are how an organisation makes a difference, and who it makes a difference for. These are reflected in an organisation's mission, vision, values and objectives. An organisation's purpose will also be shaped by the interests of its key stakeholders. However, the way purpose is translated into strategy will also reflect the governance mechanisms in an organisation.

In this chapter we also discuss different types of stakeholder, and how their different levels of power and interest can influence strategy (for example, mission and objectives).

The chapter finishes by looking at the corporate governance structure within which organisations operate, highlighting the importance of organisations behaving in a socially responsible and ethical manner.

Topics covered in this chapter:

- Definition of purpose, vision and values
- Linkage between purpose, vision and value to each other and to strategy
- Stakeholder analysis
- Roles and responsibilities of leaders of organisations for strategy

2 Purpose, vision and values

2.1 Defining an organisation's purpose

In Chapter 1, we discussed the purpose of strategy. However, an important part of the strategic planning process is actually defining an organisation's purpose.

When thinking about an organisation's purpose, two key questions (*Johnson et al, 2017*) are:

- **How** does the organisation make a difference?
- **For whom** does the organisation make that difference?

There are four ways in which organisations typically define their purpose:

- Mission
- Vision
- Values
- Objectives

2.2 Corporate mission statement

A mission statement describes the purpose of an organisation. The mission can be thought of as a statement that covers **what** an organisation does, **who** it does it for and **how** it does it.

> **Mission statement:** 'Aims to provide employees and stakeholders with clarity about what the organisation is fundamentally there to do' (*Johnson et al, 2017*).

Real life example – Tesla

Tesla's original mission statement was 'to accelerate the world's transition to sustainable transport.' However, in mid-2016, under Elon Musk's direction, the company changed the corporate mission to 'to accelerate the world's transition to sustainable energy.' (*Tesla, 2019*)

We can see that the company's mission potentially goes far beyond electric cars.

An effective mission statement should have some of the following features:

- Describe the **purpose** and **values** of the organisation
- What business areas the organisation wants to be in ie products and markets

- Reference to key stakeholders ie customers, shareholders
- Broad outline of some of the main objectives

There is some scepticism towards corporate mission statements (eg that they become public relations exercises and are often full of generalisations which are impossible to tie down to specific objectives).

However, it is possible to give a balanced argument on their overall usefulness as follows:

- Can help strategic managers identify factors which are central to their strategy
- Can promote goal congruence across an organisation (eg are strategic plans consistent with an organisation's mission and values?)
- May provide a focal point for new strategies
- Allows the organisation to communicate core values to stakeholder groups (eg an organisation's values and principles can influence consumers' buying decisions)

Mission statements contain only **statements** of purpose and strategy, but in order for an organisation to develop a 'sense of mission' that 'mission' must be exhibited in the performance standards and values of the organisation.

2.3 Vision

A mission statement identifies what an organisation is **now**. By contrast, an organisation's vision is a statement of where the organisation wants to be in the **future**, and the future it seeks to create. **Vision statements** should answer the question of 'where do we aim to be?' or 'what do we want to achieve?'

Real life example – Amazon

Amazon's **corporate vision** is 'to be earth's most customer-centric company, where customers can find and discover anything they might want to buy online.' *(Panmore, 2019)*

An effective vision statement should have some of the following features:

- Clarity
- Description of a bright future
- Memorable and engaging
- Realistic and achievable aspirations
- Consistency with organisational values and culture

Illustration 1: Mission and vision statements

Required

Which of the following real-world statements would be described as vision statements?

A   **Avon:** 'To be the company that best understands and satisfies the product, service and self-fulfilment needs of women – globally.'

B   **Spotify:** To become 'the Operating System of music', a universal platform for listening.

C   **Microsoft:** 'To help people and businesses throughout the world realise their potential.'

D   **NatureAir:** 'To offer travellers a reliable, innovative and fun airline to travel in Central America.'

E   **Oxfam:** 'A world without poverty.'

Solution

The correct answers are:

- **Avon:** 'To be the company that best understands and satisfies the product, service and self-fulfilment needs of women – globally.'
- **Spotify:** To become 'the Operating System of music', a universal platform for listening.

- **Oxfam:** 'A world without poverty.'

Microsoft and NatureAir's statements primarily describe the current purpose of the organisations, whereas the other statements are more aspirational – describing what the organisations would like to achieve in the future.

2.4 Values

Statements of corporate values 'communicate the **underlying** and **enduring** core "principles" that guide an organisation's strategy and define the way that the organisation should operate.' (*Johnson et al, 2017, p7*)

Values help to establish **why** an organisation does what it does, and what it stands for. Therefore, values may help shape an organisation's mission statement.

An organisation's values influence the type of strategic initiatives the organisation considers or rejects – according to how well they fit with the organisation's values. (For example, one of the core values of a university could be to promote leading-edge research. As such, the university would not pursue a strategy which threatened the quality of its research.)

Real life example – Deloitte

'Our shared values are timeless. They succinctly describe the core principles that distinguish the Deloitte culture' (*Deloitte, 2018*).

- **Integrity** – we believe that nothing is more important than our reputation and behaving with the highest levels of integrity is fundamental to who we are.
- **Commitment To Each Other** – we believe that our culture of borderless collegiality is a competitive advantage for us, and we go to great lengths to nurture it and preserve it.
- **Strength From Cultural Diversity** – we believe that working with people of different backgrounds, cultures, and thinking styles helps our people grow into better professionals and leaders.
- **Outstanding Values To Markets & Clients** – we play a critical role in helping both the capital markets and our member firm clients operate more effectively. We consider this role a privilege, and we know it requires constant vigilance and unrelenting commitment.

Assessment focus point

The syllabus requires you to be able to analyse the linkage between purpose, vision and values to generating strategic options. As such, when evaluating potential strategies, an important factor to consider may be whether or not the strategy is consistent with an organisation's purpose and values, or whether it will help the organisation achieve its vision.

2.5 Objectives

Objectives: Statements of specific outcomes that are to be achieved (*Johnson et al, 2017*).

KEY TERM

2.5.1 Strategic objectives

A vision or mission statement may be vague and open-ended; an organisation's objectives should counter this, having the following properties:

- Specific
- Measurable
- Attainable
- Relevant
- Time bound

When creating a set of objectives, the organisation must consider the needs of all of its **stakeholders** (see Section 3) and ensure these are met where possible. In so doing a broad range of measures will be required, both **financial** and **non- financial**.

Increasingly, organisations are also setting objectives linked to the **triple bottom line** (see Section 5), meaning that alongside economic objectives, the organisation also sets environmental and social objectives relating to their **corporate social responsibility**.

Activity 1: Objectives

In different types of organisations, the objectives will differ due in large part to the different stakeholders each has.

Required
Describe how the objectives of a state-funded university would be different to that of BPP University, a privately run, 'for-profit' institution.

Solution

3 Stakeholders

> **Stakeholders:** 'Those persons and organisations that have an interest in the strategy of the organisation. Stakeholders normally include shareholders, customers, staff and the local community' (*CIMA*, 2005).

An organisation must consider its stakeholders when it is developing its mission and objectives.

Stakeholders can be categorised as **primary** (contractually tied to) and **secondary** (any others impacted by a decision). The reasons for doing so are:

- They may exercise great **power** over the organisation (eg trade unions)
- The organisation may be highly **dependent** on certain stakeholders due to their financial resources, knowledge, and claim over organisational assets or ownership
- Stakeholder **conflict** should be avoided where possible, by considering the needs of all stakeholders from the outset

Another way of categorising stakeholders is as one of the following:

- **Internal** – managers and employees
- **Connected** – shareholders, bankers, suppliers, partners, customers
- **External** – government, pressure groups, media, local communities, trade unions, competitors

3.1 Stakeholder mapping

A useful way of assessing stakeholders is to look at the power they exert over an organisation, and the level of interest they have in its activities.

Mendelow's matrix (*Mendelow, 1991*) enables stakeholders to be classified according to these two factors: power and interest. These factors help to define the type of relationship the organisation should seek with its different stakeholder groups and how it should view their concerns.

		Level of interest	
		Low	High
Power	Low	**Minimal effort** Casual labour	**Keep informed** Small local suppliers Core employees
	High	**Keep satisfied** Government Customers	**Key players** Key managers/employees Main suppliers

This matrix can be used to:

- **Track the changing influences** between different stakeholder groups over time. This can act as a trigger to change strategy as necessary; and
- **Assess the likely impact that a strategy** will have on different stakeholder groups.

Its aim is to assess:

- Whether stakeholders' resistance is likely to inhibit the success of the strategy; and
- What policies or actions may ease the acceptance of the strategy.

If the needs of different stakeholders conflict, the organisation will likely have to prioritise the interest of its key stakeholders (based on their level of power and interest).

In order to be successful, a strategy **must be acceptable to key stakeholders** at least. As such, it is advisable that key players are consulted during the planning process, so that any concerns they have can be addressed as a strategy is developed.

3.1.1 Non-market stakeholders

Companies will often consider the needs of those groups who can help them gain a competitive advantage eg customers, employees etc. However, it may well be that competitive advantage can be built outside of the direct market in which it operates. Non-market stakeholders include, but are not limited to:

- Governments
- Regulators
- Charities
- Pressure groups
- The media
- The public at large

Activity 2: Stakeholders

As part of a restructuring exercise AB Co has decided to outsource its home delivery service, and as such will have to make some of its distribution staff redundant.

Required

According to Mendelow, which of the following methods would be appropriate for the staff?

A   Keep informed

B   Keep satisfied

C   Key players

D   Minimal effort

Solution

3.2 Stakeholders and strategy

Identifying key stakeholders, and their interests, is very important when developing strategy, so that an organisation ensures that its strategy meets the needs of these key stakeholders.

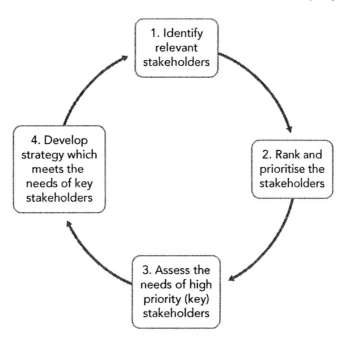

 ## Activity 3: Stakeholder evaluation

As well as assessing what stakeholders need or want *from* an organisation, it is also important to consider what different stakeholder groups provide *to* an organisation, and how the organisation can benefit from successfully managing its relationship with that stakeholder.

Required

Indicate below what the stakeholder groups want from an organisation, what they provide, and the potential benefits to the organisation from managing the relationship with that stakeholder group successfully.

(a) Customers

(b) Investors

(c) Suppliers

(d) Employees

(e) Local communities

(f) Regulators

Solution

3.3 Relationship building

An effective way to manage any group of stakeholders may be to build relationships with them. This could be achieved by:

- Building alliances eg with complementary suppliers
- Collaboration with your own suppliers eg to secure exclusive distribution
- Building loyalty with customers eg via reward cards or relationships marketing

3.4 Resolving conflicts

Cyert and March (1992) suggested four ways in which stakeholder conflict may be resolved:

- **Satisficing** – using negotiation between key stakeholder groups to find a compromise which is acceptable to all of them
- **Sequential attention** – addressing each group in turn, rather than trying to meet all their needs at the same time
- **Side payments** – making some kind of concession or payment to a group if its primary objectives cannot be met
- **Exercise of power** – a senior figure imposing a decision if there is no other way of resolving conflicting views

3.5 Corporate political activity

Government will be a 'keep satisfied' stakeholder for most businesses and as such, larger organisations may employ specialists to manage political relationships. The activities that organisations may involve themselves in to influence political decision making may include:

- **Lobbying** – dialogue with decision makers to help shape their views
- **Election funding** – financial donations to favoured candidates/parties
- **Petitions** – raising political and public awareness, and using public sentiment to influence legislation
- **Coalition building** – joining forces with competitors to increase collective influence on decision makers eg forming or joining trade associations
- **Directorships** – businesses can give board seats to influential persons such as retired civil servants or MPs (politicians), in the hope that they can use their knowledge, experience, contacts and influence to help the company
- **Legal action** – challenging laws through the courts

3.6 Stakeholders and governance

An important part of managing the relationship between an organisation and its stakeholders is ensuring that powerful stakeholder groups have confidence in the organisation's management team. The effectiveness of corporate governance in an organisation will influence stakeholders' confidence in that organisation.

Johnson et al (2017) suggest that governance and ethics form an important link between stakeholders and strategy. The interests of key stakeholders help to define the purpose of an organisation, but governance mechanisms and ethical considerations also need to be applied when translating that purpose into strategy.

The key concepts of governance include:

- **Fairness** – including equality when dealing with internal and external stakeholders
- **Openness and transparency** – providing information instead of concealing it

- **Innovation** – transforming knowledge and ideas into products and services. This requires the transformation of tacit knowledge into explicit knowledge
- **Scepticism** – keeping a questioning mind, staying alert to the threat of fraud and error
- **Independence** – ensuring that the NEDs are independent of senior management, and that all directors are free from vested interests; to ensure objective decision making
- **Probity and honesty** – ensuring honesty in all operation eg accurate financial reports
- **Responsibility** – clearly defining roles and responsibilities
- **Accountability** – accounting for group and individual actions and activities. This will require development and maintenance of risk management and control systems
- **Reputation** – taking the actions required to maintain the good name of organisation
- **Judgement** – taking decision in the best interest of the organisation
- **Integrity** – steadfast adherence to the organisation's ethical standards

(Based on *Johnson et al*, 2017; pg 133)

4 Corporate governance

> **Corporate governance:** 'The system by which organisations are directed and controlled' (*Cadbury Committee, 1992*).

However, it is important to distinguish between the purpose and the objectives of corporate governance:

Purpose of corporate governance	Objectives of corporate governance
To monitor the parties within an organisation who control and use the organisation's resources on behalf of its owners.	To contribute to improved accountability and performance in creating long-term value for the owners (long-term shareholder value).

Remember the definitions of strategy from Chapter 1; strategy helps define the direction an organisation takes to achieve competitive advantage in the long term. Corporate governance (by contributing to improved performance) plays a key part in supporting an organisation's strategy.

Effective governance should also help to increase **investors' confidence** in a company, and thereby encourage the investment and funding which may be needed to support investment and economic growth.

4.1 Elements of corporate governance

Although governance is mostly discussed in relation to large quoted companies, it is an issue for all corporate bodies, whether they are commercial or not for profit.

There are a number of key elements in corporate governance:

- The management and **reduction of risk** is a fundamental issue in all definitions of good governance, whether explicitly stated or merely implied.
- The notion that overall **performance is enhanced by good supervision andmanagement** within set best practice guidelines underpins most definitions of good corporate governance.
- Good governance provides a **framework** for an organisation to pursue its strategy in an **ethical and effective** way from the perspective of **all stakeholder groups** affected, and offers safeguards against misuse of resources, physical or intellectual.
- Good governance is not just about externally established codes; it also requires a willingness to **apply the spirit** as well as the letter of the law.
- **Accountability** is generally a major theme in all governance frameworks.

Good corporate governance involves managing risk and internal control, being **accountable to shareholders** and other stakeholders, and conducting business in an ethical and effective way.

Assessment focus point

Directors' accountability to 'other stakeholders' beyond shareholders reiterates the importance of stakeholder management. To succeed in the long term, companies need to build and maintain relationships with a wide range of stakeholders – so when evaluating potential strategies it is important to assess their impact on different stakeholder groups.

4.2 Principles of governance

The **UK Corporate Governance Code** (*FRC, 2018*) identifies the key principles of good corporate governance, which contribute to sustainable corporate success.

Of these, the principles relating to board leadership and company purpose are particularly relevant in the context of developing strategy:

(*Financial Reporting Council, 2018; p4*)

	Principles
A	A successful company is led by an effective and entrepreneurial board, whose role is to promote the long-term sustainable success of the company, generating value for shareholders and contributing to wider society.
B	The board should establish the company's purpose, values and strategy and satisfy itself that these and its culture are aligned. All directors must act with integrity, lead by example and promote the desired culture.
C	The board should ensure that the necessary resources are in place for the company to meet its objectives and measure performance against them. The board should also establish a framework of prudent and effective controls which enable risk to be assessed and managed.
D	In order for the company to meet its responsibilities to shareholders and stakeholders, the board should ensure effective engagement with, and encourage participation from, these parties.
E	The board should ensure that workforce policies and practices are consistent with the company's values and support its long-term sustainable success. The workforce should be able to raise any matters of concern.

The other principles in the Code relate to:

- **Division of responsibilities** – there should be an appropriate combination of executive and non-executive (particularly, **independent non-executive**) directors so that no one individual or small group of individuals dominates the board's decision making.
- **Composition** – the board and its committees should have a combination of skills, experience and knowledge, and the board should be evaluated annually to consider its composition, the **diversity** of its members, and how effectively those members work together to achieve objectives.
- **Risk and control** – the board should present a fair, balanced and understandable assessment of the company's current position and its future prospects. The board should also establish procedures to manage risk, oversee the internal control framework, and determine the nature and extent of risks the company is willing to take in order to achieve its strategic objectives.
- **Remuneration** – remuneration policies and practices should be designed to support strategy and promote long-term sustainable success. Executive remuneration should be aligned to company purpose and values and be clearly linked to the successful delivery of the company's strategy.

4.3 Implications of corporate governance for strategy

While corporate governance plays a beneficial role in risk management and control within organisations, it could still have some less favourable implications in relation to business strategy:

- Governance increases **shareholders' power** and prioritises shareholders' interests, potentially at the expense of other stakeholder groups.
- The increased scrutiny to which results are exposed (particularly in listed companies) may encourage a focus on short-termism and **short-term results** rather than long-term plans.
- The increased emphasis on risk management and risk reduction may make directors feel that they should accept **lower risk** (and lower return) projects in favour of ones which might generate higher returns (but which might also carry higher risk).

Real life example – Enron

Enron was once the world's sixth largest energy company, with its shares peaking at $85 in August 2000. By January 2002, the shares had fallen to below $1 (*Encyclopedia Britannica, 2019*).

The extraordinary growth of Enron over the previous seven years was largely fuelled by a series of elaborate deceptions, made possible by exploiting accounting standards, with the complicity of the company's auditors, Arthur Anderson. The most damaging deception was the practice of hiding multi-billion pound losses in so called 'off balance sheet vehicles'. These entities were subsidiary companies that were legally controlled in such a way that they were not consolidated into Enron's group accounts. The company was therefore able to transfer losses into these companies, thus hiding them from investors.

In the year before the deception came to light, Enron paid its two most senior executives $67 million and $42 million. In the months before the company crashed, many senior executives sold their shareholdings in the company, something that ordinary employees were forbidden from doing by stock market regulations, and consequently, many lost their life savings. To compound matters, many employees had pension funds that only invested in Enron shares, leaving their retirement plans in tatters.

The fall-out from Enron was huge. Several top executives were imprisoned, Arthur Anderson collapsed and the US Government enacted the Sarbanes-Oxley Act.

4.4 Roles and responsibilities of directors

The board is responsible for taking strategic decisions and major policy decisions, and for ensuring that these decisions are properly implemented by an organisation.

The UK Corporate Governance Code (*Financial Reporting Council, 2018*) identifies a number of key elements of the directors' role:

- Establish the company's purpose, values and strategy.

- Lead by example and promote the desired culture in an organisation.
- Ensure the necessary resources are in place for the company to meets its objectives.
- Ensure an appropriate framework is in place to measure the company's performance against its objectives.
- Establish a framework of controls to enable risk to be assessed and managed.

Illustration 2: Corporate governance

Required
Which of the following are features of effective corporate governance?

A   Increased risk
B   Separation of executive roles
C   Board leading by example
D   Infrequent shareholder engagement
E   Fixed remuneration for directors
F   Promoting short-term success

Solution

The correct answers are:

- Separation of executive roles
- Board leading by example

Response option	Explanation
Increased risk	Risk should be decreased by better controls.
Separation of executive roles	Eg CEO and chair
Board leading by example	The board should lead by example and promote the desired culture in an organisation.
Infrequent shareholder engagement	This should be effective not occasional.
Fixed remuneration for directors	Remuneration should contain incentives, hence cannot be fixed.
Promoting short-term success	Long-term, sustainable success should be promoted.

5 Corporate social responsibility and sustainability

5.1 Corporate social responsibility

> **Corporate social responsibility (CSR):** An organisation's obligation to maximise positive stakeholder benefits while minimising the negative effects of its actions.

Corporate social responsibility (CSR) centres on the approach taken by organisations to provide **benefits to society** in general, rather than to specific stakeholders.

The degree to which companies in particular embrace CSR is often dictated by the views of their management, with two contrasting schools of thought as follows.

- **Strong view** – a company exists for the benefit of **all its stakeholders**.
- **Weak view** – a company exists to maximise the **wealth of its shareholders**.

5.2 Types of CSR

Carroll (1991) devised a four-part model forming a pyramid, but argued an organisation only truly acts in a socially responsible manner when it satisfies all four parts:

Pyramid of corporate social responsibility (after *Carroll, 1991*)

- **Economic responsibility** – the fundamental level upon which the others are built. This requires employees to be paid fairly, shareholders to be adequately compensated and customers to receive value for money.
- **Legal responsibility** – the organisation must obey the law.
- **Ethical responsibility** – doing what is right, just and fair, even if this is not required by law.
- **Philanthropic responsibility** – the highest level of CSR, including charitable donations, contributions to local communities and providing employees with the chances to improve their lives.

5.2.1 Social responsiveness

As well as categorising the different kinds of responsibility, Carroll (1979) identified the different ways organisations can respond to social responsibility and social issues:

- **Reaction** – an organisation denies any responsibility for social issues, and either ignores calls for it to act in response to them or rejects them.
- **Defence** – an organisation accepts a basic responsibility for social issues but does only the minimum required to defend its current position.
- **Accommodation** – an organisation accepts responsibility for social issues and does what is asked of it by the stakeholder groups affected.
- **Proaction** – an organisation makes considerable effort to address social issues; actively addressing specific concerns and anticipating future issues. For example, a company which discovers a possible fault in a product and recalls the product without being forced to, and before any injury or damage is caused, acts in a proactive way.

5.3 CSR stances

- **Short-term shareholder interest** – the firm exists to make a profit for shareholders but will abide by the constraints imposed on it by government (through legislation and regulation).
- **Long-term shareholder interest** – the firm should be prepared to go over and above its legal minimum requirements where there is a long-term shareholder benefit. The justification for social action is that it makes good business sense (eg improving brand image).
- **Multiple stakeholder obligation** – accepting that the firm exists for more than just shareholder wealth. As such the wider stakeholder groups (eg suppliers, employers, customers) are considered in the firm's activities. The firm recognises that without appropriate relationships with these groups it would not be able to function.
- **Shaper of society** – this is an ideologically driven view, resulting in financial interests being subordinate to the firm's wider vision and the benefits its actions provide to society.

Activity 4: CSR stances

Petra runs an energy firm that focuses exclusively on generating power from renewable sources. The company is not listed and any profits are reinvested in renewable energy research. Petra does not take a salary or any dividends from the company.

Required

Which of Johnson et al's CSR stances is Petra adopting?

A   Short-term shareholder interest

B   Multiple stakeholder obligation

C   Shaper of society

D   Long-term shareholder interest

Solution

5.4 The impact of technologies on CSR

The development of new technologies has impacted on organisational CSR in the following ways:

- **Quicker scrutiny** – real time data is delivering CSR news to stakeholders much more quickly. Organisations need to be able to respond more quickly to these faster data flows.

- **Greater stakeholder engagement** – stakeholder feedback now extends far beyond the traditional AGM (annual general meeting), feedback via social media has greatly increased stakeholder engagement.

- **More integrated CSR practices** – stakeholders require data on a wider range of CSR measures eg not just the organisation itself, but also relating to its supply chain and ecosystem.

- **Improved measurement** – development in areas such as big data, internet of things and AI have created expectations of increased accuracy in CSR reporting.

- **Ecosystems and openness** – there are greater expectations of openness and transparency from all those who participate in ecosystems, enforcing higher levels of CSR on all those who wish to participate.

5.5 Sustainability

Sustainability can be viewed as a sub-branch of CSR. In essence it encourages an organisation to focus on the creation of long-term consumer and employee value.

Sustainability is often evidenced by the implementation of 'green' strategies.

However, sustainability doesn't relate only to environmental issues. Elkington (1997) highlights that the challenge is for businesses to deliver, simultaneously:

- Social justice
- Environmental quality
- Economic prosperity

Elkington (1997) promoted the idea that organisations will need to build sustainability measures into their corporate reporting structures. If organisations focus too much on short-term issues at the expense of the longer term, this could damage their longer-term reputation and prospects.

Elkington advocates the 'triple bottom line' approach to corporate reporting based upon capturing data around:

- People – the social justice of an organisation's operations
- Planet – the environmental impact of an organisation's operations
- Profit – the economic benefit enjoyed by the host society

6 Ethics in business

Ethics are the rules and principles of behaviour which help us decide between right and wrong.

The organisation's approach to ethics stems right back to its vision and mission since this is where organisational actions should flow from. These should be reinforced by the **corporate values**, as expressed through the vision, mission and objectives. Organisations are coming under increasing pressure to adopt an ethical approach towards:

- Stakeholders (eg employees, customers, suppliers, local communities)
- Environmental issues (eg pollution, recycling)
- Dealings with unethical companies or countries

Real life example – Google 'don't be evil'

Incorporated into Google's original code of conduct was the motto 'don't be evil'. This was intended to set the ethical standards within the company at a very high level. However, as Google grew, and became a listed company, the company found it increasingly difficult to adhere to this standard. The company has faced international criticism over a range of issues including its taxation policies, and agreeing to sensor its Chinese search engine.

In 2015 the motto 'don't be evil' was removed from the preface of the code of conduct. Google's parent company, Alphabet Inc, now uses the motto 'Do the right thing' as the opening of its corporate code, urging employees to 'follow the law, act honourably and treat co-workers with courtesy and respect' (*Alphabet, 2017*).

6.1 Ethics in the strategy process

When directors or managers make decisions, these could be influenced by a variety of ethical influences:

- **Individual** – relating to the person's own ethical code
- **Organisational** – guided by the values, code of ethics or code of conduct of their organisation, and/or their professional body (eg CIMA)
- **Societal** – guided by the laws, cultures and traditions of their home country
- **International** – guided by the laws, customers and traditions of foreign countries (in the context of multinational organisations).

6.1.1 The importance of ethics

It is important that ethics are embedded in an organisation's business model, and corporate ethics should be considered at each and every stage of the strategic decision-making process.

Ethics can have a significant impact on a business. For example, strong ethical policies – that go beyond simply upholding the law – can add value to a brand and can assist an organisation's ability to thrive in the long term.

Conversely, failing to act ethically can cause social, economic and environmental damage, and in doing so can undermine an organisation's long-term reputation and prospects.

Real life example – Huawei

The Chinese telecoms company has been accused of embedding spying software into its devices as a way of stealing secrets from western governments. On top of this, its Chief Financial Officer (CFO) was arrested in 2018 and faced extradition to the US on charges of breaching international sanctions. These allegations of unethical behaviour are having a material effect on the company as EU member states, alongside the US and Canadian Governments look set to ban the company from supplying infrastructure to support the roll-out of 5G networks.

Assessment focus point

The syllabus requires you to be able to analyse the role of business ethics in the context of generating strategic options. Even though a strategic option might appear financially or commercially attractive, before you recommend that option you also need to assess whether it raises any ethical issues. You should not recommend strategies which are unethical or could lead to an organisation being perceived as unethical.

Activity 5: Rational model

A multinational operator of a coffee shop franchise is performing a complete review of its corporate strategy.

Required
For each stage of the Rational Model (covered in Chapter 1) give ONE reason as to why ethics ought to be a consideration.

Solution

6.2 CIMA fundamental ethical principles

CIMA expects its members to maintain the highest ethical standards at all times, remembering their roles as business professionals, and the trust placed in them.

To assist its members, CIMA produces a Code of Ethics (*CIMA, 2017*), based on the International Federation of Accountants (IFAC) Code of Ethics.

The Code identifies five key principles of ethical behaviour (which can be arranged to form the mnemonic 'OPPIC').

- **Objectivity** – not allowing bias, conflict of interest, or the undue influence of others to override professional or business judgements.
- **Professional competence and due care** – maintaining professional knowledge and skill at the level required to ensure that a client or employer receives competent professional services, based on current developments in practice, legislation and techniques, and in accordance with applicable technical and professional standards.
- **Professional behaviour** – complying with relevant laws and regulations in order to avoid any action that would discredit the profession. Treating people dealt with in a professional capacity with courtesy and consideration.
- **Integrity** – acting honestly, straightforwardly and truthfully in all professional and business relationships. Not being associated with information which you know to be false or misleading.
- **Confidentiality** – respecting the confidentiality of information acquired through professional and business relationships, not using that information for their personal advantage nor disclosing any such information to third parties without proper authority, unless there is a legal or professional duty to do so.

Many organisations have their own code of ethics, or code of conduct. A code of conduct typically contains a series of statements setting out an **organisation's values**, the **behaviours** it expects from its staff, and explaining how it sees its **responsibilities** towards stakeholders.

The purpose of any code of ethics is to promote good behaviour among staff, regardless of their function, and discourage bad behaviour at the same time.

6.2.1 Threats to ethical principles

As well as identifying the ethical principles, CIMA's Code of Ethics also identifies five categories of threat which could compromise the accountant's ability to comply with one or more of the principles:

- **Self-interest** – the threat that a financial or other interest will inappropriately influence the professional accountant's judgement or behaviour eg the threat of a conflict of interest.
- **Self-review** – the threat that a professional accountant will not appropriately evaluate the results of a previous judgement made by themselves, or by another individual within their organisation, but will rely on that judgement as part of a service they are currently providing.
- **Advocacy** – this threat arises if a professional accountant is promoting a client or employer's position or opinion to the extent that the accountant's subsequent objectivity is compromised.
- **Familiarity** – if an accountant develops too close a relationship with a client or employer the accountant could become too sympathetic to the interests of the client or employer such that their professional judgement becomes compromised.
- **Intimidation** – an accountant is deterred from acting objectively by actual or perceived threats, including attempts to exercise undue influence over the accountant.

CIMA Code of Ethics, Section 100.12 (CIMA, 2017)

6.2.2 Resolving ethical conflicts

The CIMA Code imposes a positive duty on members (and student members) to take positive action in the event of uncovering a breach of ethics. The Code advises that conflicts can be resolved as follows:

(a) Gather all relevant facts

(b) Establish the ethical issue(s) involved

(c) Refer to the relevant fundamental principles

(d)   Follow established internal procedures

(e)   Investigate alternate courses of action

(f)   Consult with appropriate persons within the firm

(g)   Obtain professional advice from CIMA/lawyer

(h)   Consider resigning

Chapter summary

```
┌─────────────────────────────────────────────────────┐
│      Organisational purpose, governance and ethics    │
└─────────────────────────────────────────────────────┘
```

Purpose, vision and values

Purpose
- How does organisation make a difference?
- Who does it make a difference for?

Mission

Helps to describe purpose:
- What organisation does
- Who it does it for
- How it does it

Values
- Communicate an organisation's core principles
- Help to define the way an organisation should operate

Objectives
- SMART qualities
- Should consider the needs of stakeholders

Stakeholders

Consider stakeholders when setting mission and objectives

Stakeholder management

Related to power and interest
- Low power; low interest: minimal effort
- Low power; high interest: keep informed
- High power; low interest: keep satisfied
- High power; high interest: key players

Relationship building
- Alliances
- Collaboration with suppliers
- Customer loyalty

Stakeholders and governance
- Effectiveness of governance influences stakeholders' confidence in an organisation
- Quality of decision-making can affect competitive advantage

Corporate governance

- Purpose: monitor parties who control and use organisational resources on behalf of owners
- Objectives: improved accountability and performance

Elements of corporate governance
- Management and reduction of risk
- Performance is enhanced by effective supervision and management
- Pursue strategy in an effective and ethical way
- Accountability

Roles and responsibilities of directors
- Establish purpose, values, strategy
- Lead by example; promote desired culture
- Ensure resources are available to meet objectives
- Measure performance against objectives
- Establish framework of controls to assess and manage risk

Corporate social responsibility and sustainability

Ethics in business

Corporate social responsibility (CSR)

- Maximise positive stakeholder benefits while minimising negative effects of actions
- Strong view – benefits for all stakeholders
- Weak view – benefits for shareholders only

Types of CSR (Carroll)

- Economic responsibility
- Legal responsibility
- Ethical responsibility
- Philanthropic responsibility

CSR stances

- Short-term shareholder interest
- Long-term shareholder interest
- Multiple stakeholder obligation
- Shaper of society

Sustainability

Triple bottom line:
- People
- Planet
- Profit

- Difference between right and wrong
- Relevant at all stages of strategic planning, implementation and control
- Should be reinforced by corporate values

CIMA Code of Ethics

- Objectivity
- Professional competence and due care
- Professional behaviour
- Integrity
- Confidentiality

Key terms

Mission statement: 'Aims to provide employees and stakeholders with clarity about what the organisation is fundamentally there to do' (*Johnson et al, 2017*).

Objectives: Statements of specific outcomes that are to be achieved (*Johnson et al, 2017*).

Stakeholders: 'Those persons and organisations that have an interest in the strategy of the organisation. Stakeholders normally include shareholders, customers, staff and the local community' (*CIMA, 2005*).

Corporate governance: 'The system by which organisations are directed and controlled' (*Cadbury Committee, 1992*).

Corporate social responsibility (CSR): An organisation's obligation to maximise positive stakeholder benefits while minimising the negative effects of its actions.

Activity answers

Activity 1: Objectives

The correct answer is:

(a) No mention of profitability

(b) No reference to financial stakeholders (and the underlying need to generate value for shareholders)

(c) More reference to efficiency, effectiveness and economy ('value for money')

(d) Absence of reference to competitive environment

(e) Higher emphasis given to contributing to society/research

Activity 2: Stakeholders

The correct answer is:

Keep informed

The staff will have a high level of interest in the decision (because it directly affects them) but they are likely to have little power to be able to influence it, not least because AB Co has already decided that it has to make some of its staff redundant, so it seems very unlikely that they will be able to prevent redundancies occurring.

The appropriate method for managing relationships with stakeholders with a high level of interest but a low level of power is to keep them informed about potential strategies.

Activity 3: Stakeholder evaluation

The correct answer is:

Stakeholder	What they want	What they provide	Benefit to the organisation
Customers	• Products/services that meet their needs	• Revenue • Loyalty • Advocacy	• Maintaining revenue • Brand value
Investors	• Return on investment • Confidence in board/ management team	• Capital	• Funding to support growth • Lower cost of capital
Suppliers	• Continuing business • Loyalty	• Resources; inputs	• Resource availability • Quality/reliability of inputs
Employees	• Job security • Job satisfaction • Training and development	• Skills and productivity • Know-how	• Productivity • Quality of service to customers • Motivation, loyalty
Local communities	• Employment • Economic benefits (jobs, investment) • Care for environment	• Infrastructure • Support • Permission to operate	• Higher brand value/reputation

Stakeholder	What they want	What they provide	Benefit to the organisation
Regulators	• Compliance with rules and legislation • Compliance with social norms	• Permission to operate	• Permission to operate • Lower cost of operations

Activity 4: CSR stances

The correct answer is:

Shaper of society

Petra's firm has a primary focus that is not financial, and the success of the firm is used to sustain this.

Activity 5: Rational model

The correct answer is:

Mission and Objective: Objectives could include ethical targets eg eliminate unfairness in the supply chain via payment of a living wage.

Position Audit: The company's value chain could be analysed to see where ethical improvements can be made.

Environmental Analysis: Ethical rivals could be used as a benchmark for improvement.

Corporate Appraisal: Where poor ethics is identified as a weakness in the SWOT, the company could create strategies to convert this to a strength in the future.

Strategic Options Generation: Ethical options should be encouraged.

Strategic Evaluation and Choice: Ethics should be included under the headings of Suitable and Acceptable when options are assessed.

Strategic Implementation: Ethics should be embedded within implementation eg if construction firms are used to fit out new outlets they should follow the highest safety standards (re: health and safety in the workplace).

Review and Control: Any metrics used to measure strategic progress should include ethical measures eg reduction in carbon footprint.

Test your learning

1 Required

Which of the following statements aims to provide employees and stakeholders with clarity about what an organisation is fundamentally there to do?

A   Mission

B   Objectives

C   Values

D   Vision

2 Required

Is the following statement true or false?

An organisation's values can help to shape its mission statement.

A   True

B   False

3 Required

Which one of the following is NOT a feature of poor corporate governance?

A   Lack of dialogue with shareholders

B   The directors come from a wide variety of backgrounds

C   Lack of involvement of the board in strategic decisions taken by a company

D   The board is dominated by one person

4 Required

What is corporate social responsibility?

5 You have been working with the finance director preparing a presentation for your company's shareholders. You have noticed that the FD's presentation makes the company's performance look significantly more favourable than it actually is, because the FD has excluded the results from a poorly performing division from the presentation.

When you mentioned this omission to the FD, he replied that he was already aware of it, and he had deliberately chosen to exclude the division's results.

Required

Which fundamental ethical principle is being threatened here?

A   Objectivity

B   Integrity

C   Professional behaviour

D   Professional competence and due care

E   Confidentiality

Analysing the organisational ecosystem

Syllabus learning outcomes

Having studied this chapter you will be able to work through the following syllabus outcomes:

Syllabus Area B: The organisational ecosystem
1   The elements of the ecosystem
a - b   Markets and competition and society and regulation

Exam context

In the exam, you will be expected to demonstrate competence in the following representative task statements:

- Perform or review a SWOT (strengths, weaknesses, opportunities and threats) analysis to analyse an organisation's internal and external options related to overall strategy
- Prepare, or review, a Porter's five forces analysis to analyse an organisation's competition
- Prepare, or review, a Porter's Diamond analysis to analyse an organisation's position related to national competitive advantage
- Perform a PESTEL (Political, Economic, Social, Technology, Legal and Environment) analysis to analyse the impact of society on an organisation

Chapter overview

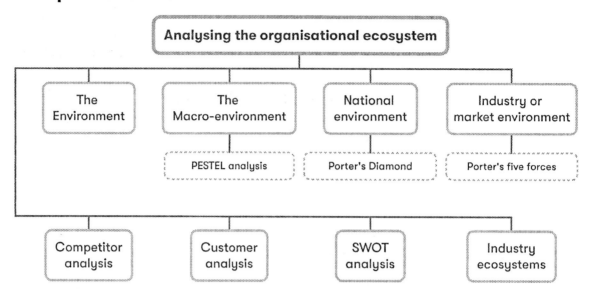

1 Introduction

An organisation needs to analyse the environment in which it operates in order to gain an understanding of its current strategic position, and to develop future strategies.

The external environment is a source of opportunities and threats to an organisation, which can influence an organisation's ability to survive and grow. Changes in the environment may mean that the organisation needs to change its strategy in response: either to take advantage of opportunities, or to protect itself from potential risks and threats.

In this chapter we will look at the different models and frameworks an organisation can use to analyse its environment, and how the choice of model depends on the level at which the environment is being analysed.

The topics covered in this chapter are:

- PESTEL analysis (macro-environment)
- Competitor analysis
- Industry ecosystems (Porter's five forces)
- Wider ecosystems (including national competitive advantage – Porter's Diamond)
- Customer analysis
- SWOT analysis

2 The environment

The environment can be described as everything which is beyond the organisational boundary.

It comprises a number of different elements, illustrated by the concentric rings in the diagram below:

Adapted from *Johnson et al, 2017*, p33

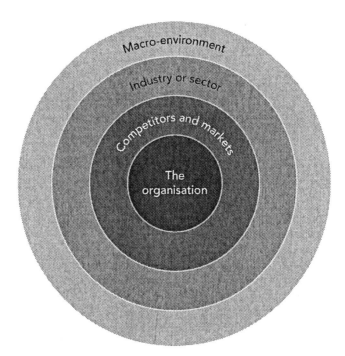

Ansoff (1965) summarised the importance of the external environment to an organisation when he said: '... the firm is a creature of its environment. Its resources, its income, its problems, its opportunities and its very survival are generated and conditioned by the environment...' (*Ansoff, 1965*).

The external environment is a source of **opportunities** (external changes which a business could exploit to its advantage), but also **risks** and **threats** (external changes which could damage a business).

Note. This diagram and the majority of our discussion in this chapter are based on a model of business in which organisations act separately and compete with other organisations. However, as we will see in the next chapter, organisations are also now collaborating in ecosystems, which can extend across different markets and sectors.

2.1 Levels of the external environment

The external environment can be analysed in terms of the broad factors which affect all businesses (**macro-environment**) or those relevant to a specific industry or market (**micro-environment**).

Macro-environment

The macro-environment includes broad factors which could affect all businesses; for example, political or economic factors, or technological change. These can be assessed using **PESTEL analysis**.

Micro-environment

The micro-environment relates to the factors which affect an organisation's ability to operate effectively in its chosen industry or **market sector**. Key factors here are: customers, competitors, distributors and suppliers. These can be assessed using **Porter's five forces**.

The two levels of the external environment can also be viewed in terms of **society** and **markets**.

Society

Society regulates the conduct, activities and operations of organisations through laws and moral norms. It provides the social, economic and legal infrastructure that enables business activities to take place (*Tagoe, 2016*).

Markets

The market is the environment in which organisations interact with their customers, suppliers, partners and competitors. Its defining characteristics are exchange, competition and profit (*Tagoe, 2016*).

Historically, organisations have tended to prioritise markets over society (eg focusing on profits for their shareholders). More recently, the increased importance of environment, social and governance (ESG) issues (eg sustainability) has shown the increasing importance of society for organisations when they are determining their business models and strategy.

3 Analysing the macro-environment

3.1 PESTEL analysis

Organisations can use PESTEL analysis as a framework for analysing the general business environment (macro-environmental), and the opportunities and threats present in the environment.

Political	**Economic**	**Social**
How do changes in government policy (international; national; local) affect an organisation? eg government decisions and policies, such as changes in competition policy or consumer policies	How do economic factors affect an organisation's ability to generate value? eg impact of the economic cycle (recession, or economic growth); inflation; interest rates; tax rates; foreign exchange rates	How do social and cultural factors affect customers' needs and requirements? eg demographics; changes in tastes or culture. (Demographic changes can affect workforces as well as consumers.)

Organisation – opportunities and threats

Technological	**Environmental (or Ecological)**	**Legal**
How do changes in the technological environment affect production and consumption? Changes in technology that affect ways of working, or the types of products and services demanded	How do environmental issues, such as pollution, climate change, environmental regulation, consumer attitudes to products affect a company? (eg environmentally friendly products; sustainability of resource use)	What laws and regulations (or changes to them) affect a company's activities? eg employment law; health and safety; data protection

Activity 1: Environmental analysis

You are a management accountant for an organic fruit farm in Teeland. The farm grows apples and produces apple juice, both of which it sells at local markets and to retail companies.

The farm's management team are considering its future strategy and have asked for your help in assessing its macro-environment.

Organic farming and the food industry in Teeland

Organic food must be produced using environmentally friendly farming methods, so no genetically modified (GM) crops, growth enhancers or artificial pesticides and fertilisers may be used. Any farmer claiming to be organic must be certified by a government-approved body, such as the Teeland Soil Association. Food producers must also comply with government-approved regulations regarding the production, packaging and labelling of food.

Regulatory bodies have the authority to forbid the use of misleading labels and product descriptions and can issue fines for inappropriate production. In extreme cases, regulatory bodies can close down operations which regularly fail to comply with regulations for production, packaging and labelling of their products.

Consumers increasingly want food that is healthy and is sourced both ethically and locally. Consequently, although organic food was initially perceived as a luxury niche product, it is now increasingly seen as a lifestyle choice by those consumers who regard non-organic products as more harmful to health and the environment. Major supermarkets in Teeland have started to stock more organic and locally grown food.

A key issue for all farmers is the weather, which significantly affects the volume (yield) and quality of a crop and hence the market price. Organic farmers are unable to use artificial fertilisers or pesticides, so have developed alternative high-tech farming methods to improve profitability and cash flow. Weather information systems help plan planting, harvesting and irrigation. Climate-controlled growing tunnels and stores provide a pest-free environment with temperature, light and humidity control. These methods increase yields, extend the possible growing season and allow crops to be stored for longer before usage or sale, with no loss of flavour or quality.

Required

Using the information provided, analyse the THREE key factors in the environment which are likely to have most impact on the farm.

BPP
LEARNING
MEDIA

Solution

Assessment focus point

The syllabus requires you to be able to perform a PESTEL analysis to analyse the impact of society on an organisation.

It is important to remember that external factors (eg PESTEL factors) are sources of **opportunities** and **threats** to an organisation. So a key question in any analysis could be: how might any changes in the environment affect an organisation, and its ability to operate successfully (eg by changing demand for its products/services, or affecting the way they are produced or distributed)?

4 National environment

Assessing the opportunities and threats which are present in different countries can be particularly important for multinational companies which are thinking about investing in a new country.

However, another key consideration in the investment decision could be how competitive the country is.

4.1 Porter's Diamond

Michael Porter (1990) observed that some nations' industries are more successful than others', and he identified four key factors which collectively determine a country's attractiveness for a given industry:

(Porter, 1990)

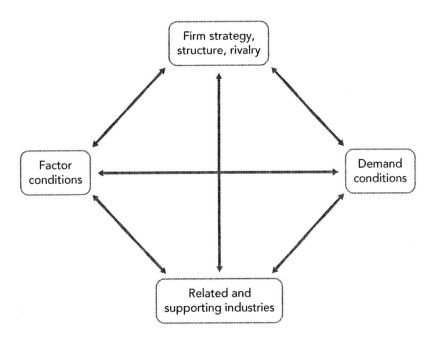

4.2 Components of the diamond

The inter-related elements that can be used to assess a nation's competitive advantage are:

- Factor conditions – relate to a country's resources (so in effect are 'supply side' factors). These can be categorised as:
  - Basic factors – for example, natural resources, climate, semi-skilled or unskilled labour. Basic factors are pre-conditions for an industry to be successful but, by themselves, do not provide any sustainable competitive advantage.
  - Advanced factors – for example, infrastructure and communications, higher education, and skilled employees (eg skilled scientists or engineers to support high-tech industries. In contrast to basic factors, the presence of advanced factors can help to promote competitive advantage.
- Demand conditions – a tough domestic market is likely to encourage competitiveness, as firms have to produce cost-efficient, high-quality goods to satisfy the requirements of their domestic customers. The experience a firm gains from meeting domestic customers' needs will then allow it to compete successfully on an international scale.
- Related and supporting industries – industries need to be supported by a good local supply chain, which contributes to quality and cost advantages.
- Firm strategy, structure and rivalry – cultural factors, social attitudes and management styles can all lead to competitive advantage in certain industries. Intense domestic rivalry among firms means they need to perform well to survive (eg through cost reduction or quality improvement and innovation). Intense domestic rivalry may also encourage firms to look for export markets.

4.3 Clustering

The combination of these elements can create a 'cluster' of extremely competitive firms that are well-placed to compete internationally.

Clustering helps to reinforce the factors in the diamond – for example, by providing a concentration of advanced factor conditions, and related/supporting industries (as with the high-tech electronics industry in Silicon Valley, California.)

4.4 Government policy

Government policy can also be important in nurturing the elements of the diamond, for example, by investing in infrastructure and higher education.

The tax regime and government's attitudes to foreign investors could also affect a multinational company's decision about whether or not to invest in a country.

Activity 2: Porter's Five Forces

Porter's analysis of the competitive advantage of nations identifies basic and advanced factor conditions that contribute to a nation's success in producing a particular good or service.

Required

Identify whether the following factors are basic or advanced.

Input	Advanced/basic
A well-respected university education system, with a focus on technology	▼
Availability of unskilled labour	▼
High-speed broadband service	▼
Temperate climate	▼

Picklist:

Advanced

Basic

Solution

Assessment focus point

The syllabus requires you to be able to prepare or review a Porter's Diamond analysis to analyse an organisation's position related to national competitive advantage. It is important to recognise that Porter's Diamond looks at the factors which affect the competitiveness of different **nations**, while Porter's Five Forces model (which we look at next) looks at the factors which affect the profitability of different **industries**.

5 Industry or market environment

An organisation's strategic position and performance are affected not only by the macro-environment (PESTEL factors) but also by factors specific to its industry or market sector.

Porter (1980) argues that the level of profit which can be sustained in an industry is influenced by the state of competition in that industry ('Porter's five forces'). The stronger the five forces, the lower the level of profit which can be sustained in the industry.

5.1 Using Porter's five forces model

The five forces model has three main uses:

- Analysing the inherent profitability (and therefore attractiveness) of a particular industry or market segment. If possible, companies should aim to invest in industries where the five forces are in their favour and high returns can be made.
- Identifying actions relating to the different competitive forces on an organisation that:
  - mitigate their damaging effects (**threats**); and/or
  - promote the beneficial effects (**opportunities**).
- Considering whether all competitors are affected equally by the forces. For example, higher buyer power may mean that small competitors cannot raise prices, giving an advantage to large ones who can, or who can afford to operate on lower margins.

5.2 Porter's five forces model

Porter's Five Forces

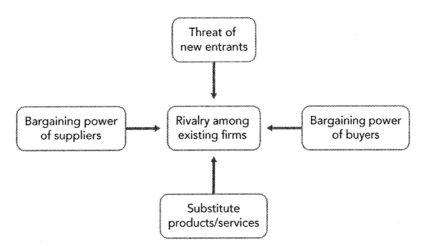

Activity 3: Five forces

The airline industry has historically accumulated large financial losses, often underwritten by national governments to support national infrastructure. This indicates that the five forces are very strong within the industry.

Required

Using the airline industry as an example, identify THREE factors that influence the strength of each of the five forces in a given industry.

Solution

In some industries, it is relevant to consider a 'sixth force', organisations that are complementors. This means an organisation that 'enhances your business attractiveness to customers or suppliers' (*Johnson et al, 2017, p69*). For example, app developers are complementors to smartphone and tablet providers because apps make the devices more useful. These organisations need to be taken into account in assessing the environment.

The notion of complementors is also particularly significant in the context of ecosystems, which we will look at in the next chapter.

> **Assessment focus point**
>
> The syllabus requires you to be able to prepare, or review, a Porter's five forces analysis to analyse an organisation's competition. An important point to remember here is that the intensity of competition in an industry (ie the strength of the forces) will affect the level of profit which can be maintained in that industry, and therefore how attractive that industry could be for an organisation to participate in.

5.3 Triggers for change

Changes in the industry environment can change the strength of the competitive forces; for example:

- Arrival of new entrants into the market; or mergers/acquisitions between existing competitors
- Slowdown in the market growth rate
- Innovations or technological developments leading to the emergence of new substitutes
- Consolidation in supply chain or distribution networks (eg mergers/acquisitions between suppliers)

Changes like these could affect the profitability of the industry, and therefore prompt an organisation to reconsider its strategic position (in relation to opportunities and threats) and its future strategy.

6 Competitor analysis

As well as assessing the overall competitive forces in an industry or market, an organisation should also seek to understand its competitive advantages/disadvantages in relation to its competitors' strategies – through competitor analysis. In order to be successful, an organisation needs to provide greater customer value and satisfaction that its competitors do.

> **Competitor analysis:** The 'identification and quantification of the relative strengths and weaknesses (compared with competitors or potential competitors) which could be of significance in the development of a successful competitive strategy' (*CIMA, 2005*).

Competitor analysis could also provide valuable insights into competitors' strategies, which an organisation could use to develop, or modify, its own strategies to achieve advantage over its competitors.

6.1 Questions to ask in competitor analysis

The following are key questions to ask in competitor analysis:

- Who are the competitors?
- What are the competitors' goals or strategic **objectives** (eg maintaining profitability, increasing market share)?
- What assumptions do the competitors hold about themselves and the industry (eg trends in the market, products and consumers)?
- What **strategies** are the competitors currently pursuing? (eg are they competing on the basis of low cost/low price or on quality? Are they trying to serve the whole market or a specific niche?)
- What are the competitors' **strengths** and **weaknesses**? What key **resources** and **capabilities** do the competitors have (or not have)?
- How is the competitor likely to **respond** to any strategic initiatives the organisation introduces? (eg if an organisation reduces prices in order to try to increase market share, will competitors also reduce their prices?)

6.2 Identifying competitors

One of the dangers organisations face when identifying competitors is that they adopt too narrow a definition of who their competitors are.

For example, an organisation might only consider other organisations offering technically similar products and services as its competitors. However, this ignores companies that produce substitute products which could perform a similar function, or those which solve a problem in a different way.

In addition, as well as considering existing competitors, organisations need to scan the environment for potential new entrants into the industry, or potential disruptors to the industry.

6.3 Levels of competitors

- **Brand** – competitors are perceived as firms offering a similar product or service, to the same customers, and at similar prices (eg Coca-Cola vs Pepsi).
- **Industry** – all firms supplying the same product or class of products are perceived as competitors, even if they serve different markets (eg Tesco vs Carrefour). Competitors are not necessarily a similar size or structure.
- **Product or 'Form'** – competitors are seen as all firms providing products or services that meet the same customer need, although the products themselves are different (eg bowling alleys vs cinemas as leisure activities).
- **Generic** – competitors are seen as all firms who compete for the same consumer expenditure (eg holidays vs home improvements).

> **Assessment focus point**
>
> It is important to remember that competitor analysis does not simply involve finding out information about competitors. An organisation also needs to consider how it can use the information it has gathered to help shape its own strategies.

6.3.1 Competitor responses

Once an organisation has analysed its competitors, it can then begin to assess their likely response to its strategies or tactics.

We can identify four types of competitor response (*Kotler, 1997*):

- **Laid-back:** competitor does not respond, even though it has seen and recognised your move.

- **Selective**: competitor only responds to certain types of attack. However, unlike 'Unpredictable' competitors (see below), 'Selective' competitors tend to be consistent in their responses; so, if they respond to price discounting on one occasion, they will do so on all occasions.
- **Retaliatory** (or 'Tiger'): competitor reacts and responds aggressively to any attack.
- **Unpredictable** (or 'Stochastic'): impossible to predict how competitor will react. Sometimes they will react aggressively; other times they will not respond at all.

7 Customer analysis

To be successful, a company needs to meet customer needs more effectively than its competitors. To be able to do this, a company first needs to understand its customers, and the markets in which it is competing, in order to develop appropriate strategies.

Real life example – Tesco

In its 2018 Annual Report, Tesco identifies that its business model is organised around three key pillars: customers, product and channels (ie how products are made available to customers).

In relation to 'customers', the Report (Tesco, 2018) states: 'Tesco exists to serve customers – listening to them and acting on what is most important [to them], however they choose to shop with us.'

7.1 Customer segments

The range of products and services available to contemporary consumers, coupled with the variety of needs and expectations which those consumers have, mean that very few products or services can satisfy all the consumers in a market.

At the same time, customers are becoming increasing discerning and demanding in their relationships with organisations; for example, they expect to receive marketing communications which are relevant to them.

Therefore, organisations can serve their customers more effectively if they target different products or services to particular market segments. To do this, organisations need to understand their different customer segments.

Customer segmentation	Industrial segmentation
Psychological – common mental characteristics	Company size – large/small
Purchasing – volume/frequency of purchases	Purchasing – volume/frequency of purchases
Demographics – rich/poor, old/young	Company type – retail/wholesale/own use
Geographic – regional analysis	Geographic – regional analysis
Benefit – health/enjoyment eg breakfast cereals	Benefit – reliability, versatility, safety

Market segmentation: The division of the market into homogeneous groups of potential customers who may be treated similarly for marketing purposes.

Segmentation enables an organisation to get a better understanding of customer requirements in a segment (eg based on age, lifestyle, location) so that the organisation can tailor its product to meet the needs of those customers as effectively as possible.

Market segmentation can also be useful when attempting to spot opportunities and threats. As customers' requirements change, new segments emerge. If a company can identify a 'new' segment before its competitors, this could be a source of growth.

7.2 Segment validity

A segment will only be valid if it is worth developing a unique marketing mix for that segment.

The following could affect the validity of a segment:

- Can the segment be measured?
- Is the segment big enough to be profitable?
- Can the segment be reached through the organisation's promotion and distribution channels (eg physical; online)?
- Can the segment be reached **profitably**?
- Does the segment respond differently to other segments? (If not, there is no point having a different marketing mix for the segment)

Tagoe (2016) suggests attractive segments typically have customers who are frequent shoppers, regularly respond to special offers and promotions, regularly leave product reviews, and use social media to tell friends about their purchases.

7.3 Marketing

Managing customers is sometimes referred to as 'downstream supply chain' management. One of the main objectives of marketing is to help attract customers and enhance the organisations image amongst them. In order to do this the organisation needs to understand who it markets to. Payne (1997) identified six different markets:

(a) **Customer markets** – selling directly to the customer

(b) **Referral markets** – selling to an intermediary, who sells onwards to the consumer

(c) **Supplier markets** – working with suppliers to generate customer interest in the product eg mobile device manufactures working with chip suppliers to jointly promote mobile technologies

(d) **Recruitment markets** – employers working with labour suppliers (universities, professional bodies) to ensure a steady supply of talented employees

(e) **Influence markets** – using public relations to drive demand for goods/services

(f) **Internal markets** – setting up internal markets so that divisions become customers and suppliers of each other

Once the market has been identified the overall approach to marketing can be determined. Put simply, the organisation can view customer acquisition as being merely transactional (focus on the sale) or as the first step in relationship building. The difference is 'relationship' versus 'traditional' marketing have been summarised in the table below:

Traditional marketing	Relationship marketing
Focus on the product/service	Focus on customer retention
Little interest/knowledge of the customer	Visible commitment to the customer
Product/service quality is critical	Ongoing customer contact
Customer retention neglected	Service quality is paramount
Focus on winning the first sale	Long-term relationship is the aim
Sales focus around product/service quality	Customer benefits are built and stressed

7.3.1 Understanding customer behaviour

A successful marketing approach will be underpinned by understanding the needs and behaviours of customers. In an industrial context the major characteristics of buyers include:

- **Motivation** – the buyer is trying to satisfy the needs of their organisation rather than their own needs. It pays to know why a customer is placing a specific order, eg the customer is desperately low on inventory.

- **Who makes the decision** – although a buyer may place the order, this may be at the behest of a wider group, eg a buyer may place orders on behalf of a group of companies or a group of departments.
- **Organisational influences** – these can affect a buyer's discretion eg are they bound by formal requisition processes?
- **Reciprocal buying** – is an order being placed to secure future orders from the supplier?
- **Purchasing power** – industrial purchasers will be likely to seek discounts based upon volumes, especially if competitors aggregate to purchase together eg all car manufactures may order common components together.

It is important to note that, when dealing with buyers, dissonance will occur when an individual's attitudes and behaviours are not consistent. For instance, cognitive dissonance occurs when a buyer regrets a purchase after it has been made, perhaps feeling that they did not get value for money or the opportunity to purchase a better item has been lost. In these circumstances it will be difficult to persuade the customer to place repeat orders. It is therefore the job of the marketing team to identify and eliminate aspects of the product/service/experience that can cause dissonant emotions to occur eg the makers of a luxury item may try and reassure the customer that the produce is 'reassuringly expensive' in order to overcome the guilt associated with a decadent purchase.

7.3.2 Customer acquisition via e-marketing

Assuming that the organisation is following the relationships approach to marketing, then the next step after acquisition is search engine marketing – optimising search outcomes by embedding links to improve the search engine ranking of your organisation/products/services/brands. Alternatively, sponsored searches with 'PPC' (pay per click) can see your results listed alongside relevant searches.

- **Online PR** – traditional public relations can be ported online eg using social media feeds, news alerts, forums, blogs to feed relevant news stories into the digital marketplace
- **Online partnerships** – mutually beneficial relationships between sellers can be built online via:
  - **Link-building** – reciprocal links on organisations' websites
  - **Affiliate marketing** – paying commission to see your company's products sold on a website eg listed on Amazon
  - **Sponsorship** – sponsoring trusted website is perceived to have more integrity that outright advertising online
  - **Co-branding** – low-cost advertising is possible where products are labelled with two brands eg Nike and Apple work together to promote fitness apparel and apps
  - **Aggregators** – comparison sites offer greater choice to consumers, especially for homogenous products such as insurance
- **Interactive adverts** – adverts that pop-up on a website or appear around the website's content. These may launch videos or direct links through to a company website
- **Opt-in email** – although strictly controlled by privacy legislation, these allow companies to directly market to consumers
- **Viral marketing** – using social media to distribute promotional messages via humorous/clever/shocking viewing content

7.3.3 Customer retention

Assuming that the organisation is following the relationships approach to marketing, then the next step after acquisition is to manage the ongoing relationship with the customer. Customer relationship management (CRM) consists of processes focused on the retention and development of the customer relationship. Key to this will be understanding and delivering the drivers of customer satisfaction, and in turn loyalty. These will include:

- **Tangibles** – the physical appearance of goods and packaging, or, for service providers any physical facilities, personnel or communication that customers receive
- **Reliability** – the dependability of goods/services provided
- **Responsiveness** – how willingly, and quickly, customer requests are dealt with

- **Assurance** – the ability to generate the trust and confidence of your customers
- **Empathy** – delivering a caring and personalised level of service

There are a number of technologies that organisations can deploy to develop these characteristics:

- **Personalisation** – marketing messages are tailored to promote products/services that the customer wants or needs
- **Mass customisation** – delivering customised content by using AI to understand your customers
- **Extranets** – allowing customers to build their own products/services via a sales portal
- **Online communities** – gathering feedback on products/services, which can be used to drive innovation

Other technologies that can be used to manage customer relationships include:

- **Electronic Data Interchange** – EDI links together the sales and purchasing systems, which automates processes, and also builds exit barriers for the customer
- **Cloud computing** – allows customers to place and track orders on the move
- **E-commerce** – online sales opens up more markets
- **Intelligence gathering** – Big Data can improve customer understanding leading to improvements in goods/services as well as personalisation and customisation

The increased power of technology has encouraged companies to harness intranets and extranets as methods to reduce costs, gather more information and improve customer service. In some instances, this has led to structural changes via:

- **Disintermediation** – intermediate companies can be eliminated from the supply chain eg Spotify removes the need to visit a record shop
- **Reintermediation** – it is sometimes possible to introduce an intermediary eg some insurance companies set up their own comparison sites in order to intercept other providers' customers
- **Countermediation** – where established firms create their own intermediaries to combat established intermediaries eg where a traditional 'bricks and mortar' retailer sets up a website to compete against online retailers

8 SWOT analysis

> **SWOT analysis:** Summarises the key issues from the external environment (opportunities, threats) and the strategic capabilities of an organisation (strengths, weaknesses) that are most likely to shape strategy development.

We have already identified that the external environment (society, markets) is a source of **opportunities** and **threats**. Organisations that identify and exploit the opportunities and respond effectively to risks and threats are able to generate value for their stakeholders.

However, in order to develop and evaluate potential strategies, an organisation's **internal capabilities** (strengths, weaknesses) need to also be assessed, alongside external opportunities and threats.

SWOT analysis provides a framework for analysing an organisation's current strategic position, looking at its strengths and weaknesses as well as the opportunities and threats it faces. These elements (S, W, O, T) all need to be considered together, in order to develop and assess potential strategies.

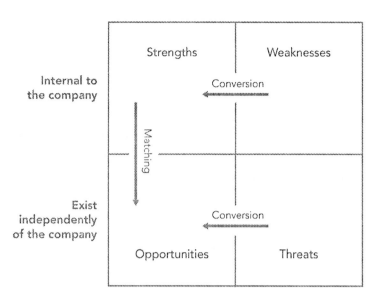

Potential strategies following a SWOT analysis include:

- Matching – strengths with opportunities
- Conversion – turning a weakness into a strength, or a threat into an opportunity

Assessment focus point

The syllabus requires you to be able to perform or review a SWOT analysis to analyse an organisation's internal and external options related to overall strategy. When performing a SWOT analysis it is important to remember that strengths and weakness are internal factors, relating to an organisation's own resources, capabilities, products/services.

By contrast, opportunities and threats are external, and reflect the environment (market; society) in which the organisation operates.

Be careful to classify factors correctly, according to whether they are internal or external.

Illustration 1: SWOT

Vidlen Co manufactures and retails luxury consumer goods, including watches, jewellery and handbags. It has customers across a number of different countries worldwide.

Vidlen has recently analysed its strategic position and has identified a number of factors which it believes could affect its future strategy and performance.

Required

Identify whether each of the following factors is a strength, weakness, opportunity or threat:

Input	SWOT
Two of Vidlen's competitors have launched popular new ranges of jewellery	▼
Excellent reputation for product design	▼
Reliance on a very small number of suppliers for key raw materials	▼
Increased consumer spending on premium brands globally	▼

Picklist:

Strength

Weakness

Opportunity

Threat

Solution

The correct answer is:

Input	SWOT
Two of Vidlen's competitors have launched popular new ranges of jewellery	Threat
Excellent reputation for product design	Strength
Reliance on a very small number of suppliers for key raw materials	Weakness
Increased consumer spending on premium brands globally	Opportunity

9 Industry ecosystems

Commentators are suggesting that economies and businesses are in the middle of a 4th industrial revolution (Industry 4.0), in which physical and digital technologies are combining through analytics, artificial intelligence, cognitive technologies, and the internet of things (IoT) to create digital enterprises capable of quicker and more informed decision making (*Girzadas, 2018*).

Industry 4.0 is increasing the pace of change and is also raising concerns that the digital era is too complex for companies to compete in isolation. Instead, they are looking increasingly to apply a 'collective' philosophy to their business strategies – and collaborating with other companies in the context of ecosystems. We will look at ecosystems in more detail in Chapter 4.

9.1 Ecosystems and environmental analysis

The context of increased collaboration and co-operation (inherent in ecosystems) also raises new questions for an organisation to consider when thinking about its strategy and strategic position:

- **Strategic position:** When assessing their company's strategic position, executives need to assess the ecosystem's strengths and weaknesses, as well as the company's own; for example, is the company linked with the best suppliers and partners (distributors, retailers)?

- **Competitors:** Competitors could also be analysed from an ecosystem perspective. What customer and supplier relationships have competitors developed? What are the nature and benefits of those relationships? How do they compare to the company's own relationships?

- **Innovation:** What new innovations might make the current business obsolete? What would it take to develop a cluster of fresh ideas into a new, more competitive business ecosystem?

10 Supply chain management

The supply chain refers to all of the activities and information flows necessary for the provision of an organisation's' goods and services. The traditional 'push' model of buying enough material to satisfy the production needed to meet forecast sales demand is being overtaken by the 'pull' model, where the whole process of sales, production and purchasing is 'pulled' through by customer orders. The pull system is being driven by constant improvements in technology eg cloud computing allows customers to order 'on the move', requiring manufacturers to develop more flexible and responsive manufacturing techniques to meet this instant demand, or they risk losing their customers to more agile competitors.

Flexibility in the 'upstream' supply chain requires manufacturers to considers factors such as:

- Sources – where are the raw materials coming from?
- Suppliers – is single or multisource more cost-effective?

BPP LEARNING MEDIA

- Cost and quality – customer requirements must be met
- Make or buy – is it more effective to insource or outsource?

The pull model may also require a cultural reset, as traditional supply relationships were antagonistic eg manufacturers tried to use their buyer power to get the lowest price from their suppliers and vice versa. This involved competitive tendering, penalty clauses and threats to switch suppliers to keep prices as low as possible. The pull model however relies on partnerships to ensure reliable and flexible supply chains, able to cope with less predictable demand patterns. Given the increased demands on both parties this may require a comprehensive service level agreement.

In the fourth industrial revolution we are seeing technology play an increasing role in downstream supply chain management. Common aspects of e-procurement include:

- E-sourcing – using technology to find new suppliers, and to manage tenders and quotes
- E-purchasing – systems used to requisition and despatch items
- E-payments – electronic invoicing and payments

The benefits of e-procurement can be easily identified, and include:

- Reduced labour costs
- Reduced inventory holdings and greater inventory controls
- Greater transparency, as new technologies such as blockchain can created more trusted ledgers
- Faster, more responsive ordering systems

The risks however are also easily identified:

- Technology risks – system malfunctions, hacking
- Organisational risks – staff not adapting to new systems
- Costs exceed benefits – costs may be understated, and benefits overestimated

Chapter summary

Analysing the organisational ecosystem

The Environment

- Factors affecting all businesses (Macro-environment)
- Factors affecting competition in a given market or sector (Micro-environment)

The Macro-environment

PESTEL analysis

Framework for analysing potential opportunities and threats:

- Political
- Economic
- Social
- Technological
- Environmental
- Legal

National environment

Porter's Diamond

Factors affecting a country's attractiveness for different industries or types of organisation

- Factor conditions (Basic; advanced)
- Demand conditions
- Related and supporting industries
- Firm strategy, structure and rivalry

Industry or market environment

Porter's five forces

Factors affecting the profitability, and attractiveness, of different industries or markets

- Threat of new entrants
- Substitutes
- Bargaining power of customers
- Bargaining power of suppliers
- Competition and rivalry

- Also need to consider 'complementors'

Competitor analysis

Assess organisation's strategic position in relation to its competitors, in order to help develop strategy

- Who are competitors?
- What are competitors' goals or objectives?
- What assumptions do competitors hold?
- What strategies are competitors pursuing?
- What are competitors' strengths and weaknesses?
- How are competitors likely to respond to organisation's strategic initiatives?

Customer analysis

- Understand customers and their needs in order to develop strategies to meet those needs more effectively than competitors do
- Market segmentation: helps an organisation tailor its product / service to meet the needs of particular groups of customers more effectively

SWOT analysis

- Strengths
- Weaknesses
- Opportunities
- Threats

- S, W = internal
- O, T = external

Industry ecosystems

- Impact of digitisation and automation on the competitive environment
- Increased collaboration and cooperation
- Competition between ecosystems, rather than between companies?

Key terms

Competitor analysis: The 'identification and quantification of the relative strengths and weaknesses (compared with competitors or potential competitors) which could be of significance in the development of a successful competitive strategy' (*CIMA, 2005*).

Market segmentation: The division of the market into homogeneous groups of potential customers who may be treated similarly for marketing purposes.

SWOT analysis: Summarises the key issues from the external environment (opportunities, threats) and the strategic capabilities of an organisation (strengths, weaknesses) that are most likely to shape strategy development.

Activity answers

Activity 1: Environmental analysis

The correct answer is:

(a) **Social** – consumers' attitudes to organic food are changing because of concerns about health and the environment. Organic food is perceived as more socially responsible than non-organic alternatives. These changing consumer attitudes will increase industry demand from organic farms. However, farmers' accountability – and compliance with organic certification – is necessary to maintain consumer confidence in buying organic produce.

Note. You could also have included these points in relation to the 'Environmental/Ecological' aspect of the PESTEL model – because a key factor in the growth of the organic farming industry has been the drive for more environmentally friendly products.

(b) **Technological** – the industry needs to use technology (such as sophisticated weather management systems and atmospherically controlled tunnels) to avoid using fertilisers and pesticides. Technological developments will increase yields, and also reduce problems of seasonality and perishability by extending the life of the product through storage. This will benefit farmers' cash flows.

(c) **Legal (regulatory)** – there is significant regulation in the food industry generally, and particularly in relation to organic produce. Organic farms need to obtain the relevant certification before they can start selling produce as organic; and then they need to comply with all the appropriate regulations regarding production, packaging and labelling. There are severe sanctions for breaching regulations. As a result, compliance is very important, and the associated costs of compliance are likely to be high.

Any changes in regulations or standards in the future could lead to additional compliance costs.

However, the existence of strict regulations should help to ensure consumer confidence in the industry.

Activity 2: Porter's Five Forces

The correct answer is:

Input	Advanced/basic
A well-respected university education system, with a focus on technology	Advanced
Availability of unskilled labour	Basic
High-speed broadband service	Advanced
Temperate climate	Basic

Advanced factors are ones which help to promote competitive advantage. The quality of the higher education system (producing high-skilled employees) and the quality of the infrastructure and communications networks are advanced factors.

Basic factors are the 'threshold' factors which are needed to be successful, but don't, in themselves, provide any sustainable competitive advantage. Unskilled labour is a basic factor (in contrast to high-skilled labour, which is an advanced factor).

Activity 3: Five forces

The correct answer is:

Threat of new entrants

- Cost of buying/leasing planes
- Availability of landing slots
- Getting a licence from the aviation regulator

Bargaining power of suppliers

- Pilots – tend to be more applicants than jobs
- Choice of plane – Airbus vs Boeing vs Bombardier etc, may help reduce price of airplanes
- Destination airports – can use out of town locations like budget carriers to reduce landing fees

Bargaining power of buyers

- Customers may have lots of choice depending on destination and other carriers
- Lots of freely available information via internet comparison sites like Skyscanner
- Loyalty can be encouraged via frequent flyer schemes

Substitutes

- No effective substitute for long-haul flights
- Short-haul competes with car/trains, which may be quicker given no need to check in
- In the holiday market, flying competes against other leisure activities such as cruise ships

Rivalry among existing firms

- Lots of companies in the market, often with routes overlapping
- Some carriers are state-owned so this may distort competition if they are subsidised
- Co-operation is common via 'code sharing' and alliances such as 'One World' to reduce flight overlaps

Test your learning

1   **Required**
    Which TWO of the following are classifications in PESTEL analysis?

    A   Economic

    B   Ecosystems

    C   Political

    D   Substitutes

2   TWS is one of the 'Big Four' supermarket companies in Essland. Collectively, the 'Big Four' account for over 80% of the market share.

    Like the other 'Big Four' TWS has supply contracts with a number of different suppliers, and its business represents a high proportion of these suppliers' total sales.

    Required
    With reference to Porter's five forces model, indicate whether the following are 'high' or 'low' in relation to supermarket industry in Essland.

    Threat of new entrants: [▼]

    Bargaining power of suppliers: [▼]

    Picklist:

    High

    Low

3   **Required**
    Which of the following models is most appropriate to use for analysing the relative attractiveness of different countries as a potential location for a company?

    A   PESTEL analysis

    B   Porter's five forces

    C   SWOT analysis

    D   Porter's Diamond

4   **Required**
    Identify which of the following statements are true.

    A   Competitor analysis helps managers to understand their company's competitive advantages and disadvantages compared to its competitors.

    B   Competitor analysis helps to provide an informed basis to assist a company in developing its own competitive strategies.

5   **Required**
    In a SWOT analysis, which of the classifications relate to factors which are internal to an organisation?

    A   Strengths

    B   Weaknesses

    C   Opportunities

    D   Threats

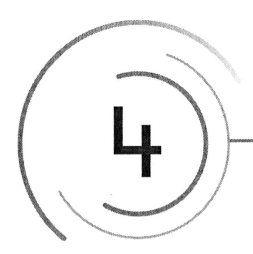

Impact of the ecosystem on organisations and strategy

Syllabus learning outcomes

Having studied this chapter you will be able to work through the following syllabus outcomes:

Syllabus Area B: The organisational ecosystem	
2	The drivers of change in ecosystem.
a-e	Institutional/systemic, social, market, technology, and sustainability.
3	The impact of the ecosystem on organisational strategy.
a	The impact of strategic networks and platforms on organisational strategy.

Exam context

In the exam, you will be expected to demonstrate competence in the following representative task statements:

- Analyse the drivers of change in an ecosystem including globalisation, geopolitical impact, demographics, customer empowerment, digital technology, automation, and sustainability

- Analyse what an organisation can do to create value in an ecosystem and how that organisation can capture the value they helped to create

- Analyse the participants and interactions in networks and platforms and their associated roles, reach, capabilities, rules, connections, and courses

- Analyse how technologies such as cloud computing, social media, mobile, and analytics impact ecosystem

- Analyse how technologies that create a more open, connected and complex business environment impact corporate social responsibility

Chapter overview

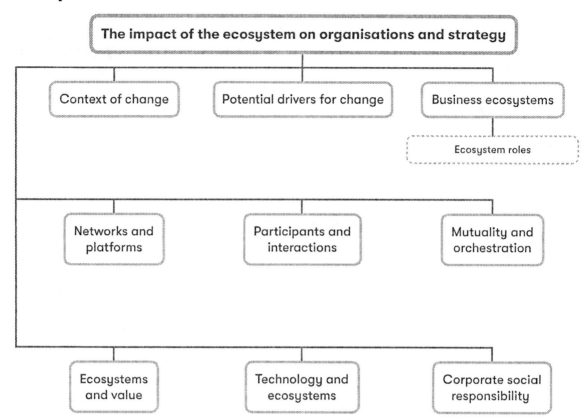

1 Introduction

As we have seen in Chapter 3, the external environment has an impact on organisations by providing **opportunities** and **threats** (eg from society – **PESTEL**; in markets – **Porter's five forces**).

However, events in the external environment can also act as drivers for change in an organisation. We begin this chapter by looking at some of the key factors which are leading to disruption and change in the contemporary business environment.

In recent times, technology (especially digitisation) has been the most significant source of disruption for many organisations, for example affecting the way products/services are produced and delivered. One specific consequence of this has been the increased collaboration between organisations within **business ecosystems**.

In Chapter 3, we mainly considered the 'ecosystem' as the wider business environment in which an organisation operates. However, business ecosystems can be, more specifically, 'dynamic networks of entities interacting with each other to create and exchange sustainable value for participants' *(Panetta, 2017)*, and we will look at this idea of business ecosystems in more detail in this chapter.

Rather than trying to meet customer needs by themselves, organisations are looking to become part of these platform-based ecosystems, which leverage the skills and capabilities of different entities within their network to deliver products, services and experiences that would be too difficult – or too costly – for individual organisations to deliver on their own.

In this chapter, we will look at the key characteristics of business ecosystems, the different roles organisations can play in those ecosystems, and the way organisations can create value within an ecosystem.

We will also consider the importance of digital technologies, such as cloud computing, in facilitating the development of ecosystems, by significantly reducing the cost and effort required for organisations to connect and collaborate.

Topics to be covered:

- Globalisation
- Geopolitics
- Demographics
- Customer empowerment
- Digital technology
- Automation
- Sustainability
- Value creation in ecosystems
- Participants and interactions in networks and platforms
- Technology enablers in networks
- Process of creating networks and platforms
- Stakeholder analysis in networks
- Corporate social responsibility

2 Context of change

Events in the external environment can act as drivers for change in an organisation, and PESTEL analysis and Porter's five forces model could both be useful ways of identifying drivers for change.

Activity 1: Environmental analysis

F2U is a long-established manufacturer and retailer of domestic furniture such as sofas and dining sets (tables, chairs). All goods are made to order and are typically delivered with a lead-time of 6–12 weeks. All products costing more than $500 come with the offer of three years' interest-free credit.

Required
Using the PESTEL and five forces frameworks, identify aspects of F2U's environment that could change.

Solution

Real life example – Industry 4.0

'Industry 4.0' (the 4th Industrial Revolution or the digital revolution) reflects the way that technology and digitisation are fuelling systemic changes: transforming entire systems, across companies, industries and society.

In a relatively short space of time, digital disruptors (such as Airbnb, Uber or Alibaba) have begun to reshape their industries. Boundaries between industries are being blurred and re-shaped. Competition is coming from new and unexpected sources.

3 Potential drivers for change

The syllabus lists some specific drivers for change: globalisation, geopolitical impact, demographics, customer empowerment, digital technology, automation and sustainability.

We will discuss each of these in turn.

3.1 Globalisation

Historically, business environments have been perceived on a national basis (eg Porter's Diamond looks at national competitive advantage). However, business is now increasingly becoming unrestricted by borders. Reductions in transportation, information and communication costs, coupled with the growth of new technologies and e-business have changed the geography of world trade.

The main characteristics of globalisation are:

- Multinational / multi-company supply chains
- Offshoring work (relocating business activities from one country to another)
- Increasing mobility (of capital, resources)

This has implications for firms in terms of how they grasp new opportunities and combat new threats, and, for countries, in terms of how they invest to nurture their industries eg investing in advanced factors as seen in Porter's Diamond.

Globalisation involves the entry of foreign markets, with this move often driven by factors such as:

- Shareholder pressure – requiring increased returns
- Saturated home markets – shrinking growth rates
- Opportunities – emerging economies offer the potential of untapped markets
- Trade barriers lowering – free trade agreements make international trade easier

The emergence of global trading does however offer contrasting benefits and risks:

Benefits	Risks
Greater economies of scale	Marketing mix complications/adaptations needed
New cultural developments	Cultural barriers
Cheaper raw materials	Varying cost structures (not always cheaper abroad)
Market development opportunities	New competitors
Risk reduction via diversified markets	Exchange rate/political volatility
Political incentives to encourage inward investment	Entry requirements – legal barriers

3.2 Geopolitics

The increasing interconnectedness of markets and supply chains across the global economy also increases the importance of thinking about risks relating to geopolitical issues around the world, which could affect multinational businesses.

Geopolitics: The way a country's geography, economics and politics affect its power and relationships with other countries.

Geopolitical events could include: general elections/regime change; economic policy announcements; rising tensions with other nations; wars; immigration and mass population movements; natural disasters (eg flooding, drought); and the threat of terrorism.

As with globalisation, the changing nature of geopolitics can create both opportunities and threats.

Natural resources have traditionally been a key driver of geopolitical relations – eg access to resources such as water or oil has been a source of conflict between countries. However, **technology** can now also affect the geopolitical landscape.

'Technology has long been an ingredient in how states gain, use or lose power. But today, three interconnected elements – innovation, talent and resilience [to disruption] – increasingly determine whether states are well-positioned to advance their own security and wellbeing' (Engelke, 2018).

3.3 Demography

Demographic factors relate to the structure of a population, and include the following:

- **Ageing populations** – altering the consumer market and government tax and spending plans.
- **The rise of the millennial generation** – people born between the early 1980s and early 2000s are typically more adept at using digital technologies. They are digital natives, so have different expectations from customers of previous generations. They also think how technology can be used to improve their lives, making them harder to surprise with new products or services.
- **Growth of the middle classes** – especially in developing countries. The rise of the middle class provides potential opportunities for multinational companies to expand into developing countries.

3.4 Customer empowerment

As a general trend, consumers are getting smarter and more demanding (*IBM, 2010*), but to remain successful organisations need to ensure they respond effectively to customer requirements.

3.4.1 Characteristics of customer empowerment

The following are characteristics of customer empowerment, and changing customer demands:

- Convenience – customers value convenience, or 'instant gratification' and also expect effortless and smooth experiences when dealing with a company. (Technology needs to help, not hinder, customers' quest to get what they want, where and when they want it.)
- Information – customers use the increasing amounts of information available to them to find the 'best' product, or the best price. This includes social media – and negative comments about a product or service can influence consumers' purchasing decisions.
- The price of a mistake is high – customers are less loyal than in the past.
- Personalisation – customers expect personalised experience, rather than simply 'products' or 'services'. In addition, they want better value, quality and variety. So an important question for companies is how they can enhance the value proposition they offer to customers.
- Collaboration – consumers are increasingly happy to collaborate with producers in designing new products and services that meet their needs. This collaboration is sometimes referred to as 'co-creation'.

Real life example – Lego

LEGO© has encouraged the co-creation of products with its customers for a number of years now. 'LEGO Ideas' is an online community where members can submit their own designs for new LEGO sets, and review designs submitted by other members (*LEGO, 2018*). Members can give feedback and vote for the designs they like. If a project gets 10,000 votes, LEGO reviews the idea and selects a winner from all the projects to be created and sold worldwide. The creator of the design earns a percentage of the revenue it subsequently generates.

Illustration 1: Customer empowerment

Required

Identify which of the following statements are true.

A Customer empowerment has resulted in an increase in customer loyalty.

B A characteristic of customer empowerment is that customers expect personalised experience, rather than just products and services.

C Customers are increasingly collaborating with producers in the design of products and services.

Solution

The correct answers are:

- A characteristic of customer empowerment is that customers expect personalised experience, rather than just products and services.
- Customers are increasingly collaborating with producers in the design of products and services.

Customer empowerment has meant that customers are more critical of mistakes an organisation makes, resulting in a decrease in customer loyalty, not an increase.

3.5 Digital technology

Digital technology can have a number of different dimensions, and its impact on society and markets is immense:

- Changing products or services – eg audio and video streaming services to replace physical products such as CDs and DVDs
- Transforming delivery – eg e-commerce instead of physical shops, or software as subscription rather than a one-off licence
- Automation of operations and processes to increase productivity and efficiency – eg automated reordering across the supply chain
- Enabling 'customers' to be linked – eg via crowd-sourcing platforms, eliminating the need for traditional business intermediaries
- New forms of interaction – eg social media

Increasing penetration of the internet and smartphones means consumers are increasingly becoming used to a world in which they have access to products, services and experiences at any time, and on-demand. E-commerce (and the ability to access global markets, and source products from around the world) also increases competition among retailers and manufacturers.

We discuss digital transformation and digital technologies in more detail in Chapters 11 and 12. However, it is important to recognise 'digital' as a major driver for change. In a rapidly expanding digital marketplace, legacy companies without a clear digital transformation strategy are being left behind.

3.6 Automation

New technologies are going to dramatically change the nature of work across industries and occupations. However, one major uncertainty is the extent to which automation will substitute for human labour. How long with this take, and how far will it go?

Schwab (2016) highlights two competing effects that technology could have on employment:

Technology-fuelled disruption and automation substitute capital for labour, forcing workers to become unemployed or reallocate their skills elsewhere

The destruction effect is accompanied by a capitalisation effect in which the demand for new goods and services increases and leads to the creation of new occupations, businesses and even industries.

Schwab (2016) acknowledges that there is considerable uncertainty about the extent to which the 'capitalisation' effect will follow the 'destruction' effect. What is much more certain though is that many categories of work – particularly those which are repetitive and process-driven – have already been automated, and many others will follow.

Where the 4th Industrial Revolution creates jobs, these are likely to be cognitive and creative, but the market for routine and repetitive jobs is likely to be greatly diminished.

Activity 2: Automation

Automation will not affect all jobs equally.

Required

Assess, with reasons, how susceptible the following job roles are to automation:

- Data entry clerk
- Doctors/surgeons
- Plumbers

Solution

3.7 Sustainability

In recent years, there has been increasing public concern for the natural environment, corporate social responsibility and sustainability. This has also led to an increased focus on the potential impact that businesses have on the natural environment, eg the potential exhaustion of supplies of natural resources and climate change.

KEY
TERM

> **Environmental footprint:** A measure of the impact that an organisation's activities have on the environment, including its resource use and its environmental and pollution emissions.
>
> **Social footprint:** A measure of the impact or effect that an organisation can have on a given set of concerns or stakeholder interests.

Social footprint reflects the impact an organisation has on people, society and the wellbeing of communities. Impacts can be positive – such as job creation and community benefits – or negative – such as when a plant closure increases unemployment and the local community suffers. This can be measured via the Triple Bottom Line approach seen in Chapter 2.

Activity 3: E-Zee

E-Zee plc operates a chain of convenience supermarkets. The company is concerned that its business model is failing to address the environmental concerns of many of its customers, so it is considering investing in a sustainability strategy.

Required

Which of the following is LEAST likely to result from E-Zee plc adopting a sustainability strategy?

A   Lower energy consumption

B   Lower prices for customers

C   Lower emissions

D   Lower transportation costs

Solution

Assessment focus point

The syllabus requires you to be able to analyse the drivers of change in an ecosystem including globalisation, geopolitical impact, demographic, customer empowerment, digital technology, automation, and sustainability. An important part of this analysis could be how the drivers of change create opportunities or threats for an organisation, and what the implications of these could be for different organisations.

4 Business ecosystems

As we noted earlier, new technologies mean the world is becoming more connected. Companies are also recognising the need for more relevant customer engagement, and many are using digital transformation initiatives to try to create better experiences for their customers.

However, this increasing connectedness also means that companies will look to collaborate, rather than always competing as standalone entities. In particular, the focus of innovative organisations is expected to shift from being 'organisation-centric' to becoming increasing 'ecosystem-centric' (Davidson et al, 2014).

> **Business ecosystem:** 'A complex web of interdependent enterprises and relationships aimed at creating and allocating business value' (*Davidson et al, 2014*).

Companies need to rethink how their business environment operates, how they partner, and how they interact with customers. For example, Amazon's ecosystem provides sellers with access to a much larger pool of customers than they might be able to achieve by operating on their own; and the online food order and delivery service Just Eat provides customers with the widest choice of food outlets, enabling restaurants to reach many more customers than they would be able to operating alone.

Real life example

Relationships – when a mobile phone company, such as Samsung or Huawei, launches a new phone, it needs to engage not only with users but also with the carriers that own and manage mobile networks and the major app providers such as Google. When a user buys a phone, their decision is likely to be influenced by the number and type of apps that are available on the platform.

Platforms – internet-based companies like Airbnb, Spotify and Uber have changed industry dynamics and competition with their new business models. A key feature of these business models is that they involve more complex relationships than traditional models which just feature a 'buyer' and a 'seller'. For example, Uber itself does not own any taxis, but its business model involves co-ordinating customers who want to book a taxi with available taxis – and earning a commission for doing so.

4.1 Benefits of ecosystems

Two important ways organisations can drive value from ecosystems are:

- Improved access and lower cost of skills – allowing organisations to access critical capabilities that would otherwise be impossible or very difficult to obtain
- Using the ecosystem to expand the scope of strategic business opportunities and initiatives – opening up new market segments or geographies; creating new types of products, potentially combining capabilities and assets from different organisations.

Real life example – Nest

Nest, a US-based home automation company, leveraged a single product based on remotely managing home heating and air conditioning systems to form a new technology platform for connected devices. Nest achieved this by forming partnerships with brands such as LG and leveraging the capabilities of these partners to create new experiences for home owners (*Giesen et al, 2017*)

4.2 Ecosystem roles

To be successful in an ecosystem environment, organisations need to understand how they can add value within their network.

There are four main ways they can do this, or 'roles' they can play (*Giesen et al, 2017*):

- **Experience providers** – they provide specialist competences in differentiated or unique functions.
- **Asset providers** – they provide or manage assets used for production, either within the supply chain or for other activities within the ecosystem.
- **Process providers** – they manage processes and service-level agreements across shared services and activities to increase the seamlessness and agility of processes within the ecosystem (eg making a platform easy for customers to use and find what they want on it).
- **Platform providers** – they provide the environment that supports the ecosystem and enables it to operate (eg by providing a platform which matches buyers and sellers). A key success factor

for platform providers is the ability to attract and retain stakeholders on their platform (eg by providing greater access to customers).

Organisations can play more than one role in an ecosystem, for example being both a platform provider and a process provider (eg eBay provides a platform matching buyers and sellers, and also provides the process for hosting a sale or auction).

However, to sustain a valuable role, an organisation needs to match its own capabilities with the roles or activities needed in the ecosystems in which it participates.

Assessment focus point

The syllabus requires you to be able to analyse what an organisation can do to create value in an ecosystem. Part of this analysis could require you to identify what capabilities an organisation could contribute to the ecosystem, and what role it can play in the ecosystem.

Illustration 2: Platforms

Required

Identify which of the following statements are true:

A   Process providers create integrated environments that support and enable ecosystems to operate.

B   Platform providers need the ability to obtain and retain stakeholders on their platform in order to be successful.

Solution

The correct answer is:

Platform providers need the ability to obtain and retain stakeholders on their platform in order to be successful.

Response option	Explanation
Process providers create integrated environments that support and enable ecosystems to operate.	Platform providers (not process providers) create the integrated environments that support and enable ecosystems to operate.
Platform providers need the ability to obtain and retain stakeholders on their platform in order to be successful.	Successful platform providers possess the ability to obtain and retain stakeholders on their platform, eg through the greater capability or sophistication of their platform.

Activity 4: Ecosystems

In 2015, Audi, BMW and Daimler bought the 'HERE' mapping business from Nokia.

Mapping is increasingly important for automobile companies and acquiring HERE means the car companies have an accurate source of information for maps in their cars without having to depend on external technology providers like Google.

Required

What role does 'HERE' play in the automobile companies' ecosystem?

A   Platform provider

B   Asset provider

C   Experience provider

D   Process provider

Solution

5 Networks and platforms

Networks and platforms are key elements of digital ecosystems.

5.1 Networks

> **Network:** 'A set of connections that enables people or things to connect, share information, and exchange products, services or insights' (*Libert et al, 2016, pix*).

A fundamental principle of networks is that value expands with the number of connections in the network. This can give the largest company an advantage which is very difficult for other networks to overcome.

There are two types of network effect (*Reddy, 2018*):

(a) Direct network effect: the value of a product or service to a user increases exponentially with the number of other users using the same product. Increasing supply means more demand, which leads to more supply (for example, as with eBay or Skype).

(b) Indirect network effect: the value of a product or service increases with the complementary products or services that add to it (for example, as with Microsoft Windows or Google Android).

5.2 Platforms

Platforms are the business models which support and enable these networks. In effect, platforms are business models that use technology to connect people, organisations and resources.

The 'platform' is typically created and owned by a single business but designed to attract the active participation of large numbers of other actors. (*Kelly, 2015*)

The platform model is the basis of some of the most successful companies operating today, for example Google and Amazon.

> **Platform:** A 'business based on enabling value-creating interactions between external producers and consumers. The platform provides an open, participatory infrastructure for those interactions and sets governance conditions for them' (*Parker et al, 2016*, p5).

The overriding purpose of platforms is to connect participants, thereby facilitating the exchange of goods, services or information between those participants. For example, AirBnb 'matches' a traveller's need for somewhere to stay with available rooms in their desired location.

A platform has two key functional elements (*World Economic Forum, 2017*):

- Interactions – suppliers/producers, consumers and platform orchestrators collaborate in the creation, consumption and compensation of units of value (eg physical goods, services, information, currency or labour).

- Infrastructure – relates to the underlying technology and architecture which provides functionality for the platform. Key issues include security, reliability and interoperability between platforms.

5.3 Delivering value

Network business models also fundamentally change the way that firms deliver value.

Libert et al (2016) suggest that traditional business models can be classified into three types:

- Asset builders: make, market, distribute and sell physical goods (eg Ford, Tesco, BP).
- Service providers: employ skilled people to provide services to customers (eg Accenture, JP Morgan Chase).
- Technology providers: develop and sell intellectual property, such as software, analytics, pharmaceuticals (eg Microsoft, Oracle, Pfizer).

However, we can now add a fourth type of business model:

- Network orchestrators: create a platform that participants use to interact or transact with other members of the network. They deliver value through connectivity (eg eBay, Facebook, Uber, TripAdvisor).

Real life example – Airbnb

In one sense, Airbnb is in the same business as hotel chains like Hilton or Marriott. Like the hotels, it uses pricing and booking systems designed to allow guests to find, reserve and pay for rooms as they need them.

However, unlike Hilton or Marriott, Airbnb doesn't own any rooms. Instead Airbnb applies a platform model. It maintains the platform which allows individual participants to provide the rooms directly to consumers. In return, Airbnb takes a transaction fee for every rental arranged through the platform.

5.4 Platforms and value creation

Digital platforms are the foundation of the network orchestrator business model. The 'platform' enables parties to interact with, and contribute to, the product/service offering.

Platforms create value in their own right, for example:

- By allowing consumers to access value created on the platform (eg YouTube videos)
- By allowing producers access to a community or market (eg sellers on Amazon)
- By ensuring that users find it easy to make matches that produce significant value for them (eg passengers finding an available ride on Uber)

In turn, platforms can then monetise this value – for example, by charging a commission or transaction fee; or by charging for access or enhanced access to the platform (eg users can access a basic version of LinkedIn free, but if they pay a monthly fee they can access a premium version).

6 Participants and interactions

Ecosystems, like other business environments, are made up of participants and interactions (*Davidson et al, 2014*):

- Participants are the individual organisations within the environment.
- Interactions are the products or services exchanged among participants.

The IBM Institute for Business Value (*Davidson et al, 2014*) recommends that participants can be defined in relation to three components:

- Role played within the environment eg supplier, customer or facilitator
- Reach through the environment eg participants' ability to extend their activities or interactions
- Capability or key value proposition eg what the participant will be contributing to the ecosystem eg expertise, finance

Similarly, interactions can also be defined with reference to three components:

- Rules governing the environment – the principles, either formal or informal, governing conduct within the environment
- Connections of elements – the linkages across the environment; connecting elements of products and services, but also sharing data and knowledge
- Course of interactions – the speed and direction at which content or value is shared between participants

(*Davidson et al, 2014*)

Assessment focus point

The syllabus specifically mentions that you should be able to analyse the roles, reach, capabilities, rules, connections and courses of participants and interactions in networks and platforms. Therefore, it is important that you are familiar with all the terms used here, so that you could apply them as necessary in your analysis.

Activity 5: InStep

InStep, is rapidly gaining market share, and developing a favourable reputation as the platform of choice in the market for high-end fashion footwear. InStep provides people and companies with an online portal which is comprehensive as well as easy to use, through which they can design and produce their own customised shoes. InStep facilitates production and logistics from a number of high-quality footwear manufacturers in Italy and serves customers around the world.

Required

Identify the components which each of the following factors in InStep's success reflect.

Instep facilitates production from a number of high-quality manufacturers and has access to a customer base around the world: [▼] , [▼] and
[▼] .

The comprehensiveness and ease of use of the website: [▼] ,
[▼] and of course [▼] .

Picklist:

Reach

Connections

Capability

Connections of elements

Course of interactions

Solution

7 Mutuality and orchestration

The existence of participants and interactions is not unlike the framework of traditional markets (with buyers/sellers and transactions). The defining characteristics of an ecosystem, which distinguish it from traditional 'markets' are mutuality and orchestration (*Davidson et al, 2014*).

7.1 Mutuality

> **Mutuality:** An enhanced level of co-ordination with formally or informally shared ideals, standards or goals (*Davidson et al, 2014*).

Traditional, market-based business models comprise organisations which operate out of self-interest. By contrast, in an 'ecosystem' entities operate together to produce something of greater value, benefiting both the organisation and the ecosystem as a whole (ie there is a mutual benefit). The underlying reason for ecosystems is that participants can deliver more value by acting together within the ecosystem than they could acting individually.

7.2 Orchestration

Orchestration refers to the formal or informal co-ordination of interactions between participants in the ecosystem.

> **Orchestration:** The co-ordination, arrangement and management of complex environments (*Davidson et al, 2014*).

Every ecosystem requires 'orchestration' by someone who understands the network. The orchestrator needs to know the ecosystem's key customers (and their requirements); participants; their value propositions, and the drivers of progress.

In some cases, orchestration may be informal – for example, through cultural practices agreed among the participants. However, orchestration can also be formal, with an organisation taking on the role of orchestrator to manage interactions between other participants.

Activity 6: Alpha

Alpha is a start-up business developing software for autonomous cars. Beta makes hardware for intelligent systems, with its products currently being used in a range of industrial products. Gamma is a management consultancy that offers its clients bespoke solutions, with its unique selling point (USP) being its unparalled range of industry contacts, and track record for helping companies work together. Epsilon manufacturers domestic white goods but is looking to move into the production of driverless cars.

Required
Which of these companies is most likely to be the orchestrator of an ecosystem to develop driverless cars?

A   Alpha

B   Beta

C   Gamma

D   Epsilon

Solution

7.3 Stakeholders in networks and platforms

We have already identified the importance of **participants** and **orchestrators** in ecosystems. However, organisations need to manage their relationships with the other participants in a network as well as the orchestrator (eg as we noted earlier, Samsung or Huawei need to engage with the owners of mobile networks, and app providers).

Customers are another key stakeholder in ecosystems, as in traditional business models.

7.3.1 Relationships with customers

Customers' relationships with organisations are influenced by the following:

- More information is available to consumers, giving them more choices and the ability to make more informed choices. (Social media also allows customers to provide feedback on products and services, which in turn could influence the products and services being offered.)

- Customers have increasing expectations of their interactions with companies (linked to customer empowerment).

- Decreasing brand loyalty. Consumers have less patience with unsatisfactory experiences (eg slow response times, failing to address individual requirements) and are willing to switch interchangeably between brands (IBM, 2014).

8 Ecosystems and value

Value creation in traditional markets tends to be linear – think, for example, of a supply chain; where an organisation receives inputs from its suppliers, adds value to them, before selling them on to the end consumer. By contrast, in an ecosystem, instead of flowing in a 'straight line' from producers to consumers, value is created in an iterative way across the ecosystem as a whole.

The nature of ecosystems means that value creation is networked, as **organisations collaborate** to deliver something of **mutually beneficial** value. Organisations create value through their engagement within the system as a whole. Rather than interacting with individual organisations within a particular ecosystem, customers may pay for access to the system as a whole, or for the benefits it provides.

Traditional value network (based on *Porter*, 1985, p35), Ecosystem (based on *Davidson et al*, 2014, p2)

Traditional value network

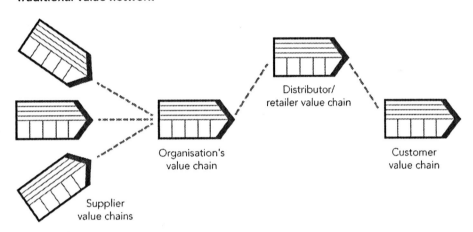

Ecosystem

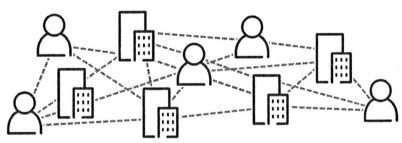

 ### Real life example – DBSchenker

Historically, when a dispatcher for DBSchenker trucking in Europe needed a load of cargo picked up and delivered, they ordered it, with a message instructing a specific truck to pick up a specific load.

Now, Schenker uses a web-based brokerage platform. When a dispatcher needs a load of cargo picked up, they place a request for this on the platform ('Drive4Schenker') and an available carrier agrees to pick it up.

The difference between ordering a supplier to do something and influencing an ecosystem partner to take action (based on an event, such as pick up request) is one of the key differences between ecosystems and previous business models.

One of the key success factors in the logistics business is operating with fully loaded trucks; empty or half-full trucks are not profitable to run. The benefit of the 'Drive4Schenker' platform is that it allows carriers to pick the load that best fits their needs – for example, in terms of available space, pick-up location, destination – increasing the chance of them operating with fully loaded trucks (*Pemberton, 2017*).

8.1 Co-creation with customers

Another factor which is contributing to the difference between traditional value networks and ecosystems is that, in ecosystems, customers are taking a larger role in the creation of products and services. (We already mentioned the idea of co-creation earlier in the chapter, in relation to the LEGO example).

Co-creation redefines the boundaries between businesses and their customers, and again undermines the idea of value creation as a linear process, in which businesses create value which they 'push out' to their customers.

For example, home appliance and electronics maker, Haier, focuses on customer-driven innovation as an important part of its strategy. The company has created an open innovation platform that enables users to communicate with suppliers and other customers searching for new business opportunities. Similarly, packaging provider Weig is integrating its customers into the production process and working with them to co-invent the perfect materials for their needs (*Reddy, 2018*).

Assessment focus point

In a 'traditional' business model, an organisation's supply chain helps it create value for its customers. However, a supply chain is essentially linear. While an ecosystem involves organisations working together to create value for customers, a key distinction between ecosystems and traditional business models is that the relationship is not linear: ie organisations in an ecosystem play a wider range of roles than simply 'producer' and 'consumer'.

8.2 Value creation and value capture

Two key questions about value in ecosystems are:

Value creation – what can organisations do to create value in an ecosystem?

Value capture – how do organisations capture the value they have helped to create within an ecosystem?

8.2.1 Value creation

Participants can create value by innovating products, services or experiences, and we have already looked earlier at the different roles an organisation can play in an ecosystem.

To be successful, an ecosystem needs its participants to collaborate to create and deliver something of mutually beneficial value (eg ecosystem orchestrators can add value by improving customer experience, or by sharing customer insights among other participants).

To create value, organisations need to identify opportunities, develop competencies and leverage synergies and complementary strengths within the ecosystem. The more essential and unique the activity an organisation can fulfil within an ecosystem, the more sustainable their position and role will be within the ecosystem.

8.2.2 Value capture

Participants can either capture value directly through transactions, or indirectly from an orchestrator:

- Direct – value capture is instantaneous and reflects the individual transaction amount (eg a consumer buys a single ticket for a journey on public transport. The consumer gains value from being able to make the journey, while the transport company captures the monetary value of the consumer's fare).
- Indirect – the orchestrator captures value from consumers, who pay for access to the ecosystem, or for a bundled array of goods and services provided by the ecosystem ('pay-to-play'). The orchestrator allocates payment to participants, to incentivise them to continue participating in the ecosystem (eg a consumer buys a pass which allows them unlimited trips on trains, buses or subways in a city in a given time period).

Indirect value capture will typically be associated with strong, explicit orchestration, while direct value capture will be associated with weaker forms of orchestration.

Real life example – Uber

The basis of Uber's business model is in providing a matching service, helping potential passengers find drivers, and vice versa.

By connecting passengers and drivers Uber creates value for both groups, and in doing so Uber is acting as a network orchestrator.

However, Uber also captures value for itself by taking a commission from all the fares paid by passengers.

8.3 Strategies for capturing value

Two key factors which shape an organisation's strategy for capturing value in an ecosystem are: the level of complexity in the activities undertaken, and the extent and formality of the orchestration in the ecosystem (*Davidson et al, 2014*).

Complexity depends on:

- The number and diversity of participants
- The sophistication of activities within the ecosystem
- How secure the participant's role is in the ecosystem (eg how difficult it is to replicate their capabilities, barriers to entry)

Formality of orchestration:

- Reflects the degree of enforceability and compliance in the ecosystem
  - Tight orchestration – orchestrators have an ability to influence behaviour across the entire ecosystem (eg in regulated industries, like financial services).
  - Loose orchestration – no individual participant has significant influence across the ecosystem; there isn't a strong central co-ordinator (eg in many places, individuals are free to express themselves as they want on the internet).

The IBM Institute for Business Value (*Davidson et al, 2014*) argues that by combining the different levels of complexity and orchestration, we can identify a range of potential ecosystem types:

(Davidson et al, 2014, p10)

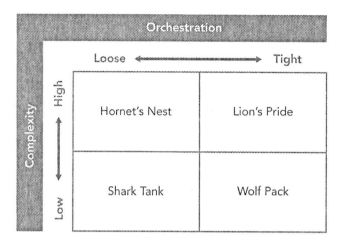

An organisation's strategy for value creation should depend on the environment in which it finds itself:

Shark Tank (low complexity, low barriers to entry, loose orchestration)

Organisations need to work to differentiate themselves as much as possible from competitors, and to reduce the perception of them being a 'commodity' player. This should help to make their role less contested.

Wolf Pack (low complexity, low barriers to entry, strong orchestration)

Participants in the Wolf Pack are continually at risk of new or existing competitors disintermediating their role in the ecosystem. As well as building differentiators (such as brand), participants need to build and sustain strong relationships with the orchestrator, who has the power to save or destroy them. This promotes collaboration in the ecosystem, because if the orchestrator is displeased with a participant, their role and position in the ecosystem could be under threat.

Real life example – Alibaba

The Alibaba Group handles around 80% of e-commerce transactions in China. Therefore, the threat of exclusion presents a serious challenge to any firm conducting business online. (*Parker et al, 2017*).

Hornet's Nest (high complexity, high barriers to entry, loose orchestration)

In the absence of strong orchestration, Hornet's Nest participants need to find their own ways of capturing value – seeking opportunities, meeting needs and building relationships. The more they can build the capabilities to deliver goods and services that are demanded by consumers, the more successful they are likely to be. This is likely to lead to fragmented competition in the ecosystem.

Lion's Pride (high complexity, high barriers to entry, strong orchestration)

To optimise their success, Lion's Pride participants should work to align their strategic objectives with those of the orchestrator. They should also look to differentiate themselves from potential competitors, to reduce the risk of them being disintermediated in the ecosystem.

9 Technology and ecosystems

Technologies such as social media, mobile, cloud computing, analytics are all shifting the competitive landscape.

Real life example – Domino's Pizza

Between 2009 and 2017, Domino's Pizza delivered a share price increase that, in percentage terms, beat Google and Facebook.

A key ingredient in Domino's success was a digital transformation of the food-ordering process. Being able to order a pizza using an app, tweet, or voice-activated personal assistance resonated with young people who spent much of their time online. By 2018, more than 60% of Domino's orders were received via digital channels rather than by phone.

We will look at the impact of digital technologies on businesses in more detail in Chapter 12, but key characteristics of the new landscape include it being:

- Connected and open – the proliferation of mobile devices (eg smart phones, tablets) and internet access means communication between companies, partners and consumers becomes constant and immediate eg through social media.

- Intelligent – organisations leverage analytics and insights to drive intelligent and predictive, data-driven, decision making (eg using predictive analytics).

- Fast and scalable – modern businesses need to be agile. Digital ecosystems use shared, scalable resources which helps them respond to changing market conditions with greater speed and efficiency than traditional 'stand-alone' business could – for example, by collaborating with new, additional suppliers to offer new products or services.

The amount of data available to companies is now also greater than ever before, so the ability to collect and analyse that data will be important in developing products, services or experiences that customers value. In this respect, the notion of fast and scalable also highlights the importance of cloud computing in enabling ecosystems and digital platforms.

Cloud computing allows organisations to buy additional storage space from a cloud service provider. Therefore, if the ecosystem expands, it can scale up seamlessly – buying additional computing power and storage as needed – rather than having to upgrade its own hardware and software capabilities.

Assessment focus point

The learning outcomes identify that you need to be able to analyse how technologies such as cloud computing, social media, mobile and analytics impact ecosystems. An important point to note here is the way that new technologies have helped to enable the development of ecosystems – for example, by enabling organisations to capture and share increasing amounts of information.

10 Corporate social responsibility

Being part of an ecosystem complicates an organisation's ability to manage its CSR commitments. One area of particular concern is shared custody of **privacy and data protection**. As companies gather increasing amounts of data about customers (eg from loyalty cards, smart devices, or wearable devices) so it is important that the data is collected and **used responsibly** (eg personal data is not shared with third parties without authorisation by the customer) and **held securely**.

The extent to which users of a platform trust a platform could be crucial for the long-term success of that platform. This highlights the importance of building trust-based platforms.

10.1 Trust-based platforms

The World Economic Forum (*WEF, 2017*) identifies six key principles for building trust-based platforms:

- Security – cyber-security measures are essential, as platforms operate on shared network infrastructure, and handle valuable transactions.

- Accountability – important in encouraging actors to trust the platform. There are three elements of this:
    - A platform must be reliable and function as expected eg fulfilling orders and transferring payments.
    - All participants must comply with accepted standards.
    - Operators must be held responsible if the platform is to fulfil its promises.
- Transparency – platforms need to provide stakeholders with meaningful information to understand relationships and transactions.
- Auditability – transactions and data flows across an array of stakeholders and jurisdictions should be externally audited, verified and monitored.
- Fairness – ensuring fairness in value allocation. Regulators and consumer protection agencies will be concerned with preventing anti-competitive tactics and collusion between ecosystem partners eg price-fixing.
- Ethics – unethical (or even illegal) activities could severely damage trust in a platform and the brands associated with it.

10.2 Platforms and regulation

Another more general concern being raised about hyperscale platforms (eg Amazon) is their potential impact on regulation and the structure of economies.

The small-scale traders who sell through a platform rely on that platform to be able to trade. As the proportion of transactions which take place through platforms increases, the platform providers can set the rules which govern an increasing large part of the economy.

As such, some concerns have been raised about the extent to which technological giants could usurp the state's traditional role as rule-maker and regulator. So, the concern is that, in effect, the market leading platforms will increasingly regulate the markets in which they operate: for example, Amazon will regulate the retail market; Google the market for digital content; and Uber the market for urban automotive transport.

Activity 7: Platforms

Concerns have been raised that as large platforms grow, their bargaining power over participants increases, and participants have to accept business terms they would otherwise consider unacceptable.

Required
If platforms change their business terms in this way, which of the principles of building trust-based platforms could be threatened?

Solution

> ## Assessment focus point
>
> It is important to recognise that although ecosystems can have a number of benefits, there could still be potential concerns around them. In relation to this, the syllabus requires that you are able to analyse the impact that technologies could have on corporate social responsibility.

Chapter summary

The impact of the ecosystem on organisations and strategy

Context of change

Events in external environment can act as drivers for change

Possible frameworks for analysing them:
- PESTEL
- Porter's five forces

Potential drivers for change

- Globalisation
- Geopolitics
- Demographics
- Customer empowerment
- Digital technology
- Automation
- Sustainability

Business ecosystems

Ecosystem: a web of interdependent enterprises and relationships

Key features:
- Connectedness
- Collaboration

Ecosystem roles
- Experience providers
- Asset providers
- Process providers
- Platform providers

Networks and platforms

Networks:
- Connections that enable the exchange of information, products or services
- Value increases with the number of connections in the network

Platforms:
- Technology and infrastructure that underpins networks
- Key elements of platforms:
  - Interactions
  - Infrastructure
- Digital platforms are the foundation of the network orchestrator business model
- Platforms monetise value by charging a transaction fee or by charging for access

Participants and interactions

Ecosystems = made up of participants and interactions

Components of participants:
- Role
- Reach
- Capability

Components of interactions
- Rules
- Connections
- Course

Mutuality and orchestration

Mutuality:
Participants in an ecosystem work together to produce outcomes of value

Orchestration:
Orchestrator coordinates the interactions between participants

Ecosystems and value

Value creation in traditional business models = linear

Ecosystems = iterative
Value creation = networked; collaborative

Organisations need to identify:
- How they can create value
- How they can capture value

Strategies for capturing value depend on complexity and level of orchestration
- Lion's pride
- Wolf pack
- Hornet's nest
- Lion's pride

Technology and ecosystems

Key characteristics of the new digital landscape:
- Connected and open
- Intelligent
- Fast and scalable

Corporate social responsibility

Privacy and data protection = vital

Key principles for trust-based platforms:
- Security
- Accountability
- Transparency
- Auditability
- Fairness
- Ethics

Key terms

Geopolitics: The way a country's geography, economics and politics affect its power and relationships with other countries.

Environmental footprint: A measure of the impact that an organisation's activities have on the environment, including its resource use and its environmental and pollution emissions.

Social footprint: A measure of the impact or effect that an organisation can have on a given set of concerns or stakeholder interests.

Business ecosystem: 'A complex web of interdependent enterprises and relationships aimed at creating and allocating business value' (*Davidson et al, 2014*).

Network: 'A set of connections that enables people or things to connect, share information, and exchange products, services or insights' (*Libert et al, 2016, pix*).

Platform: A 'business based on enabling value-creating interactions between external producers and consumers. The platform provides an open, participatory infrastructure for those interactions and sets governance conditions for them' (*Parker et al, 2016, p5*).

Mutuality: An enhanced level of co-ordination with formally or informally shared ideals, standards or goals (*Davidson et al, 2014*).

Orchestration: The co-ordination, arrangement and management of complex environments (*Davidson et al, 2014*).

Activity answers

Activity 1: Environmental analysis

The correct answer is:

Possible examples	
PESTEL (Macro-environment, 'social' factors)	• Changes in economic cycle (eg economic downturn), either domestically or internationally • Changes in rate of market growth • Changes to interest rates • New laws or regulations eg product fire safety • Changes in customer expectations and tastes • Changes in product or process technology • Changes in distribution channels (eg growth of e-commerce and mobile)
Porter's five forces (Micro-environment, 'market' factors)	• Arrival of new entrants into a market, or mergers between existing competitors • Customers start to shop around on the internet to find better value • Suppliers consolidate and raise prices • Changes to consumer demands for styles and perhaps more sustainable furnishings eg sustainably sourced wood for dining sets

Activity 2: Automation

The correct answer is:

- **Data entry clerk:** Highly susceptible. Data entry involves routine and repetitive work, with well-defined tasks. Clerical and administrative functions are among the most vulnerable to automation.
- **Doctors/surgeons:** Relatively low risk of automation. Although AI and robots could have an important role in healthcare in future, this is more likely to be working alongside human doctors than replacing them, because there is still a need for social skills in a doctor's relationship with their patient.
- **Plumbers:** Relatively low risk of automation. While some manual tasks may be simplified or automated using new technology, plumbing cannot be easily automated as it needs to be done on-site and involves a number of different problem-solving skills.

Activity 3: E-Zee

The correct answer is:

Lower prices for customers

Prices charged to customers could be higher, due to costs of sustainability initiatives, such as paying a 'fair price' (to suppliers) for goods.

Lower energy consumption: simple steps such as better insulation will reduce the environmental impact.

Lower emissions should be achieved as the company will need to switch to renewable energy sources.

Lower transportation costs: sustainability will encourage more local produce to be sourced, in order to help reduce the company's environmental footprint.

Activity 4: Ecosystems

The correct answer is:

Asset provider

HERE is providing a software asset, which the car manufacturers can incorporate into their cars.

Activity 5: InStep

The correct answer is:

Instep facilitates production from a number of high-quality manufacturers and has access to a customer base around the world: **Reach, Connections of elements** and **Capability.**

The comprehensiveness and ease of use of the website: **Capability, Connections of elements**and of course **Course of interactions.**

InStep's role in the ecosystem is as a platform provider. InStep's overall success comes from its ability to obtain and retain stakeholders on its platform; eg through its comprehensiveness and ease of use for customers, as well as for the manufacturers who ultimately produce the shoes. This ability to attract and retain stakeholders is a key **capability** for a platform provider.

The access InStep has to a number of leading manufacturers and customers worldwide could be seen as an illustration of the platform's **reach.** However, we could also suggest that this access to producers and customers contributes to InStep's overall ability to obtain and retain stakeholders, in which case we could argue it reflects InStep's capability as a network orchestrator.

We could also argue that Instep's ability to provide information to the manufacturers who make the shoes reflects the **connections** in the ecosystem. Similarly, the ease of use of the website, allowing customers to find out about products and to make orders quickly and easily, could also reflect elements of the **connections** of elements or the **course** of interactions.

Activity 6: Alpha

The correct answer is:

Gamma

Every ecosystem requires 'orchestration' by someone who understands the network. The orchestrator needs to know the ecosystem's key customers (and their requirements); participants; their value propositions, and the drivers of progress. This fits with the description of Gamma as a management consultancy able to use its contacts to bring the other companies together to collaborate in the development of driverless cars.

Activity 7: Platforms

The correct answer is:

The primary issue here appears to be one of fairness.

The threat here is that platform-owners use their bargaining power to make other participants accept business terms which create an unfair allocation of value between the platform-owner and the other participants. (For example, if a platform-owner, such as Amazon, increases the commission it charges vendors to sell products through its platform, this could result in an unfair allocation of value. The platform-owner knows that the vendors are likely to have to accept the higher commission rates because they cannot afford to be excluded from the platform, due to the platform's dominance in the market place. In extreme circumstances, a platform-owner could potentially secure a monopoly position in a market and could then be seen to be abusing its monopoly position if it changes the business terms for the other participants).

Test your learning

1 **Required**
What is geopolitics?

2 The syllabus identifies a number of drivers of change in the ecosystem: globalisation, geopolitics, demography, customer empowerment, digital technology, automation, sustainability.

   Required
   In which category of a PESTEL analysis would it be most appropriate to include drivers of change reflecting demography and customer empowerment?

   A   Political

   B   Economic

   C   Social

   D   Technological

   E   Environmental

   F   Legal

3 Three of the four 'roles' an organisation could play to create value in an ecosystem are: asset provider, process provider, platform provider.

   Required
   What is the fourth 'role' missing from this list?

4 **Required**
Which of the following refers to the formal or informal co-ordination of interactions between participants in an ecosystem?

   A   Mutuality

   B   Orchestration

   C   Infrastructure

   D   Platform

5 **Required**
Which of the following is NOT one of the components which can be used to define participants in an ecosystem?

   A   Role

   B   Reach

   C   Rules

   D   Capability

6 The level of complexity in the activities undertaken is one of the key factors which shape an organisation's strategy for capturing value in an ecosystem.

   Required
   Which one of the following is NOT one of the factors which influence complexity?

   A   The number and diversity of participants

   B   How difficult it is to replace a participant's capabilities in the ecosystem

   C   The degree of enforceability and compliance in the ecosystem

   D   The sophistication of activities within the ecosystem

Generating strategic options

Syllabus learning outcomes

Having studied this chapter you will be able to work through the following syllabus outcomes:

Syllabus Area E3: Strategic options

2	Option generation
a-b	Key strategic questions and an organisation's starting position

Exam context

In the exam, you will be expected to demonstrate competence in the following representative task statements:

- Prepare or review Porter's generic strategies, Ansoff's matrix, and method of growth for establishing a choice of possible future strategies

Chapter overview

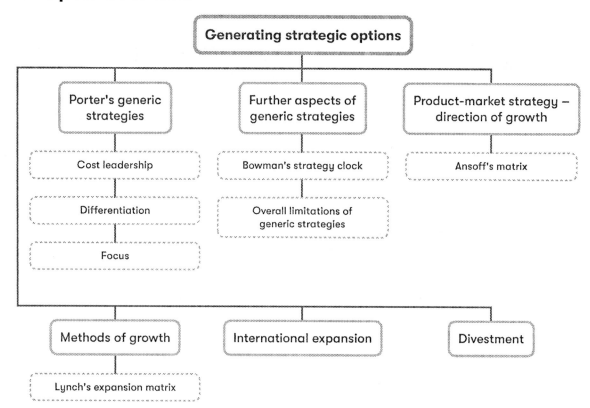

1 Introduction

On the assumption that an organisation is following the rational approach to strategy, once it has established its mission and objectives, and analysed its current strategic position (eg environment analysis and SWOT analysis) it will then need to consider its strategies for the future, and how it intends to grow.

There are three key aspects to these strategies: how to compete, where to compete (direction of growth) and method of growth.

The choice of how to compete relates to the generic competitive strategies which a firm can choose – identified by Porter as cost leadership or differentiation.

The choice of where to compete relates to the mix of products and markets an organisation serves (as illustrated by Ansoff's product-market matrix (*Ansoff, 1987*).

Choices around the method of growth relate to whether an organisation looks to grow organically or externally. External growth could be through acquisition, or some kind of strategic alliance.

Topics covered in this chapter:

- Generic strategies
- Product/market matrix

2 Porter's generic strategies

Following on from his five forces analysis, Porter (1980) argued that, in order to remain profitable in the long run, a firm needs to possess a sustainable competitive advantage which enables it to combat these forces better than its rivals.

The concept of competitive advantage is concerned with anything which gives one organisation an edge over its rivals.

Note. As we noted in the last chapter, organisations are increasingly collaborating through ecosystems, as well as competing individually. However, in this chapter, we are looking primarily at the competitive strategies pursued by individual organisations.

2.1 Generic strategy and competitive advantage

Porter (1980) argues that an organisation needs to adopt an appropriate competitive strategy which will help it achieve a competitive advantage. Porter referred to these strategies as 'generic strategies'.

Porter (1980) suggested that an organisation firm must first decide upon its competitive basis, being either to compete on the basis of lowest cost, or to differentiate. Porter argued that to do neither and be 'stuck in the middle' would lead to an inability to compete over the long term, as illustrated below.

Cost leader	Stuck in the middle	Differentiator

Porter (1980) argues that once an organisation has decided its competitive basis (cost leader or differentiator), it then needs to determine its **competitive scope**:

(a) Narrow target (focus) – aimed at a defined market group only

(b) Broad target – available to the market as a whole

The outcome of this process is the choice of the following four strategies.

		Competitive basis	
		Cost driven	Differentiation driven
Competitive scope	Broad	Cost leadership	Differentiation
	Narrow	Cost focus	Differentiated focus

KEY TERM

Cost leadership: Means being the lowest cost producer in the industry as a whole.

Differentiation: Involves providing uniqueness in a way which is sufficiently valued by customers across the industry to allow a price premium.

Focus: Involves a restriction of activities to only part of the market (a segment). Focus can involve providing goods and/or services at the lowest cost in that segment (cost focus) or providing a differentiated product or service (differentiation focus).

2.2 Cost leadership

Porter (1980) suggests that under a cost leadership strategy an organisation aims to become the lowest cost producer in the industry as a whole. By producing at the lowest cost, the organisation can compete on price with every other producer in the industry and earn higher unit profits than them. This might be particularly beneficial if the products or services the organisation sells are price sensitive.

Implications of cost leadership

- Establishes a barrier to entry
- Enables firm to remain profitable in price cutting phase of mature industry
- Allows price cuts to win market share
- Increases margins when market prices are higher

How to achieve overall cost leadership

- Establish economies of scale
- Use the latest, most efficient technology to reduce costs and/or enhance productivity.
- Exploit the learning curve effect
- Get favourable access to sources of supply and buy in bulk wherever possible (to obtain discounts for bulk purchases)
- Minimise overhead costs
- Reduce direct costs (for example, by using cheaper raw materials, or cheaper labour)
- Relocate to cheaper areas (possibly in a different country)

2.3 Differentiation

Porter (1980) argues that a differentiation strategy assumes an organisation can achieve competitive advantage through particular characteristics of its products and/or services, which differentiate them from rival offerings, deliver value to customers, and enable it to command a premium price.

How to differentiate:

- Build up a brand image.
- Give the product special features to make it stand out.
- Exploit other activities of the value chain (for example, quality of after-sales service or speed of delivery).
- Use IT and innovation to create new services or product features.
- Build customer relationships through effective branding and marketing.
- Create complementary products and/or services; for example, Apple's app store allows the users of its phones and tablets to download apps.

Advantages of this approach include:

- Creates a barrier to entry through product differentiation
- Reduces the impact of price competition from rivals through switching competitive emphasis away from price
- Increases customer loyalty and switching costs

Assessment focus point

Although a 'differentiation' strategy implies an organisation seeks to be different from its competitors, simply 'being different' isn't a basis for competitive success. To be successful, a strategy also needs to deliver value – by meeting customers' needs more effectively than competitors, for example, through greater product reliability, easier use, aesthetic appearance, faster delivery, greater convenience, or superior service.

2.4 Focus

If a firm lacks the resources to dominate the broad (or mass) market, it can seek to dominate a niche within the markets. This is known as market segmentation.

Porter (1980) notes that a focus strategy requires an organisation to concentrate its attention on one or more particular segments (or niches) of the market and does not try to serve the entire market with a single product.

- A cost leadership focus strategy: aim to be a cost leader for a particular segment. This type of strategy is often found in the printing, clothes manufacture and car repair industries.

- A differentiation focus strategy: pursue differentiation for a chosen segment. Luxury goods suppliers are the prime exponents of such a strategy.

Porter (1980) suggests that a focus strategy can achieve competitive advantage when 'broad-scope' businesses succumb to one of two errors:

- Underperformance occurs when a product does not fully meet the needs of a segment and offers the opportunity for a differentiation focus player.
- Overperformance gives a segment more than it really wants and provides an opportunity for a cost focus player.

A focus strategy can be used in a variety of ways:

- Meeting the needs of a particular buyer group
- Focusing on excellence in a particular technology or stage in the production process
- Limiting operations to a small geographical area

Advantages of a focus strategy

- A niche is more secure and an organisation can insulate itself from competition.
- The organisation does not spread itself too thinly.
- Both cost leadership and differentiation require superior performance – life is easier in a niche, where there may be little or no competition.

Drawbacks of a focus strategy

- The organisation sacrifices economies of scale which would be gained by serving a wider market.
- Competitors can move into the segment, with increased resources (eg the Japanese moved into the US luxury car market, to compete with German car makers).
- The segment's needs may eventually become less distinct from the main market.

2.5 Stuck in the middle

Although there is a risk with any of the generic strategies, Porter (1980) argues that an organisation must pursue one of them; otherwise it will be 'stuck in the middle'.

A **stuck-in-the-middle** strategy is almost certain to make only low profits. Porter (1980) argues that a firm which is stuck in the middle 'lacks the market share, capital investment and resolve to play the low-cost game, the industry-wide differentiation necessary to obviate the need for a low-cost position, or the focus to create differentiation or a low-cost position in a more limited sphere.'

2.6 Limitations of Porter's model

In practice, it is rarely simple to draw hard and fast distinctions between the generic strategies as there are conceptual problems underlying them.

2.6.1 Problems with cost leadership

The following are potential issues with the concept of cost leadership:

- **Internal focus:** Cost refers to internal measures, rather than the market demand. It can be used to gain market share: but it is the **market share that is important**, not cost leadership as such. Economies of scale are an effective way to achieve low costs, but they depend on high volumes. In turn, high volumes may depend on low prices which, in turn, require low costs. There is a circular argument here.
- **Only one firm:** If cost leadership applies across the whole industry, only one firm will pursue this strategy successfully. However, more than one firm might **aspire** to cost leadership, especially in dynamic markets where new technologies are frequently introduced. Firms competing across the industry as a whole might have different competence or advantages that confer cost leadership in different segments.
- **Higher margins can be used for differentiation:** Having low **costs** does not mean you have to charge lower prices or compete on **price**. A cost leader can choose to invest higher margins in R&D or marketing. Being a cost leader arguably gives producers more freedom to choose other competitive strategies.

There is often confusion about what cost leadership actually means. In particular, cost leadership is often assumed to also mean low price. However, **'cost leadership'** and **'low price'** are not **necessarily the same thing.**

2.6.2 Problems with differentiation

Porter assumes that a differentiated product will always be sold at a higher price.

- However, a **differentiated product** may be sold at the same price as competing products in order to increase market share.
- **Choice of competitor.** Differentiation from whom? Who are the competitors? Do they serve other market segments? Do they compete on the same basis?
- **Source of differentiation.** This includes all aspects of the firm's offer, not only the product. For example, restaurants try to distinguish themselves from their competitors through their ambience and the quality of their service as well as by serving high-quality food.

2.6.3 Problems with focus

Focus probably has fewer conceptual difficulties, as it ties in very neatly with ideas of market segmentation. In practice, most companies pursue this strategy to some extent, by designing products/services to meet the needs of particular target markets.

'Stuck in the middle' is therefore what many companies actually pursue quite successfully. Any number of strategies can be pursued, with different approaches to **price** and the **perceived added value** (ie the differentiation factor) in the eyes of the customer.

In this way, Porter's model no longer reflects the full range of competitive strategies an organisation can choose from.

Activity 1: Gear Co

Gear Co manufactures and sells motor vehicles. Several years ago, Gear invested in a new production facility, to reduce production costs and improve quality.

Gear's major rivals have also upgraded their production facilities in recent years.

Gear produces a wide range of cars that are tailored to different market segments. The prices of Gear's vehicles are similar to those of its competitors in any given market segment.

Gear has recently decided to undertake a major advertising campaign. It feels its brand is already widely recognised but wants to increase the desirability of the Gear brand, because it feels this could allow it to increase the prices of its vehicles while still maintaining its overall sales volume.

Required
According to Porter's generic strategies model, which of the following most accurately reflects Gear's current strategy?

A   Cost leadership

B   Differentiation

C   Focus

D   Stuck-in-the-middle

Solution

3 Further aspects of generic strategies

A successor to Porter's model is Bowman's **strategy clock** (*Bowman and Faulkner, 1997*).

The strategy clock acknowledges a key weakness of Porter in that firms may succeed with a **'hybrid'** strategy that combines cost leadership and differentiation.

3.1 Hybrid strategies

If a hybrid strategy is just compromising Porter's generic strategies then it is still likely to fail.

However, it may succeed in the following circumstances:

- **Greater sales volumes** – it yields economies of scale in the supply chain that can be passed on to customers in the price; eg **Tesco** has almost twice the market share of any of its rival supermarkets in the UK giving it unrivalled purchasing power.

- **Differentiation may lie in the core competences themselves** – this allows costs to be saved elsewhere; eg **IKEA** differentiates on product range, design and branding, but saves costs as customers collect and build their own furniture.

- **Market entry** – charging low prices to buy market share may allow a differentiator to establish a foothold, ensuring customer loyalty and supporting higher prices thereafter.

Bowman's strategy clock

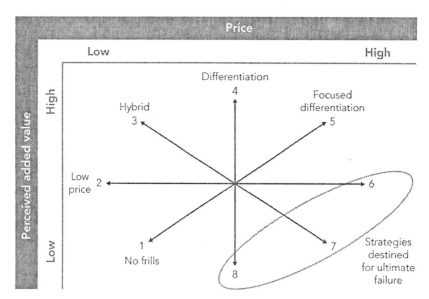

Strategies 6 to 8 are collectively known as failure strategies and are to be avoided unless a monopoly can be established.

3.2 Overall limitations of the generic strategy approach

Problems in defining the 'industry' – Porter's model depends on clear notions of what the **industry** and **firm** in question are, in order to establish how competitive advantage derives from a firm's position in its industry. However, identifying the industry and the firm may not be clear, since many companies are part of larger organisations, and many 'industries' have boundaries that are hard to define. For example, what industry is a car manufacturer in? Cars, automotive (cars, lorries, buses), manufacturing, transportation?

Defining the strategic unit – as well as having difficulties in defining the industry, we can have difficulties in determining whether strategies should be pursued at **strategic business unit (SBU)** or **corporate level**, and in relation to exactly which category of products. For example, the Volkswagen-Audi Group owns the Seat, Audi, Bentley and Skoda car marques, but should it pursue the same strategy for all of them?

Porter's theory states that if a firm has more than one competitive strategy this will dilute its competitive advantage. But does this mean that the Volkswagen-Audi's strategy for Skoda needs to be the same as for Bentley? Clearly not, and this is a major problem with Porter's theory.

3.3 Generic strategies and digital

The issue of 'defining the industry' a company operates in could be a particular problem in trying to apply Porter's generic strategies to digital business models – where companies like Amazon or Alibaba operate across different industries.

Scale – perhaps even more importantly, the importance of 'ecosystems' in digital business models highlights the importance of **scale** and **network effects** as being key elements of competitive advantage. Sites like Facebook or Snapchat are successful because of the number of people using them (scale).

Therefore, for digital business, we might argue the need to add 'scale' as a competitive basis, in addition to the two in Porter's original model (cost leadership or differentiation).

3.3.1 Basis of differentiation

We will look at digital operating models in more detail in Chapter 12, but two of the key elements of digital operating models are that they are:

- **Customer-centric** – focused on making customers' lives easier; and
- **Data-powered** – built around analytics and software intelligence.

The extent to which a company delivers these attributes successfully could be a factor which differentiates it from its competitors.

4 Product-market strategy – direction of growth

Having considered **how** organisations compete, we can now move on to consider the strategic choices facing organisations in respect of their product-market strategies.

Product-market strategies involve determining which products should be sold in which markets, by market penetration, market development, product development and diversification. Diversification is assumed to be risky, especially diversification that is entirely unrelated to current products and markets.

4.1 Ansoff's matrix

Ansoff (1987) developed a growth vector matrix, describing the directions of growth open to a firm.

		Product	
		Present	**New**
Market	**Present**	Withdrawal Consolidation Market Penetration	Product development
	New	Market development • Geographical • New Segment • New Use	Diversification • Related • Unrelated

- Market penetration means increasing market share of existing products via promotions, price reductions, increasing usage etc. It represents a relatively low-risk strategy since it requires no capital investment. As such, it is attractive to the unadventurous type of organisation. This approach can also apply to an organisation which simply wants to maintain or even reduce its position in a market.

- Market development means seeking new customers for existing products, eg new geographical markets (exporting), selling to new market segments or via new distribution channels. Risk here is still reasonably low.

- Product development is selling new products to existing customers ('cross-selling'). This strategy is riskier than both market penetration and market development since it is likely to require major investment in the new product development process and, for physical products, in suitable production facilities.

- Diversification, selling new products to new customers, may offer significant growth potential but it is risky as it may require significant investment and new competences.

4.2 Types of diversification

Diversification can be **related** or **unrelated**.

> **Related diversification:** Strategy development beyond current products and markets but within the capabilities or value network of the organisation (*Johnson et al, 2017*).

Related diversification can be achieved through:

- **Vertical integration:** an organisation expands backwards or forwards within its existing value network and therefore become its own supplier (backwards) or distributor (forward). For example, a milk processing business acquiring its own dairy farms rather than buying milk from independent farmers would represent **backward vertical integration**. A cloth manufacturer producing shirts instead of selling its cloth to other shirt manufacturers would be **forward vertical integration**.

- **Horizontal integration:** an organisation moves into activities that are competitive with, or complementary to, its existing activities. This is often achieved by merging with, or acquiring, an industry rival.

Unrelated (or 'conglomerate') diversification

Here the organisation seeks new businesses, which have no obvious relationship to its current activities.

Advantages of unrelated diversification	Disadvantages of unrelated diversification
Escape from constraints of the present business.	Lack of common identity and purpose in a conglomerate organisation.

Advantages of unrelated diversification	Disadvantages of unrelated diversification
Spreads risk by entering new products into new markets.	Lack of management experience may reduce their ability to run the new business effectively.
Uses a company's image or reputation in one market to develop into another.	Increased risk (entering a new market, producing a new product).
	Failure in one of the businesses can drag down the rest of the group.

4.3 Growth strategies and digital

One of the key themes in contemporary business strategy is the way 'digital' is disrupting traditional business models but providing new opportunities for growth.

Considering a digital focus can also be relevant in relation to the product-market matrix. The matrix below shows some possible aims a company might have in relation to its product-market strategies. If the company then preceded each of these with **'How can we use digital to...?'** this would help it to identify ways 'digital' could help support its growth.

Using 'digital' in growth strategies (Adapted from: *Duffy Agency, 2015*)

Product		
	Present	**New**
Market / Present	**Market penetration:** • Increase rate of consumption • Gain market share from competitors	**Product development:** • Add more value to existing products • Develop entirely new products
Market / New	**Market development:** • Develop new segments in current markets • Reach new segments in new geographical markets	**Diversification:** • Develop new products for a new market segment • Develop new products for new geographical markets

Illustration 1: Ansoff

A company is looking to achieve growth by selling its existing product range into new markets.

Required

According to Ansoff, what type of strategy is the company pursuing?

A   Market development

B   Market penetration

C   Product development

D   Related diversification

Solution

The correct answer is:

Market development

A strategy based around existing products and new markets would be classified as market development in Ansoff's matrix.

Activity 2: Flinding

Flinding is a business that sells a range of household furniture (eg sofas, beds) through its nationwide network of stores.

Flinding has recently started a new television advertising campaign offering discounts to customers if they spend more than a certain amount in one of its stores. Flinding regularly uses television as an advertising medium.

Required
According to Ansoff, which type of product-market strategy is Flinding pursuing in this scenario?

A Market development

B Market penetration

C Product development

D Related diversification

Solution

Assessment focus point

The syllabus requires you to be able to prepare or review Ansoff's matrix as a basis for establishing a choice of possible future strategies. The skill level required is 'analysis'. Therefore, while it is important that you know the different categories in the matrix, it is also important that you appreciate their key characteristics, and therefore how appropriate they might be in different situations. (For example, would a diversification strategy be appropriate for an organisation whose shareholders and/or management are risk averse?)

5 Methods of development

Once an organisation's management have decided the basis of competition (generic strategies) and the direction of growth (product-market matrix), they then have to decide how to implement their chosen strategies.

Factors to consider when choosing a method of growth are:

* **Resources**: does a company have sufficient competences to expand itself, or does it have plenty of resources to invest? Are there other businesses with complementary skills?
* **Speed**: how quickly does a company need to expand?
* **Control**: does a company wish to retain control of a product or process?
* **Cultural fit**: combining business involves integrating people, systems and organisational culture.

5.1 Expansion method matrix

Lynch's expansion method matrix (*Lynch, 2015*) identifies a range of ways in which an organisation can implement chosen strategies, according to: (i) whether growth is organic or involves combining with other organisations; and (ii) whether growth is sought in the organisation's home country or internationally.

Company		
	Internal development	External development
Home country	Internal development	Merger Acquisition Joint venture Alliance Franchise/Licence
Abroad	Exporting Overseas office Overseas manufacture Multinational operation Global operation	Merger Acquisition Joint venture Alliance Franchise/Licence

(New location)

5.2 Internal development (organic growth)

Internal development (sometimes referred to as organic growth) is achieved through developing and expanding an organisation's own internal resources, rather than combining with other organisations.

Activity 3: Internal development

Required

Indicate whether each of the following is an advantage or a disadvantage of internal development (organic growth) as a means of strategic expansion.

Input	Advantage/disadvantage
Burden of risk associated with a strategy	▼
Developing a new product allows a firm to understand the product and its market	▼
Maintaining corporate culture	▼

BPP
LEARNING
MEDIA

Input	Advantage/disadvantage
Barriers to entry	▼
Level of disruption to existing business	▼
Time taken to get to market	▼
Lack of suitable target companies	▼
Exploiting the firm's technological innovations	▼

Picklist:

A   Advantage

B   Disadvantage

Solution

Internal development is probably ideal for market penetration, and suitable for product or market development, but it might be a problem with extensive diversification projects.

5.3 External development

Where entities look to grow through external development, the type of relationships between two or more firms can display differing degrees of intensity:

- **Formal integration:** acquisition and merger
- **Formalised ownership/relationship:** eg joint venture
- **Contractual relationships:** eg franchising

5.4 Acquisitions and mergers

A business combination occurs when an entity enters into a formal, legal relationship with another entity through some form of joint ownership.

Acquisitions and mergers are common types of business combination.

- Acquisition involves the purchase of one entity by another.
- Merger involves two separate organisations joining together to form a single entity.

5.4.1 Rationale for acquisitions and mergers

The rationale often given for acquisitions and mergers is that they provide greater opportunities for business growth than if the entities had remained independent of one another.

Other possible reasons for acquisitions and mergers could be:

- Buy in a new product range, or obtain greater production capacity
- Buy a market presence (particularly if acquiring or merging with a foreign entity)
- Buy in technology, intellectual property and competences
- Spread risk
- Gain undervalued assets

5.4.2 Advantages and disadvantages of acquisitions

Advantages

- Speed – can provide rapid access to resources and competences
- Cost savings from economies of scale, or savings in shared overheads
- Can develop strengths/exploit opportunities, or remedy weakness, by acquiring technology, competences etc
- May reduce competition from a rival (subject to approval by competition authorities)
- Can aid expansion into a new geographical area, avoiding potential barriers to entry which could affect a 'new' entrant
- Buy market size and share

Disadvantages

- Cost – they might be too expensive, especially if resisted by the target organisation (meaning a premium has to be paid)
- Incompatibility – problems of assimilating employees, systems and cultures following the acquisition
- Firms rarely take into account the non-financial factors which can affect the success of an acquisition (HR issues are a major reason which affects the success of acquisitions)
- High risk if the 'wrong' company is acquired (eg due to a lack of 'fit' between the acquirer and the acquired)

5.5 Partnering

As well as formal business combinations, entities can also work together in partnering arrangements. **Joint ventures, alliances** and **franchises** are all forms of partnering in which an entity establishes arrangements with external third parties with a view to achieving a common purpose.

A key feature in any joint arrangement is **sharing** – of costs, benefits and risks – among the entities working together.

> **Joint venture:** An arrangement where two (or more) entities join forces to create a separate entity which has a purpose which is distinct from the entities that established it, although it usually shares some of the assets and skills of the parent entities.

5.5.1 Advantages and disadvantages of joint ventures

The following are potential advantages and disadvantages of joint ventures:

Advantages

- Costs and risks are shared between venture partners
- Specialisation – each partner brings their respective technical expertise to the venture. Enable specialist expertise to be built up quickly

LEARNING
MEDIA

- Cheaper than acquisition
- Can be used where outright acquisition is not feasible (eg due to regulatory restrictions)

Disadvantages

- Profits have to be shared between the venture partners.
- Prone to conflicts of interest between the partners
- Control is lost to some extent (because decisions are taken collectively by partners).
- Need to share potentially sensitive commercial information with partners (which they could subsequently use for their own benefit)

Joint ventures work best where the venture partners contribute different skills and specialisms to the venture eg the world's first colour screen mobile phone was a collaboration between Sony (colour screens) and Ericson (handsets).

5.6 Strategic alliances

An **alliance** is a looser form of co-operation between two or more organisations, which falls short of the formation of a separate entity. It will often involve the sharing of resources and activities between entities to pursue a given strategy. It often also involves a detailed legal agreement setting out how firms will work together.

5.7 Advantages and disadvantages of alliances

The following are potential advantages and disadvantages of strategic alliances:

Advantages

- Can build close contacts with alliance partners.
- Share development costs (eg in relation to research and development projects). Alliances can also help to spread the risk attached to research projects and new technologies.
- Alliances can be 'learning' exercises, where partners can learn as much as possible from each other.
- Lock out other competitors (who are not part of the alliance) or work together to compete more effectively against a dominant player in the market.
- By working together, alliance partners may be able to exploit synergies between their different businesses.

Disadvantages

- Disputes over control of strategic assets, leading to a breakdown of trust and co-operation between partners.
- Need to share potentially sensitive commercial information with partners (which they could subsequently use for their own benefit).
- A number of alliances end in takeover (possible after one of the organisations has gained knowledge from their partners). Firms entering an alliance need to be aware of this risk.
- Because the partners in alliances remain separate entities this may limit the level of integration or synergies they achieve (eg economies of scale).

5.8 Franchises

A franchise is a form of licensing agreement, in which the franchiser gives the franchisee the rights to use its trade-name and certain business processes to provide a good or service. (The fast food chain, McDonald's, is one of the most well-known franchisers).

Franchising enables the franchiser to expand a business using less capital than would otherwise be possible, because franchisees not only pay a capital lump sum to the franchiser to enter the franchise, but also bear some of the running costs of the operations.

Activity 4: Franchising

Franchisers and franchisees provide different inputs into a business.

Required

Identify whether each of the following is contributed by the franchiser or the franchisee.

Inputs	Franchiser/franchisee
Payment for rights and support services	[▼]
Capital, personal involvement and local market knowledge	[▼]
Support services, such as advertising, training, research and development	[▼]
Name and any goodwill associated with it	[▼]
Responsibility for day-to-day running of the operations	[▼]
Systems and business methods, business strategy and managerial know-how	[▼]

Picklist:

Franchiser

Franchisee

Solution

5.8.1 Advantages and disadvantages of franchises

Advantages

- Reduces capital requirements compared to organic growth (because franchisees contribute capital)
- Reduces managerial resources required – eg franchisees supply the staff required for day-to-day operations, and manage them
- Reduced capital and resource requirements enable faster growth than through internal development
- Reduces risk – franchiser can judge the profitability of different sites without incurring a significant business risk (because the franchisee incurs the majority of the risk of failure in a given site)

Disadvantages

- Profits have to be shared (with the franchisee)
- Dependent on the quality of the franchisee
- Risk to reputation (eg franchisee can damage the public perception of a brand by providing inferior goods or services)
- Time and cost involved in searching for competent franchisees, and then controlling them
- Likely to need an established brand name in order to attract franchisees – so typically not suitable for small, new businesses

5.9 Licensing

A licensing agreement is similar to a franchise. The licenser gives the licensee the right to exploit a product or process in exchange for certain payments. For example, many beers and lagers in the UK are brewed 'under licence' – meaning that the company that originally developed them (Fosters, Heineken) receives a share of the proceeds from the local brewer which actually produces them.

Assessment focus point

The syllabus requires you to be able to analyse methods of growth in order to establish a choice of possible future growth strategies. In this respect it is important to understand the potential advantages and disadvantages of potential growth strategies, in order to assess how appropriate they might be in different situations.

5.10 Digital business models and growth

We will look at digital business models in more detail in Chapter 12, but one of the issues companies face is deciding how to implement a digital business model.

The methods of growth we have already discussed (**organic, acquisition, partnership**) can still be used in the context of implementing a digital business model, but companies could also consider two further options: **invest** and **incubate**.

(Based on: *World Economic Forum, 2016*)

Option for growth	Comments
Build (ie organic growth)	• May be the best approach if the digital opportunity is related to the company's core business • But is the slowest option and is only suitable if there is sufficient time for the company to respond to market changes • Company must be able to hire the necessary talent (to implement its digital strategy)

Option for growth	Comments
Buy (ie acquisition)	• Is likely to be appropriate if it is strategically important to 'own' a market • May be necessary if a rapid response is needed to market change, or if it is not possible to hire the necessary talent in-house • May be appropriate if new opportunities have few links to the company's current business model • But potential issues (time, effort, cost) in trying to integrate the acquisition's operations into the existing company • May be more appropriate to retain the entrepreneurial culture of the innovative company, rather than trying to integrate
Partner	• Partnering with a digital native can help an incumbent learn more about the market and the partner's model • Can be appropriate if there is no immediate need to 'own' a market, and there is time to identify emerging opportunities • Can be a stepping-stone to deeper partnerships or acquisitions in future
Invest (in a digital start-up)	• Incumbent can connect with the skills and capabilities of the digital company (start-up) • Start-up retains its agility, entrepreneurial nature, and attractiveness to young, digital talent (contract with acquisition) • But corporate venture capital (CVC) activity can be risky. CVCs should look to aim to develop a good portfolio of investments.
Incubate/accelerate	• Similar to investment, but with a closer relationship between the funding company and the start-up • Funding company may provide capabilities, infrastructure and resources to the start-up • Funding company can benefit from access to new technologies • Incumbent needs to commit capital and leadership (including leaders with entrepreneurial experience)

5.10.1 Digital partnerships

Digital partnerships are becoming increasingly common, with non-technology companies joining with digital start-ups. These partnerships allow the companies to draw upon each other's expertise to create innovative or complementary products and services, and to extend these offerings to reach wider audiences and markets (*Accenture, 2016*).

Real life example – Banks and digital disruptors

As digital competition intensifies among financial institutions, banks are finding that the start-ups they once considered threats can be valuable strategic and operational allies. Many are moving to increase collaboration with fintech companies, rather than developing solutions in-house. This enables the banks to gain access to innovative technologies and business models that are more efficient and offer greater convenience for customers. Other advantages associated with such partnerships include: new customers, lower costs, and exposure to an innovative culture that might help the banks reinvent themselves (*Datesh et al, 2018*).

6 International expansion

The expansion method matrix highlights that one of the key ways organisations can look to expand is through international growth, and we have already mentioned in Chapter 4 that globalisation opens up opportunities to shift production internationally, or to sell to customers in new countries.

6.1 International production

There are two main reasons for moving production to a new country:

Cost or competence-led location: a country provides the best value or most cost-effective location – for example, due to low labour costs. The cost reduction opportunities must be sufficient to overcome any costs in subsequently transporting products to market though.

Market-led location: a company locates some of its production activities inside a particularly attractive market, in order to benefit from customer demand in that market. Locating in a country could also be important in enabling a company to avoid trade barriers (such as tariffs or import quotas).

6.2 Reasons for international growth

Firms may be pushed into international expansion by domestic adversity or pulled into it by attractive opportunities abroad.

- **Life cycle:** International expansion may allow sales growth since products are often in different stages of the product life cycle in different countries. For example, if a product is at the mature stage of its life cycle in a firm's home market the potential for sales growth will be limited. Therefore, it could be beneficial to expand into an emerging market where the product may be at the introductory or growth stages of its life cycle, so the opportunities for growth should be greater.

- **Competition:** Intense competition in an overcrowded domestic market sometimes induces firms to seek markets overseas where rivalry is less keen.

- **Reduce dependence:** Many companies wish to diversify away from an overdependence on a single domestic market. Increased geographical diversification can help to **spread risk**.

- **Economies of scale:** Technological factors may be such that a large volume of sales is needed either to cover the high costs of plant, equipment, or R&D.

- **Cheaper sources of raw materials:** Access to cheaper raw materials, or cheaper labour, could be a source of competitive advantage for an organisation, particularly if it is pursuing a cost leadership strategy.

- **Financial opportunities:** Many firms are attracted by favourable opportunities such as:
  (i)   The development of lucrative emerging markets (such as China and India)
  (ii) Corporate tax benefits offered by particular countries

6.3 Evaluating international expansion

Before expanding internationally, the company must evaluate the decision, as it would any other strategic decision. Key questions to consider are:

- Does the expansion fit with the company's overall mission and objectives? Could there be any CSR implications?
- Will the expansion make a positive contribution to shareholders' wealth?
- Does the organisation have (or can it raise) the resources necessary to exploit effectively the international opportunities?

7 Divestment

So far we have looked at growth and acquisition strategies. However, not all growth strategies prove successful. In particular, companies which have pursued diversification strategies may find they need to refocus on their core competences rather than trying to maintain a wider range of interests. As such, groups may need to divest (dispose of) the business units which no longer fit into their corporate portfolio.

Methods of divestment are:

- **Sale as a going concern**: a business unit is sold to another business (in return for cash and/or shares). This option allows the business to continue, and so should allow staff to keep their jobs. It should also provide continuity for customers.
- **Assets are liquidated**: the business is closed and its assets are sold. This is likely to create job losses. While this option may be necessary if no buyer can be found, it can create negative publicity. For example, if the business being closed is part of a group, it may raise questions about the group as a whole.
- **Demerger**: see below
- **Management buy-out**: see below

7.1 Demerger

Demerger refers to the splitting of one company into two or more separate companies, leaving shareholders with a stake in each of the new companies.

The reasons **for** demerging may include:

- To focus on core competences, product/market knowledge
- To enable a higher P/E ratio to be established for the division of the business with growth prospects, making raising capital easier
- To enable shareholders to realise their investment in divisions of the company whose strategies they do not support
- To raise capital to pay off the debt burden or enable investment in the core business

Reasons **not to** demerge include:

- Lost synergies and economies of scale
- Splitting assets, resources may prove problematic
- Legal, accounting, tax hurdles may exist
- Can the new companies establish effective systems and controls?

7.2 Management buy-out (MBO)

KEY TERM

> **Management buy-out (MBO):** The 'purchase of a business from its existing owners by members of the management team, generally in association with a financing institution. Where a large proportion of the new finance required to purchase the business is raised by external borrowing, the buy-out is described as leveraged' (*CIMA, 2005*).

This option may appear attractive to managers because it gives them the chance to **control their own business,** with the absence of any head office constraints.

Moreover, it removes any concerns about **redundancy or imposed changes** if the business is sold to a new owner.

Finally, the management team should know the **business's potential,** and if they think it is profitable they should be well positioned to maximise that profitability.

However, the MBO option may also be attractive for the divesting company because it can present the MBO as being an opportunity for the business to **develop its own talent.**

The managers put in some of their own capital but obtain the rest from venture capital organisations and hope to make a bigger success of the business than the company which is selling it off.

Chapter summary

Generating strategic options

Porter's generic strategies

Cost leadership
- Low costs and low prices
- Creates barrier to entry
- Allows profits to be made in mature markets
- Can cut prices to increase market share (whilst still making a profit)

Differentiation
- Characteristics of products/ services which are valuable to customers allow premium prices to be charged
- Creates barrier to entry; reduces price pressure; builds customer loyalty

Focus
- Can focus on basis of low cost or differentiation
- Market segmentation (eg buyer groups; geographical area)

Further aspects of generic strategies

Bowman's strategy clock
- Hybrid strategies can be successful (contrary to Porter's generic strategies)
- Range of strategies: no frills; low price; hybrid; differentiation; focused differentiation

Overall limitations of generic strategies
- Problems of defining the industry
- Problems of defining the strategic unit

Product-market strategy – direction of growth

Ansoff's matrix
- Market penetration (existing products; existing markets)
- Market development (existing products; new markets)
- Product development (new products; existing markets)
- Diversification (new products; new markets)

Diversification can be:
- related (horizontal/vertical integration)
- unrelated (conglomerate)

Methods of growth

Factors to consider:
- Resources/capabilities available
- Speed
- Control

Lynch's expansion matrix
- Choices:
  - Home country vs abroad
  - Internal vs external development
- Home & internal: organic growth
- Abroad & internal: exporting; foreign manufacturing; multinational/global operation
- External (home or abroad):
  - Merger/acquisition
  - Joint venture
  - Alliance
  - Franchise/Licence
- Each method has potential advantages and disadvantages

International expansion

Two main reasons to move production:
- Cost/competence led
- Market led

Divestment

Potential methods:
- Sale as a going concern
- Liquidation of assets
- Demerger
- Management buy out

BPP
LEARNING
MEDIA

Key terms

Cost leadership: Means being the lowest cost producer in the industry as a whole.

Differentiation: Involves providing uniqueness in a way which is sufficiently valued by customers across the industry to allow a price premium.

Focus: Involves a restriction of activities to only part of the market (a segment). Focus can involve providing goods and/or services at the lowest cost in that segment (cost focus) or providing a differentiated product or service (differentiation focus).

Related diversification: Strategy development beyond current products and markets but within the capabilities or value network of the organisation (*Johnson et al, 2017*).

Joint venture: An arrangement where two (or more) entities join forces to create a separate entity which has a purpose which is distinct from the entities that established it, although it usually shares some of the assets and skills of the parent entities.

Management buy-out (MBO): The 'purchase of a business from its existing owners by members of the management team, generally in association with a financing institution. Where a large proportion of the new finance required to purchase the business is raised by external borrowing, the buy-out is described as leveraged' (*CIMA, 2005*).

Activity answers

Activity 1: Gear Co

The correct answer is:

Differentiation

Gear is trying to use its brand name and reputation to differentiate itself from its competitors, and to be able to charge a price premium for its vehicles.

The fact that Gear produces a wide range of vehicles, across different market segments, suggests Gear is looking to compete across the market as a whole, rather than adopting a 'focus' strategy and only competing in a single market niche.

Activity 2: Flinding

The correct answer is:

Market penetration

The advertising campaign is designed to help Flinding sell more of its existing products (ie to increase market share).

The campaign uses an advertising medium Flinding has regularly used before, meaning it is not designed to target new markets, or new market segments.

Therefore, in terms of Ansoff's matrix, Flinding's strategy is based around existing products, and existing markets, making it a market penetration strategy.

Activity 3: Internal development

The correct answer is:

Input	Advantage/disadvantage
Burden of risk associated with a strategy	Disadvantage
Developing a new product allows a firm to understand the product and its market	Advantage
Maintaining corporate culture	Advantage
Barriers to entry	Disadvantage
Level of disruption to existing business	Advantage
Time taken to get to market	Disadvantage
Lack of suitable target companies	Advantage
Exploiting the firm's technological innovations	Advantage

Reasons for pursuing internal development (Advantages)	Problems with internal development (Disadvantages)
Learning process. The process of developing a new product gives the firm the best understanding of the market and the product.	**Time taken to get to market** – it takes longer for a firm to grow organically than, for example, to acquire another firm. This may be a particular problem in an industry which is changing rapidly.

Reasons for pursuing internal development (Advantages)	Problems with internal development (Disadvantages)
Innovation. It might be the only sensible way to pursue genuine technological innovations and exploit them.	**Barriers to entry** – if a firm is looking to enter new markets it may lack access to key supplier or distribution networks. Also, it will not have the brand awareness of established firms.
Internal development can be planned more meticulously and **offers little disruption.**	**Resource needs** – the firm will have to acquire the resources it needs independently.
The same style of **management and corporate culture** can be maintained.	**Risk of failure** – the firm has to bear all the risk of any strategies; but, for example, in a joint venture risk would be shared with the venture partner.
There is **no suitable target** for acquisition.	
The organisation has **sufficient resources and competences** to finance and deliver growth itself.	

Activity 4: Franchising

The correct answer is:

Inputs	Franchiser/franchisee
Payment for rights and support services	Franchisee
Capital, personal involvement and local market knowledge	Franchisee
Support services, such as advertising, training, research and development	Franchiser
Name and any goodwill associated with it	Franchiser
Responsibility for day-to-day running of the operations	Franchisee
Systems and business methods, business strategy and managerial know-how	Franchiser

Test your learning

1   A car manufacturer makes all its cars by hand and only serves a very small part of the market. Its target market is car enthusiasts who like cars with a traditional design but high performance, resembling that of a sports car. Because cars are hand-made, they are expensive to buy.

Required
What kind of generic strategy is the car manufacturer pursuing?

A   Cost leadership

B   Differentiation

C   Cost leadership – focus

D   Differentiation – focus

2   **Required**
Which one of the following will be the growth strategy pursued by an entity that wishes to continue selling to its current markets, but wants to increase its product range and start selling new products?

A   Market development

B   Product development

C   Market penetration

D   Diversification

3   A confectionery manufacturer has recently acquired one of the dairy farms which supplies the milk it uses to make its chocolate.

Required
Which of the following best describes the growth strategy used by the confectionery manufacturer?

A   Backward vertical integration

B   Horizontal integration

C   Forward vertical integration

D   Conglomerate diversification

4   **Required**
Which of the following are possible disadvantages of a joint venture arrangement?

(i)   Disagreements between the venture partners over management and marketing strategy.

(ii)   Profits have to be shared among the venture partners.

(iii)   Confidential information about the partners could get shared between them.

A   (i) and (ii) only

B   (i) and (iii) only

C   (ii) and (iii) only

D   (i), (ii) and (iii)

5   **Required**
Which of the following is NOT a valid advantage of acquisitions as a method of growth?

A   Speed in providing access to resources and competences

B   The potential for cost savings from economies of scale

C   Avoiding the problems of cultural change associated with organic growth

D   Avoiding potential barriers to entry into a new geographical market

Forecasting and scenarios

Syllabus learning outcomes

Having studied this chapter you will be able to work through the following syllabus outcomes:

Syllabus Area E3: Strategic options	
2	Option generation
c	Potential organisational operating ecosystem
d	Frameworks to generate options

Exam context

In the exam, you will be expected to demonstrate competence in the following representative task statements:

- Use trend analysis and system modelling to forecast potential organisational operating ecosystems
- Use scenario planning and long-range planning as tools in strategic decision making
- Analyse game theory approaches in strategic planning and decision making (complex numerical questions will not be tested)
- Analyse Real Options as a tool for strategic analysis (complex numerical questions will not be tested)

Chapter overview

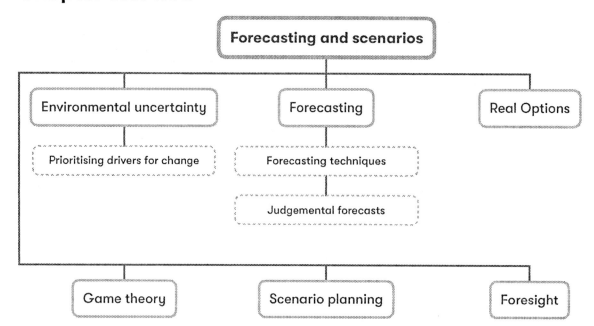

1 Introduction

In Chapters 2 and 3 we have discussed the way in which the external environment (the wider operating ecosystem) is a source of opportunities and threats which an organisation needs to be aware of when developing its strategy. Changes in the environment can also have an impact on strategy planning – for example, by creating new opportunities or presenting new threats.

As a result, organisations need to gather information about their environment to help inform their strategic choices. However, information about the environment can often be uncertain (due to its complexity and dynamism).

The topics we cover in this chapter (forecasting, real options, game theory, scenario planning, foresight) are ways an organisation can try to deal with some of the uncertainty they face in their strategic planning.

Topics covered in this chapter:

- Trend analysis
- System modelling
- Scenario planning
- Game theory perspectives
- Real options perspectives

2 Environmental uncertainty

As we have discussed in Chapter 3, external drivers for change mean that organisations operate within complex, dynamic and uncertain environments, which present opportunities and threats to them.

Illustration 1: Environmental scanning

Required
Which of the following are reasons why an organisation will need to scan its environment?

A   To identify core capabilities

B   To identify drivers of change

C   To benchmark performance

D   To identify market and product developments

E   To ensure legal compliance

Solution

The correct answers are:

- To identify drivers of change
- To benchmark performance
- To identify market and product developments
- To ensure legal compliance

An organisation's core capabilities relate to its own strengths and weaknesses, and therefore are internal factors.

However, all of the other options will require an organisation to scan its environment (eg to understand competitors' performance (for benchmarking; or to be aware of any changes in legislation and regulation, to ensure legal compliance).

Equally, organisations have to develop strategies in the face of uncertainty, and changes in the environment can undermine strategic plans by challenging their underlying assumptions.

The challenges these create for organisations include:

- Planning horizons will need to be shortened.
- Strategies may become more conservative.
- Emergent strategies may prevail over planned strategies.

2.1 Identifying key drivers for change

The complexity and dynamism in environments mean that there could be huge numbers of factors which could affect an organisation. Therefore it is necessary to step back and identify the key drivers for change: the environmental factors likely to have a high impact on industries and sectors, and the success or failure of strategies within them (*Johnson et al, 2017*).

Identifying the key drivers for change in an industry or sector helps managers focus on the factors that are most important and which must be addressed most urgently (in order to minimise threats, or seize opportunities).

2.2 Prioritising drivers of change

The exact drivers for change in any scenario will depend on the context of an organisation and its industry. However, once an organisation's leaders have identified the opportunities and threats facing their organisation they also have to prioritise them.

One useful way of prioritising drivers for change – and strategic uncertainties more generally – is in relation to their impact and immediacy.

The impact (importance) of a strategic uncertainty is related to:

- The extent to which it involves trends or events that will impact the organisation
- The importance to the organisation of the business units or products affected by the uncertainty/change
- The number of business units or products potentially affected by the uncertainty ie the scale of the impact on the organisation

The immediacy or urgency of a strategic uncertainty is related to:

- The likelihood (risk) of a trend or event occurring – if an event only has a low probability of occurring it may not be worth acting upon
- The time frame of the trends or events (eg does the event need an immediate response?)
- The time which will be available in which to react to the event, compared with the time which will be required to develop and implement an appropriate strategy to respond to that event

The order of priority for responding to environmental drivers can then be determined in relation to the relative impact (importance) and immediacy (urgency) of the different drivers. This can be illustrated in the importance/urgency matrix (*Aaker and McLoughlin, 2010*) as follows:

		Strategic importance	
		Low	High
Urgency	**High**	Lower priority	**Highest priority** (major issues)
	Low	Other issues (lowest priority)	High priority (but not as high as major issues)

Aaker and McLoughlin's (2010) strategic uncertainty matrix suggests that an organisation should then **respond to strategic uncertainties** on the basis of their urgency and importance as follows:

Strategic uncertainty matrix (Based on: Aaker and McLoughlin, 2010)

		Strategic importance	
		Low	High
Urgency	High	Monitor and analyse	Analyse in detail and develop a strategy to deal with the uncertainties
	Low	Monitor	Monitor, analyse and consider contingent strategies

3 Forecasting

To some extent, all strategic decisions involve forecasts about future conditions and outcomes.

KEY TERM

> **Forecast:** A prediction of future events and their quantification for planning purposes (*CIMA, 2005*).

In simple/static conditions, the past can be a relatively good guide to the future, and so forecasts can be made with a reasonable degree of certainty. However, in dynamic conditions, this is not the case.

Johnson *et al* (2017) suggest that while organisations may be able to make **single-point forecasts** in circumstances where there is a high degree of certainty about the future, where there is less certainty **range forecasting** – suggesting a range of possible outcomes – may be more appropriate.

Nonetheless, one of the underlying weaknesses of all forecasting models is that they are based on the assumption that the future will resemble the past.

In dynamic/complex conditions techniques such as scenario planning (see later) can be useful as they propose a number of different possible futures.

3.1 Forecasts and trends

Managers need to check that forecasts remain consistent with major trends, and they need to be alert to possible turning points. Johnson *et al* (2017) highlight three key areas for managers to focus on:

- **Megatrends** – large scale changes (eg in PESTEL factors) which affect other activities; eg demographic trends could influence trends in retail spending, housing, demand for social care (as discussed in Chapter 3).
- **Inflexion points** – moments when trends shift in direction, for instance turning sharply upwards or downwards (eg the impact of internet retail has resulted in a downturn in urban shopping in advanced economies). Inflexion points are likely to invalidate forecasts that extrapolate existing trends.
- **Weak signals** – advanced signs of future trends, which can be particularly helpful in identifying inflexion points.

Weak signals are typically pieces of information which do not fit with expected patterns or trends (eg the rise in mortgage failures in California in 2007 was a weak signal for the worldwide financial crisis that began in 2008).

However, while it is important to be alert to weak signals, it can be difficult to distinguish between them and isolated and random pieces of information ('noise') which do not have any strategic significance.

One of the indicators of a weak signal could be the emergence of some kind of pattern in information, potentially accompanied by an unexpected failure in something that had previously worked reliably.

3.2 Statistical forecasting techniques

Although it is important to be aware of the limitations of forecasts, they can be useful in helping managers plan for the future, particularly in relatively static conditions.

Statistical forecasting techniques include: trend analysis, regression analysis and econometrics.

3.2.1 Trend analysis

In trend analysis, data from past events is collected and analysed with a view to identifying a pattern, or trend, in that data, and using that trend to gain an idea of what may happen in the future. Organisations can then develop a strategy to respond to the trends, in line with their business goals.

Again, however, one of the limitations of trend analysis is that if conditions change dramatically, historical data may no longer apply.

Data analytics – drawing insights from large and complex data sets – can also be an important capability in forecasting. This uses data patterns form the past, combined with industry and entity knowledge, and can help management to anticipate the future and plan more effectively as a result.

Whereas traditional business intelligence has often be backward-looking (understanding what has happened, and why), data analytics has a **forward-looking focus** helping to make predictions about what will happen.

Market trend analytics – the process of determining whether a market is growing, stagnant or in decline and how fast that movement is occurring.

For example, if an organisation knows that its market is stagnant or declining, this could be a driver for the organisation to invest in research and development to create new products that can compete in upward trending markets while it extracts the last of the value it can from its current market (*Marr, 2016*).

3.2.2 Time series analysis

Time series analysis is a type of trend analysis. It aims to identify seasonal and other cyclical fluctuations, and to distinguish these from long-term underlying trends (for example, the UK unemployment figures are affected by seasonal variations and underlying trends).

3.2.3 Regression analysis

Regression analysis aims to identify correlation between different variables.

Regression analysis can be useful for forecasting the impact that a change in one variable is likely to have on another. (For example, if it is shown that there is a strong correlation between the price of a product and demand for it, a company can use this to assess the potential impact a change in price could have on future demand for the product.)

However, when using regression analysis it is important to remember that correlation is not causation. Simply because two variables are related does not necessarily mean one causes the other.

3.2.4 Econometrics

Econometrics studies the interrelationships between economic variables (for example, interest rates, tax rates, household income and consumer spending). Econometricians study past

relationships between variables, and then try to forecast how changes in some variables will affect others.

Leading indicators are indicators which change **before** market demand changes. For example, a sudden increase in interest rates could be an indicator of future demand for consumer goods.

3.3 System modelling

An organisation can use complex computer programs to try to model aspects of the external environment (eg economic systems, market competition) and to capture the complex interactions between the various economic and non-economic drivers in the organisation's environment.

Many large accounting packages include forecasting and analytics facilities, which can provide insights that help management make better decisions and improve performance.

However, one of the key challenges in any modelling exercise comes from identifying all the variables which need to be included and understanding how they relate to each other.

3.4 Judgemental (or intuitive) forecasts

In contrast to statistical projections and forecasts, judgemental (or intuitive) forecasts place much greater emphasis on judgement, opinions and intuition. Judgemental forecasting methods include:

Jury forecasts – a panel of experts and/or executives prepare forecasts, and a consensus forecast emerges from the panel.

Think tank – a group of experts are encouraged, in a relatively unstructured atmosphere, to speculate about future development in particular areas, and to identify possible courses of action.

Delphi method – experts respond to detailed questionnaires, anonymously giving their opinions and insights on a particular trend and how it may develop. The experts complete their questionnaires independently, and do not meet in person, to avoid any group pressure to agree with the opinions of specific known individuals. These initial results are summarised and the summary is returned to the experts who are then asked to respond again (still anonymously) once they have seen the responses of the group. This process is repeated until a consensus is achieved.

Illustration 2: Halton plc

Halton plc is attempting to forecast future events in its operating environment. To help it do this, it has asked a number of industry experts to identify what they believe will be the key potential developments in the next ten years. Halton plc wants to avoid any risk that specific experts influence the views of others, so all the experts have been asked for their responses anonymously, through a questionnaire survey.

Required

Which approach to forecasting is Halton plc using?

A   System modelling

B   Jury forecast

C   Think tank

D   Delphi method

Solution

The correct answer is:

Delphi method

Gathering responses anonymously is a key characteristic of the Delphi method; whereas in jury forecasts or think tanks the experts would be encouraged to discuss ideas among each other.

We will now look at some of the techniques which may be used to reduce the impact of uncertainty.

4 Real options

Options theory can be applied to strategic decision making, in the following ways:

- **Option to make follow-on investments** – an initial investment in a project may itself yield a negative NPV but give rise to further positive opportunities (which an organisation can only invest in if it undertakes the initial project). The follow-on investments should therefore be factored into the initial investment decisions.

- **Option to abandon** – where initial investment is high, and is followed by uncertain revenue streams, the option to abandon later may be valuable. This may occur where market acceptance of a new product/service is uncertain.

- **Option to wait** – choosing to wait before investing may allow for better information to become available. In this instance the benefit of better decision making needs to be weighed against the early cash flows foregone while waiting to invest.

In each of these instances the option can be valued via the Black–Scholes model. The resulting option value can then be added to the initial NPV of the project, allowing a more informed decision to be made.

Generally, the options will be become more valuable the longer their duration and as the level of uncertainty in a project increases.

Activity 1: Ranwem Co

Ranwem Co, a civil engineering company, has entered a fixed price contract to build a new sports stadium, and therefore faces a risk that it could make a loss on the contract if the costs associated with building the stadium increase significantly.

Ranwem's finance director has suggested making use of 'real option' theory to reduce the risk the company faces.

Required
Which type of real option is MOST useful to Ranwem in this situation?

A   Option to follow on

B   Option to abandon

C   Option to delay

D   None of them

Solution

5 Game theory

In Chapter 3 we discussed competitor analysis, and one of the elements of competitor analysis is considering how competitors might respond to an organisation's strategy.

Game-based approaches to strategy argue that, in addition to an organisation's own resources and general environment, its **competitor reactions** should be factored into strategic decision making.

In other words, game theory illustrates the problem of **interdependent decision-making** which organisations face.

> **Game theory:** A framework for shaping optimal decision making among interdependent and competing entities. The key to game theory is that the benefits one entity derives from a strategy are dependent on the strategy implemented by the other entity.

Gauging competitors' likely reaction to a strategy should increase an organisation's ability to choose a strategy that will be successful.

Illustration 3: Competitive strategies

Firms A and B are the two market leaders in the soft drinks market in a country, and between them they hold virtually 100% of the market share.

Firm A is planning to launch a major advertising campaign, because its marketing director believes this will not only increase its own sales and profit, but also reduce those of its rival (B).

However, the marketing director in Firm A has not considered B's response.

B has become aware of A's campaign and is now considering launching a campaign of its own, to restore its market share.

At the moment, both A and B make profits of $250 million per year. Firm A intends to spend $25 million on its campaign, because it wants a major campaign to generate a significant increase in revenue. The anticipated increase in revenue resulting from the campaign is $75 million.

Because A and B essentially share the market, A's revenue increase is expected to come from customers who switch to it from B (ie overall market sales will remain largely the same despite the advertising campaign).

However, B then runs its rival campaign, which also costs $25 million and generates it $75 million additional revenue (with customers switching to it from A).

Required

What impact will these campaigns have on A's and B's profits, and the overall profits earned by the soft drinks industry? What implications does this have for the firms' competitive strategies?

Solution

The correct answer is:

A's initial campaign

A's campaign leads to a revenue increase for it of $75 million, but at the same time B will suffer a revenue reduction of $75 million (as customers switch from B to A).

Consequently, at the end of A's initial campaign and in the short term, B will have suffered a reduction in profit of $75 million, while A will have enjoyed an increase in profit of $50 million ($75 million revenue less $25 million marketing costs). This is a **'win–lose'** situation, because A has 'won' while B has 'lost'.

B's campaign

B's rival campaign, also costing $25 million, generates $75 million additional revenue for it, meaning it has an increase in profit of $50 million. This time, A suffers a revenue reduction of $75 million (as customers switch from A to B).

Following the logic from before, this is now a **'lose–win'** situation because A has 'lost' and B has 'won'.

Impact on profits

The impact these campaigns have on A's and B's profits, and the overall profits earned by the soft drinks industry, are as follows:

Option	A's profit	B's profit	Industry profit
Initially (no advertising)	$250m	$250m	$500m
A advertises	$300m	$175m	$475m
B then launches counter advert	$225m	$225m	$450m

Implications

After the advertising campaigns both firms are worse off than they were before, and the industry profit has reduced by the cumulative cost of the advertising campaigns ($25m × 2 = $50m).

So, overall the advertising campaign has created a 'lose–lose' situation.

Although one of the firms can gain in the short run from a competitive strategy, in the long run both firms are likely to be better off by working together and not advertising, rather than competing with each other.

However, one of the assumptions of game theory is that the firms do not have any collusive agreements and do not know what the other is going to do. So A and B must select their strategies based solely on the outcome which they think is best for them, regardless of the decision made by their rival.

Under these circumstances, both firms will choose to advertise. Individually, they hope to increase their profits by advertising. However, as we have seen, collectively this course of action causes them each to lose $25 million (ie profits fall from $250 million each to $225 million each).

Note. This example assumes that there is no increase in the overall size of the market following the advertising campaigns. In practice, this may not be the case as the advertising campaigns might encourage additional people to start drinking soft drinks, although they had previously bought neither Firm A's nor Firm B's drinks.

5.1 Game theory and strategic choices

When implementing a strategy, the reaction of industry rivals should be simulated, to determine which of the following outcomes is likely:

- **We win – Competitors lose** – adopt this strategy
- **We lose – Competitors win** – avoid this strategy
- **We lose – Competitors lose** – avoid this strategy

5.2 Assumptions in game theory

The major assumptions of game theory are that competitors do not collude with each other or have knowledge of competitors' strategies.

However, one of the key implications of game theory is that firms may benefit from **co-operating** and **negotiating** with others in the search for optimal solutions, rather than simply working alone and **competing** with all the other players in the market. In order to create a '**win–win**' scenario, firms are likely to have to compromise and co-operate rather than always seeking to compete with each other.

In this context of networks and co-operation being preferable to constant competition, game theory can help explain the reasoning behind **strategic alliances**.

Assessment focus point

The syllabus requires you to be able to analyse game theory approaches in strategic planning and decision making. A key issue which game theory highlights is the need for organisations to consider the potential reaction of other organisations to their strategies, and how this might affect the success of the strategy. This point could be useful when evaluating strategies more generally, not just in relation to game theory.

6 Scenario planning

KEY TERM

Scenario planning: Involves constructing plausible views of how an organisation's business environment might develop in the future, based on key sets of drivers for change.

Scenario planning allows an organisation to model outcomes for its environment. These scenarios are based upon changing assumptions around key drivers for change about which there is a high level of uncertainty.

Scenarios are not forecasts and predictions, but are plausible views of possible future conditions. The aim of scenario planning is to learn rather than predict the future, so organisations are often advised to produce multiple scenarios, to maximise the learning and contingency planning if necessary.

6.1 Process of scenario planning

There are a variety of different ways of carrying out strategic planning, but the process typically involves the following key stages:

BPP
LEARNING
MEDIA

1 • **Define the scope** (eg time frame involved; products considered; markets considered) and the **major stakeholders** that drive change or affect the industry

2 • **Identify key drivers for change** and areas of uncertainty (eg based on PESTEL factors)

3 • **Construct initial scenarios**, based on the key areas of uncertainty
• Check scenarios for consistency and plausibility

4 • **Identify the implications** and impacts each scenario could have on the organisation
• Identify further information required to fill any gaps in the scenario

5 • **Develop strategies** or courses of actions which could be adopted in different scenarios if they actually happen

As well as developing strategies to respond to scenarios if they happen, organisations should also **identify indicators** that could give early warning of environmental changes (ie that some of the potential scenarios are actually happening).

6.2 Benefits and uses of scenario planning

The benefits of scenario planning include:

- Identification of key uncertainties allowing better planning around these.
- Management are forced to look externally.
- Insight is provided into the future of the industry, helping to shape strategy.
- The organisation as a whole becomes more future orientated.
- Comparing the organisation's present competences and capabilities with those to withstand or benefit from each of the scenarios, can help management identify areas where an organisation needs to strengthen its competences and capabilities.
- Fewer surprises will be encountered as more outcomes are anticipated.
- Managers are encouraged to challenge their assumptions and the ways they think about their organisations and the environment.

Activity 2: Scenario planning

A company is undertaking a scenario planning exercise.

It has constructed its initial scenarios and is checking them for consistency and plausibility.

Required

Which of the following is the next stage the company should undertake in its scenario planning?

A   Identify the major stakeholders that will drive change in the industry

B   Develop strategies that could be adopted if the scenarios actually happen

C   Identify the key drivers for change in the industry

D   Identify the implications and impacts each scenario could have on the company

Solution

7 Foresight

Scenario planning is one of the ways management can attempt to get insights into the future, and thereby prepare their organisation to deal with the opportunities and threats the future holds for it.

The rate and extent of change in the business environment means that organisations can no longer simply rely on their current business models to sustain competitive advantage. Instead they may also need to reinvent their business model in response to the opportunities and threats that lie ahead.

Foresight can be a particularly useful process for identifying possible ways in which the future could develop. It can be described as the art and science of anticipating the future.

Foresight differs from forecasting in that it does not attempt to predict the future. Instead, it aims to identify a range of possible outcomes, based on an understanding and analysis of current trends.

A further characteristic of foresight is the idea that companies try and shape their futures, rather than just waiting for them to happen. To achieve this, organisations need to improve their:

- **Communication** – providing a structure in which groups of people can exchange ideas
- **Concentration** – on long-term outcomes
- **Coordination** – enabling different groups to harmonise R&D activities
- **Consensus** – agreeing future research priorities
- **Commitment** – to research and technological advances

7.1 Foresight techniques

Foresight techniques include:

- **Scenario planning** – see section 6 earlier.
- **Issues analysis** – potentially significant events are analysed in terms of their likelihood and impact. In effect, issues analysis provides a means of developing an **impact analysis matrix**

(importance/urgency matrix) and thereby helping managers to identify and prioritise the key risks they need to consider.

- **Delphi technique** – see section 3.4 earlier.
- **Role playing** – a group of people are given a description of a hypothetical future situation and told to act as they think they would if that situation was actually happening. Analysing their actions can give useful insights into what might happen if that hypothetical situation actually occurred.
- **Cross-impact analysis** – this considers the interdependencies between different events. It involves recording events on a matrix, and at each matrix intersection questioning what impact the event in the row occurring would have on the likelihood of the event in the column occurring. In this way, cross-impact analysis provides a more systematic way of examining a range of possible future events and outcomes.
- **Morphological analysis** – all the attributes of a product or strategy are listed as column headings in a table and then as many variations of each attribute as possible are listed in each column. In effect, a matrix of components is created. One entry from each column is then chosen to create a new mixture of components. This new mixture could represent a new product or strategy.
- **Visioning** – visioning requires an organisation's management to develop a desired, but achievable, future state. A strategic plan is then developed for how to achieve that future state, and goals related to it.

As with many of the other techniques we have discussed, one of the disadvantages of foresight is that it **relies on the future being shaped by actions that can be imagined now**. It cannot take account of sudden one-off events which could dramatically change the business environment.

Nevertheless, foresight can help organisations plan for the uncertainties which they will inevitably face in the future.

7.2 Planning and digital strategy

Future planning and foresight exercises can help companies to determine not only who the key players in a market or environment are currently, but where the key players will be in the future, and how value will be created in the future.

This could be particularly useful for companies in the context of evaluating potential acquisitions, partnerships or investments designed to develop their digital strategy. (We will look at digital strategy in more detail in Chapter 11).

Equally, it could be useful in helping them to join the kinds of platforms that will underpin ecosystem development (as we discussed in Chapter 3).

However, the context of digital strategy and digital disruption could also illustrate the potential limitations of foresight. To what extent were companies able to foresee the disruption caused to markets by new digital entrants and technologies, *prior to* the first digital entrants emerging?

Activity 3: Techniques for uncertainty

Required

Match the following statements to the correct technique:

Input	Technique
There is a reliance on experts' opinions.	⬚ ▼
Analysis can be derived from regression statistics.	⬚ ▼
A range of plausible futures are developed.	⬚ ▼
This extrapolates past data but is fraught with risk.	⬚ ▼
Data is gathered anonymously.	⬚ ▼
This requires key drivers of change and areas of uncertainty to be identified.	⬚ ▼

Picklist:

Delphi technique

Forecasting

Scenario planning

Solution

Chapter summary

Forecasting and scenarios

Environmental uncertainty

Potential implications of uncertainty:
- Shorter planning horizons
- More conservative strategies
- Emergent strategies prevail

Prioritising drivers for change
- Impact/urgency matrix
- Key drivers are high impact and highly likely to happen

Forecasting

Range forecasts likely to be more appropriate than single-point in dynamic conditions

Forecasting techniques
- Trend analysis (using analytics?)
- Time series
- Regression
- Econometrics
- System modelling

Judgemental forecasts
- Jury forecasts
- Think tank
- Delphi technique

Real Options

Options to:
- Wait
- Follow on
- Abandon

Valued using Black-Scholes model

Game theory

- Simulate competitors' reactions to initiatives
- Highlights problem of interdependent decision-making
- Might be more beneficial to co-operate rather than compete

Scenario planning

Construct plausible views of future circumstances

Stages:
- Define scope
- Identify key drivers for change
- Construct initial scenarios
- Identify implications of each scenario
- Identify further information required
- Develop strategies which could be adopted if scenarios occur

Foresight

Aims to identify a range of possible outcomes

Foresight techniques:
- Scenario planning
- Issues analysis
- Delphi technique
- Role playing
- Cross impact analysis
- Morphological analysis
- Visioning

Key terms

Forecast: A prediction of future events and their quantification for planning purposes (*CIMA, 2005*).

Game theory: A framework for shaping optimal decision making among interdependent and competing entities. The key to game theory is that the benefits one entity derives from a strategy are dependent on the strategy implemented by the other entity.

Scenario planning: Involves constructing plausible views of how an organisation's business environment might develop in the future, based on key sets of drivers for change.

Activity answers

Activity 1: Ranwem Co
The correct answer is:

Option to abandon

The risk the company faces is that, if costs increase, it becomes tied into a contract which is loss-making for it.

Therefore, having the option to abandon the contract if costs rise above a certain level would be useful to Ranwem, because it could limit any losses the company will incur on the contract.

Activity 2: Scenario planning
The correct answer is:

Identify the implications and impacts each scenario could have on the company

The company should have already identified the major stakeholder, and the key drivers for change before constructing the initial scenarios.

Developing strategies that could be adopted if scenarios actually happen is the final stage of the process.

Once the company has constructed its initial scenarios and checked them for consistency (Stage 3), the next stage is to identify the implications and impacts of each strategy (Stage 4).

Activity 3: Techniques for uncertainty
The correct answer is:

Input	Technique
There is a reliance on experts' opinions.	Delphi technique
Analysis can be derived from regression statistics.	Forecasting
A range of plausible futures are developed.	Scenario planning
This extrapolates past data but is fraught with risk.	Forecasting
Data is gathered anonymously.	Delphi technique
This requires key drivers of change and areas of uncertainty to be identified.	Scenario planning

Test your learning

1 **Required**

List three types of real options that could be relevant to strategic projects.

2 An organisation follows a strategy which it thinks will be beneficial to it, but because of the response of its competitors the strategy turns out to be detrimental to both the organisation and the industry as a whole.

Required

Which one of the following does this demonstrate best?

A   Emergent strategy

B   Game theory

C   Gap analysis

D   Delphi

3 **Required**

Which of the following is NOT a stage of the scenario planning process?

A   Define the requirements of the project

B   Identify key drivers for change and areas of uncertainty

C   Construct initial scenarios and check for plausibility

D   Develop potential courses of action which could be adopted if scenarios occur

4 **Required**

Which technique for gaining insights into the future is described below?

A number of experts are asked to independently and anonymously give their opinions and insights on a particular trend and how it may develop. These initial results are summarised, and the summary is returned to the experts who are then asked to respond again once they have seen the responses of the group. This process is repeated until a consensus is achieved.

A   Delphi method

B   Cross-impact analysis

C   Morphological analysis

D   Visioning

5 **Required**

Which one of the following is NOT a benefit of scenario planning?

A   It identifies the key uncertainties to which an organisation could be exposed

B   It forces management to look externally at wider business issues, rather than only looking internally at their own organisation

C   It allows management to forecast what is going to happen

D   It can provide managers with useful insights into the future of their industry which can help shape their strategy

Resources and capabilities

Syllabus learning outcomes

Having studied this chapter you will be able to work through the following syllabus outcomes:

Syllabus Area C: Strategic options

2	Option generation
c	Frameworks to generate options

Syllabus Area D: Strategic choices

2	Choices into coherent strategy
a - b	Value analysis and Portfolio analysis

Syllabus Area E: Strategic implementation

2	Resource allocation to support strategy implementation
a - b	Resource availability and Resource allocation to strategic choices

Exam context

In the exam, you will be expected to demonstrate competence in the following representative task statements:

- Analyse value drivers (tangible and intangible) and the data needed to describe and measure them
- Prepare or review a Porter's value chain analysis to assess whether an organisation has a sustainable competitive advantage
- Recommend how to manage the product portfolio of an organisation to support the organisation's strategic goals
- Perform an analysis of key resources and capabilities needed for strategy implementation
- Perform an analysis of forecasts, trend analysis, system modelling, and in-depth consultation with experts to aid resource allocation
- Recommend how to manage the product portfolio of an organisation to support the organisation's strategic goals

Chapter overview

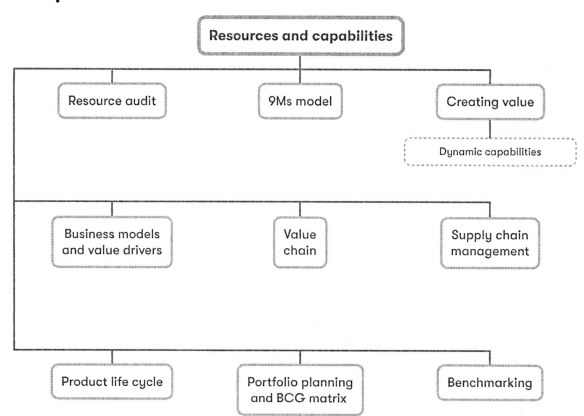

1 Introduction

The analysis stages in the rational model illustrate that, as part of understanding its strategic position, an organisation needs to analyse its own resources and capabilities as well as the external opportunities in the external environment.

In previous chapters, we have looked at the external environment in which an organisation operates. In this chapter, we will now look at the implications an organisation's own resources and capabilities could have for its strategies, and for its ability to develop and sustain a competitive advantage over its rivals.

It is very important for an organisation to understand how it creates value (and what it does well) so that it can develop strategies which build on its strengths.

The value chain can be a key model for helping to identify the sort of strategy (cost leadership, differentiation) that is likely to be appropriate for an organisation.

Another influence on an organisation's ability to sustain a competitive advantage is the products or services it has to sell. Understanding an organisation's product portfolio could be very important in identifying the potential need to develop new products (or potentially to dispose of certain products) in order to help the organisation achieve its strategic goals.

Topics covered in this chapter:

- Tangible and intangible value drivers and data to measure them
- Value chain analysis
- Managing product portfolio
- Audit of key resources and capabilities needed to implement strategy
- Matching resources to strategy

2 The resource audit

2.1 Resources and capabilities

In organisation's internal competences and capabilities affect its ability to deliver value to customers and achieve competitive advantage in an industry. A key question for an organisation to consider, in relation to implementing a strategy, is:

How, and **with what,** do we create the products, services or experiences that meet the needs of our customers?

Other important questions that affect an organisation's ability to deliver value are:

- Does the organisation have a **suitable business model** to deliver future success, based on an understanding of the sources of competitive advantage that contribute to profitability and growth across the value system of the organisation?
- Does it have the **people, processes and resources** it needs to be able to deliver this success?

Resource-based approaches to strategy focus on these **internal characteristics** of an organisation.

The resource-based view is that sustainable competitive advantage can only be attained as a result of possessing distinctive resources or capabilities.

A **resource audit** (or **position audit**) is part of the rational planning process that identifies and analyses the resources and capabilities an organisation has.

This helps management to identify the organisation's internal strengths and weaknesses, and also to identify what additional resources might be required to enable the organisation to pursue its chosen strategy.

3 9 Ms model

A useful tool for undertaking a resource audit is the **9 Ms**. This acts as a checklist of areas to assess as strengths or weaknesses as follows:

Manpower	An analysis of human resources – eg number of staff, skills
Money	An analysis of financial resources
Machinery	An analysis of operational resources such as plant and machinery – eg condition of assets, efficiency
Materials	Purchasing and supplier relationships
Markets	Issues of marketing and distribution to the customers
Management	The corporate, tactical and operational stewardship of the company – eg skills, experience and vision of senior management
Methods	Processes used to create outputs from inputs – eg in-house or outsourced? Are they 'lean'?
Make up	Organisational structure and culture (also need to consider other intangibles, such as patents and brands)
Management information systems	Strategic use of IT and IS – eg availability of information to support strategic decision making, produced on a timely basis

However, in many cases, resources alone are of little or no value to an organisation unless they are organised into processes or activities.

As Johnson et al (2017, p98) note: 'The efficiency and effectiveness of physical or financial resources, of the people in an organisation depend, not just on their existence, but on the systems and processes by which they are managed, the relationships and cooperation between people, their adaptability, their innovatory capacity, the relationships with customers and suppliers and the experience and learning about what works well and what does not.'

This highlights that resources alone are unlikely to implement a strategy successfully. An organisation also needs the capabilities to use those resources effectively.

KEY TERM

> **Capabilities:** An organisation's capabilities are the ways which enable it to use its assets effectively (Johnson et al, 2017).

3.1 Resources and digital strategy

In Chapter 4, we discussed the growth of business ecosystems, and we will also look in Chapter 11 at digital strategies.

An important question for organisations to consider, in relation to developing digital strategies will be:

- Do we have the skills and capabilities to develop and implement this strategy?

Equally, in the context of business ecosystems an important question for organisations to consider will be:

- What resources and capabilities do we have which will enable us to add value to the ecosystem?

3.2 Gap analysis

Gap analysis could be used to compare the expected supply of given resources against demand trends. In this way it helps to identify any 'gaps' in an organisation's resources and capabilities: either where the resources are not sufficient to meet future needs, or where the level of resources an organisation has exceeds anticipated demand trends.

Assessment focus point

The syllabus requires you to be able to analyse forecasts, trend analysis, system models and the results of in-depth consultations (as discussed in Chapter 6) to be able to aid resource allocation. A key issue here could be identifying, from the forecast and analysis, what quantity and type of resources are required to implement a strategy, and what implications this has for an organisation; eg does it have enough resources? Does it have the right types of resource?

4 Creating value

4.1 Capabilities

KEY
TERM

Threshold resources and capabilities: Those needed for an organisation to meet the necessary requirements to compete in a given market and achieve parity with competitors in that market (*Johnson et al, 2017*).

Distinctive resources and capabilities: Those required to achieve competitive advantage.

Strategic advantage can be driven by an organisation's capabilities in the following areas:

- Research and development
- Product design
- Operational efficiency
- Marketing
- Sales and distribution

For example, Apple has distinctive resources in mobile technology and in its powerful brand, but it also has distinctive competences in product design and in understanding consumer behaviour.

4.2 Capabilities and competitive advantage

Johnson *et al* (2017) suggest that if competitive advantage is to be achieved, resources and competences must have four qualities: value, rarity, inimitability, organisational support.

- **Value** – no matter how rare a resource or how well-developed a capability is, it cannot create competitive advantage if customers do not value it or the things it enables the organisation to do.

BPP
LEARNING
MEDIA

- **Rarity** – the importance of rarity is that a resource or capability will only confer an advantage to an organisation if its rivals do not also have access to it.
- **Inimitability** – means that a resource or capability is difficult for competitors to replicate. This quality most frequently relates to the capabilities involved in linking activities and processes in ways that both satisfy customer priorities, and which are difficult for competitors to imitate.
- **Organisational support** – focuses upon whether or not an organisation is able to support its capabilities, including its processes and systems.

4.3 Dynamic capabilities

Strategic capabilities are generally regarded as being more valuable to an organisation if they can sustain a competitive advantage for a long time. However, changes in the external environment may mean that existing capabilities become redundant, or similar capabilities may be developed by competitors – meaning they are no longer rare.

In order to maintain their competitive advantage in a changing environment, firms need to possess **dynamic capabilities**.

> **Dynamic capabilities:** An organisation's ability to renew and recreate its resources and capabilities to meet the needs of changing environments (*Johnson et al, 2017*).

Such capabilities demand the ability to change, to innovate and to learn. They can take many forms and may include such things as systems for new product development or developing new business models, to ensure that an organisation's production plans and processes are aligned with customer needs.

Teece (2018) highlights that successful firms need three key elements of dynamic capabilities:

(a) **Sensing** – organisations must constantly search for, and identify, opportunities across various markets and technologies (eg through new technological developments).

(b) **Seizing** – developing new business models (eg changing processes and activities) as necessary in order to exploit the opportunities.

(c) **Transforming** – reconfiguring its culture, structure and capabilities (eg by acquiring or developing new technologies) as necessary to successfully implement new business models.

The strength of a firm's dynamic capabilities determines its ability to align its resources – and its business model – to customer needs and aspirations, in order to respond effectively to new opportunities or threats as they arise (*Teece, 2018*).

5 Business models and value drivers

One of the issues an organisation needs to consider in its strategic planning is how it makes money, and how this might change in the future – for example, due to changes in the business environment, or the emergence of new business models.

5.1 Business models

Business models are particularly useful when explaining business interrelationships that generate value and profits for more parties than just a buyer and a seller. The concept of business models has become increasingly popular as internet-based companies like Airbnb, Spotify and Uber have disrupted markets and captured market share with their new models.

> **Business model:** 'A business model describes a value proposition for customers and other participants, an arrangement of activities that produces this value, and associated revenue and cost structures' (*Johnson et al, 2017, p229*).

Teece (2010) argues that the essence of a business model is in defining the manner by which an enterprise delivers value to customers, entices customers to pay for value, and converts those payments to profit.

There are three key elements to consider:

(a) Value creation – what is offered to what customer segment? Products/services need to be targeted at specific target segments eg Land Rovers aimed at farming communities.

(b) Value configuration – how is the value proposition structured? Consider how various resources and activities underlie the value proposition (eg technology, brands). Linkages between activities and within the value system are important here; eg Land Rover may supply the car, but a third party may provide the finance package.

(c) Value capture – why does the model generate a margin? The company needs to consider how to ensure its revenues exceed its costs, and how value is apportioned between stakeholders in the value system.

This identifies some key implications for developing strategy:

- Business model design requires deep knowledge of customer needs and the technological and organisational resources and capabilities that might meet those needs.

- It is also important to understand why customers buy particular goods and services, because this could help an organisation identify the critical success factors (CSFs) required to satisfy those customers effectively.

- Business models evolve; they need to change in response to changes in the business environment (eg new technologies) or the actions of competitors. In the longer term, the existing business models may need to be replaced.

5.2 Value drivers

The underlying aim of strategic management in companies is to **create value for shareholders**. In order to do this, managers should focus on identifying and improving a company's performance in relation to the factors or activities that are most important in creating value. These factors are value drivers.

No company can be all things to all people. Therefore, to be successful, an organisation needs to identify the needs and requirements which are most important to its customers, and then focus on delivering them.

Leveraging big data and analytics capabilities to drive insights from customer data can help organisations improve customer experiences, and potentially to develop new products or services.

Value drivers: The factors or capabilities that give a firm a competitive advantage over its rivals. Value drivers are often linked to the features of a product or service that enhance its perceived value for customers, and thereby create value for the producer.

Link to earlier topic

Porter's value chain (Porter, 1985) (which we look at later) is also an important model we can use to look at the way an organisation creates value for its customers.

Real life example – Apple

In 2018, Apple became the first public company to be valued at $1 trillion.

The catalyst for the company's success was the launch of the iPhone in 2007. Between 2007 and 2018, the value of the company's shares increased by more than 1,100%. As such, the development of the iPhone, led by the company's Chief Executive at the time, Steve Jobs, illustrates how exploiting new technologies and opportunities can drive value for an organisation.

In 2006, Apple had sales of less than $20 billion, and profits of around $2 billion. By 2017, sales had risen to $229 billion, with profits of $48.4 billion, making it the most profitable US listed company (Johnston, 2018).

The iPhone transformed Apple's fortunes, and – more widely – started the smartphone revolution that has changed the way billions of people worldwide live and work.

5.3 Types of value driver

At a high level, we can identify three main types of value driver (*L.E.K. Consulting, 2017*):

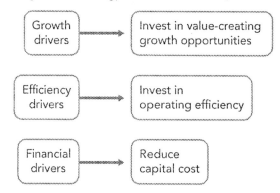

5.4 Rappaport's value drivers

Rappaport (1986) looks at value drivers in more detail, and suggests that the value of a company is dependent on seven drivers of value (based on the idea that the value, to shareholders, of an investment reflects the discounted future cash flow arising from that investment):

(a) Increase sales growth rate

(b) Increase operating profit margin

(c) Reduce tax rate

(d) Reduce incremental investment in capital expenditure

(e) Increase duration of competitive advantage (period of value growth)

(f) Reduce investment in working capital

(g) Reduce cost of capital

 Illustration 1: Value drivers

In order to maximise shareholder wealth Rappaport argues that managers need to focus on the seven drivers of value.

Required

Identify suitable data for measuring performance in each of the following value drivers:

(a) Sales growth rate

(b) Profit margin

(c) Tax payable

(d) Investment in capital expenditure

(e) Period of value growth

(f) Investment in working capital

(g) Cost of capital

Solution

The correct answer is:

Sales growth rate	% annual growth or % market share
Profit margin	% net margin or % gross margin
Tax payable	Tax paid as $ or as a % of net profit or revenue
Investment in capital expenditure	$ spent on tangible/intangible assets, relative to the increase in sales or profit generated by that expenditure

Period of value growth	Months/years added to the life of existing NPV projects
Investment in working capital	Length of cash cycle, made up of receivables, payables, inventory days
Cost of capital	Company's WACC

Remember, identifying the value drivers in a company can also be important in deciding which performance metrics are most important to measure, because a company should try to link its performance metrics to its most important value drivers.

5.5 Tangible and intangible value drivers

Although buildings, equipment and other physical property might be an organisation's most obvious assets, in many organisations the assets and value drivers which are most important in generating competitive advantages are intangible. As we have already mentioned, an organisation's dynamic capabilities – its abilities to sense and respond to changes in the business environment – could help give it a competitive advantage over its rivals.

However, the following (intangible) attributes within a business could all create value for it:

- Superior management
- Employees' skills and knowledge
- Brand and reputation
- Innovation and new product development
- Intellectual property (eg patents)
- Network relationships and linkages
- Quality management

For a high-quality restaurant – with a reputation for good food and offering customers a positive dining experience – key value drivers might include: the skill of the chefs and the quality of the cooking, the quality of the waiting staff, and the ambience of the restaurant.

For a professional services firm (eg accountants, lawyers) key value drivers might include: highly skilled staff, and the quality of the relationships developed with clients.

In both of these cases, the value drivers are **non-financial** and, therefore, the performance metrics needed to measure how well the organisation is performing against them will also need to be non-financial.

5.6 Value drivers and performance management

We discuss performance measurement systems in more detail later in this Workbook, but the need to monitor non-financial performance (as well as financial performance) is central to multidimensional performance measurement systems, such as the balanced scorecard.

An organisation's value drivers should be reflected in its **critical success factors (CSFs)**.

In turn, a firm then needs to define its **key performance indicators (KPIs)** to ensure it measures how well it is performing against its CSFs.

We will look at CSFs and KPIs in more detail in a later chapter.

Assessment focus point

The syllabus requires you to be able to analyse value drivers (tangible and intangible) and the data needed to describe and measure them. The link between value drivers, CSFs and KPIs could be important in this respect. Value drivers are the factors or capabilities that give a firm a competitive advantage over its rivals, and CSFs are the areas in which an organisation needs to outperform its competitors in order to be successful.

6 The value chain

6.1 Porter's Value Chain

Another way of looking at value creation is through the value chain.

Porter observed that an organisation is essentially a system that converts inputs into outputs, the aim being to 'add value' and thus make profits.

For Porter (1985), competitive advantage arises out of the way in which firms organise and perform value-adding activities.

> **Value chain:** The 'sequence of business activities by which, in the perspective of the **end-user**, value is added to the products or services produced by an entity' (*CIMA, 2005*).

Porter's (1985) **value chain** is a graphical representation of what a firm does to add value for the end customer. It illustrates the direct (**primary**) and indirect (**support**) activities the firm performs that allow it to turn raw materials, manpower and capital into finished goods and profits.

Porter's value chain

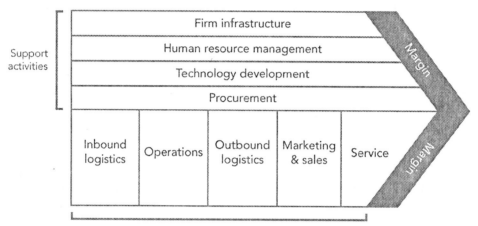

Primary activities

Components of the value chain

The margin is the excess the customer is prepared to pay over the cost to the firm of obtaining resource inputs and providing value activities. It represents the value created by the value activities themselves and by the management of the linkages between them.

6.2 Primary activities

Primary activities are directly related to production, sales, marketing, delivery and service.

- **Inbound logistics** – receiving, handling and storing inputs to the production system (warehousing, transport, inventory control).
- **Operations** – converting resource inputs into a final product or service; resource inputs are not only materials. People are a resource, especially in service industries.
- **Outbound logistics** – storing the product and its distribution to customers: packaging, delivery and so on.
- **Marketing and sales** – informing customers about the product or service, persuading them to buy it, and enabling them to do so: eg advertising, promotion.
- **After-sales service** – installing products, repairing them, upgrading them, providing spare parts and so forth.

6.3 Support activities

Support activities provide purchased inputs, human resources, technology and infrastructural functions necessary to support the primary activities.

- **Procurement** – all of the processes involved in acquiring the resource inputs to the primary activities (eg purchase of materials, subcomponents equipment).
- **Technology development** – product design, improving processes and resource utilisation.
- **Human resource management** – recruiting, training, managing, developing and rewarding people; this activity takes place in all parts of the organisation, not just in the HRM department.
- **Firm infrastructure** – planning, finance, quality control, the structures and routines that make up the organisation's culture.

Assessment focus point

The syllabus requires you to be able to prepare or review a Porter's value chain to assess whether an organisation has a sustainable competitive advantage.

Make sure you know which activities are primary activities and which are secondary, so that you can allocate them to the correct part of the chain.

However, it is also important to note the link to 'sustainable competitive advantage'. The value chain helps to identify the activities which create value for a firm's customers. In doing so, it can also help managers identify the key processes and areas where the firm has to perform successfully to secure a competitive advantage. For example, if a company is pursuing a differentiation strategy, will the way in which it carries out different activities help to support that strategy?

6.4 Value chain and competitive advantage

The value chain has the following implications for strategic management:

- It enables managers to establish the **activities** that are particularly important in **providing customers with the value they want** (ie so the organisation can exploit strengths in these activities, or address weaknesses).
- Porter argues that firms need to ensure that they adopt one of his **generic strategies** (differentiation, cost leadership). The value chain allows managers to check whether all of their processes are consistent with the relevant strategy and are aligned around adding value, or minimising cost.
- The organisation needs to ensure that it is measuring its performance in those key areas which create value for its customers (ie its **critical success factors**).

6.5 Limitations of the value chain

However, the value chain does have its critics who cite the following limitations:

- It was originally designed for use in a manufacturing context, so can be harder to apply to service companies.
- Porter's original model (published in 1985) takes little account of the increasing role of IT and digitisation in business.
- It is a complex model to implement. Making best use of the value chain idea requires adopting at least some part of activity-based costing to establish the costs of value activities. This can be time-consuming and expensive.
- The costs of analysing activities may outweigh the benefits.

Activity 1: ABC Ltd

Application of the value chain

A private college, ABC Ltd, provides training for professional accountancy qualifications. It derives most of its funds from employers and self-financing students. For most qualifications there are a number of stages that students need to go through until full accreditation; this can take up to four years.

In recent years, the college has placed emphasis on recruiting lecturers who have achieved success in delivering good academic knowledge of the syllabus in class along with good pass rates. This has led to the college further improving its reputation within the academic community, and applications from prospective students for its courses have increased significantly.

The college has good student support facilities in respect of website learning support, student helpdesks and excellent material. It has recently implemented a sophisticated online student booking system. Courses at the college are administered by well-qualified and trained non-teaching staff that provide non-academic (that is, not learning-related) support to the lecturers and students.

The college has had no difficulty in filling its courses. The college has also noted in the last year a significant increase in the number of students transferring from other training providers.

You are the college's management accountant and have been asked by the Chief Executive of the college to review the increasing rate of transfer of students to ABC's courses.

Required

For each of the following factors identify which area(s) of the value chain it is enhancing.

Input	Area		
Lecturer recruitment	▾	▾	
Good pass rates	▾	▾	
Good support facilities	▾	▾	
Online booking system	▾	▾	
Well-qualified non-teaching staff	▾	▾	▾
Improved reputation	▾		

Picklist:

Inbound logistics

Operations

Outbound logistics

Sales and marketing

Service

Firm infrastructure

HRM

Technology development

Procurement

Solution

6.6 The value system

The activities which create value for customers are not confined within a single company's boundaries. Instead, an individual company's value chain is connected to what Porter (1985) describes as a value system, and what Johnson *et al* (2017) call a **value network**.

(Adapted from: *Porter, 1985, p35*)

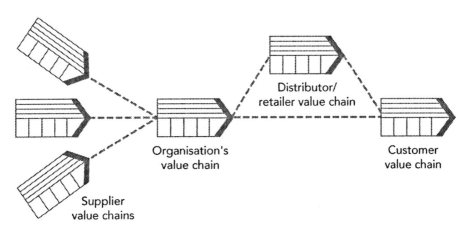

As well as managing its own value chain, a firm can help to secure competitive advantage by managing the linkages (ie relationships) with the value chains of its suppliers and customers. In this way, we can look at a value network as being similar to a supply chain.

However, whereas a supply chain shows the system of organisations, people, technology or activities involved in transforming a product or service from its raw materials to a finished product to be delivered to the end user customer, the value system (or value network) places an emphasis on the value-creating capability within the supply chain processes.

6.7 Strategic value analysis (SVA)

One of the benefits of value chain analysis for managers is that it enables them to understand how the processes they manage add value for the customer. In turn, they can then help identify where the amount of value added can be increased, or else costs lowered, with a view to enhancing the competitive position of their organisation.

However, to help it achieve and maintain a competitive advantage, an organisation also needs to to understand the entire value delivery system (eg its suppliers; its distributors), not just the portion of the value chain in which it participates.

Strategic value analysis (**SVA**) highlights the need to analyse business issues and opportunities across the entire value chain for an industry. Such analysis is critical for multi-stage industries because change in one stage will almost inevitably have an impact on other businesses all along the chain.

SVA prompts companies to ask three key questions:

(a) Are there any new or emerging players in the industry (in any portion of the value chain) that may be more successful than existing players?

(b) Are these companies positioned in the value chain differently from existing players? (In particular, are companies emerging which specialise in single activities within the value chain, eg marketing or logistics, rather than trying to cover all activities?)

(c) Are new market prices emerging across segments of the value chain? If a firm used these market prices as transfer prices in its own company, would it alter the company's perspective on any of its operating units or the way they function?

SVA is particularly relevant to vertically integrated companies, because it encourages them to consider whether it would be more profitable for them to **outsource** certain functions or activities rather than continuing to perform them all in-house.

In such a context, the decisions an organisation takes around which activities to produce in-house, and which to outsource, coupled with the way in which it manages its relationships with its outsource partners could, in themselves, help contribute to its strategic capability and competitive advantage.

6.8 Contrasting value chains and ecosystems

In Chapter 3, we discussed the idea of ecosystems and the way businesses are increasingly collaborating to create value, rather than operating on their own and competing as single entities.

In Porter's original analysis (*Porter, 1985*), the activities in a value chain were all performed by a single company. However, the business models in modern ecosystems are very different from this 'internal' model.

Real life examples – Amazon and Uber

For example, Amazon doesn't manufacture the products which it sells to customers. Instead, when a customer orders a product through Amazon, Amazon transmits that order to the company that manufactures or supplies the item, and that company then distributes the product to the customer. In effect, Amazon is positioned in the middle of a network, routing purchase orders to various parties.

6.9 IT and the value chain

In response to criticism that the value chain took no account of the increasing role of IT in business, Porter and Millar (1985) revisited the model and stressed the importance of using emerging technologies to increase linkages, both internally and externally (*Porter and Millar, 1985*).

Modern applications such as ERP systems will help achieve this and are often viewed as essential in the modern manufacturing environment. Other applications that are commonly used are shown below:

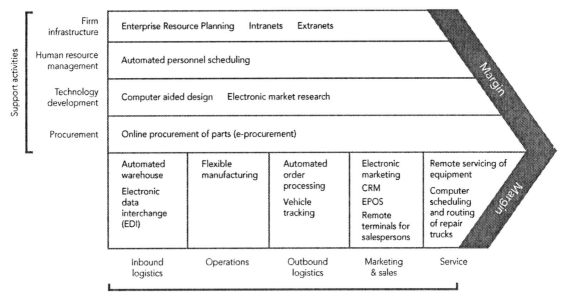

	Firm infrastructure	Enterprise Resource Planning Intranets Extranets				
Support activities	Human resource management	Automated personnel scheduling				
	Technology development	Computer aided design Electronic market research				
	Procurement	Online procurement of parts (e-procurement)				
		Automated warehouse Electronic data interchange (EDI)	Flexible manufacturing	Automated order processing Vehicle tracking	Electronic marketing CRM EPOS Remote terminals for salespersons	Remote servicing of equipment Computer scheduling and routing of repair trucks
		Inbound logistics	Operations	Outbound logistics	Marketing & sales	Service

Primary activities

6.10 Service organisations

An alternative version of the value chain that is applicable to service organisations is the **value shop** (Stabell and Fjeldstad, 1998). This model recognises that although service organisations have the same support activities as manufacturers their **primary activities are different** as illustrated below:

- **Problem-finding and acquisition**: Recording, reviewing and formulating the problem to be solved, and choosing an overall approach to solving the problem. Marketing effort could be required here as well as professional expertise.

- **Problem solving**: Professional expertise must be deployed to identify and evaluate potential solutions to the issue at hand.

- **Choice between solutions**: A preferred solution is chosen (in consultation with the client) from the alternative solutions which have been identified.

- **Solution implementation**: Communicating with the client to organise and implement the chosen solution.

- **Control and feedback**: Measuring and evaluating the extent to which the solution has solved the initial problem, to ensure the effectiveness of the solution.

7 Supply chain management (SCM)

For manufacturers in particular, inbound logistics is a key business function as there is a heavy reliance on external suppliers to ensure a smooth flow of materials into the organisation, allowing it in turn to satisfy the needs of its customers.

7.1 The supply chain and supply chain management

The supply chain is the network of organisations involved in the different activities required to transform raw materials into finished goods and services in order to satisfy the requirements of the end customer.

Supply chain management focuses on the interaction and collaborations required throughout the supply chain in order to ensure that the customers' requirements are satisfied adequately.

There are three main themes to supply chains and supply chain management:

(a) **Responsiveness** – the combination of shortening product life cycles and increasing customer expectations means firms must be able to supply their customers quickly.

(b) **Reliability** – deliveries through the supply chain must be reliable, in terms of timeliness, quality and quantity.

(c) **Relationships** – the need for responsiveness and reliability means that the members of the supply chain need to develop a mutual understanding and trust of each other.

As result, elements of effective supply chain management include:

- **Reduction in the number of suppliers** – to develop relationships with a small number of suppliers
- **Price and inventory co-ordination** – firms co-ordinate their price and inventory policies to avoid problems and bottlenecks caused by short-term surges in demand, such as promotions.
- **Linked computer systems** – EDI saves on paperwork and administrative expense. Technology also enables firms to track the status of purchases from order to dispatch and delivery.
- **Earlier supplier involvement** in product development and component design.

7.2 Supply chain management as a capability

Earlier in the chapter we discussed the idea of capabilities, and supply chain management could be seen as a capability for an organisation.

For example, Seven-Eleven Japan is a company that has used excellent supply chain design, planning and operation to drive growth and profitability (*Chopra and Meindl, 2016*). Seven-Eleven has a very responsive replenishment system which, coupled with an excellent information system, ensures that products are available at each of its convenience stores to match customer needs. The responsiveness of Seven-Eleven's system allows it to change the merchandising mix at each store by time of day, to match precisely with customer demand.

Chopra and Meindl (2016) highlight the importance of the supply chain for organisations when they note that supply chain design, planning, and operation decisions play a significant role in the success or failure of a firm. To stay competitive, supply chains must adapt to changing technology and customer expectations.

7.3 Lean supply chain

The objective of a lean supply chain is the total elimination of waste in order to achieve a competitive advantage.

The advantages of lean supply chains are:

- Reduced cost
- Improved quality leading to lower reworking and scrap costs
- Reduced inventories
- Shorter lead times

The disadvantages of lean supply chains include:

- Focus on cost rather than quality and innovation
- Lower inventory levels reduce production flexibility
- Could result in lock-in with an unreliable or unsuitable supplier

8 The product life cycle (PLC)

The product life cycle (PLC) is a description of the changing demand conditions for a product (or service) over time.

The product life cycle also indicates that products demonstrate different characteristics of revenue, profit and competition at different stages in their life cycle.

Examining where different products are in their life cycles enables a firm to examine its portfolio of goods and services as a whole.

As well as being a strategic marketing tool, the life cycle model is useful for internally assessing an organisation at three levels:

- **Industry life cycle** – to analyse the progress of the industry as a whole

- **Product life cycle** – to analyse the state of a generic product (eg cars)
- **Brand life cycle** – to analyse the state of a particular product or brand (eg a specific make of car)

8.1 Stages of the product life cycle

The four main stages in the life cycle are:

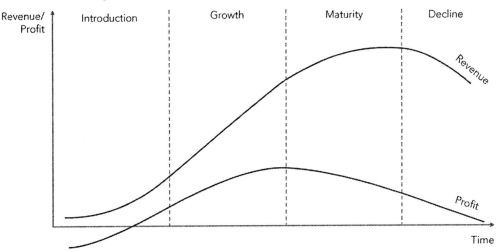

The following sections summarise the key characteristics of the different stages in the life cycle.

8.1.1 Introduction

- A new product takes time to be accepted by would-be purchasers.
- There is initially a slow growth in sales. Unit costs are high due to low output and costly promotions. High marketing costs are required in order to get the product recognised by customers.
- The product for the time being is a loss-maker and has negative cash flows.
- The product is high risk because it is new and has not yet been accepted by the market.
- The product has few, if any, competitors (because they are not willing to take similar risks).

8.1.2 Growth

- If the new product gains market acceptance, sales will eventually rise more sharply and the product will start to make profits.
- Capital investments are needed to fulfil levels of demand, meaning cash flows remain lower than profit. However, cash flows increase as sales increase and the market becomes profitable.
- Competitors are attracted with similar products, but as sales and production rise, unit costs fall (eg due to economies of scale).
- Sales for the market as a whole increase.
- Need to add additional features to differentiate from competitors as buyers become more sophisticated. New market segments may be developed.

8.1.3 Maturity

- Total sales growth in the market slows down significantly. Purchases are now based on repeat or replacement purchases, rather than new customers.
- High levels of competition, because in order to increase sales a firm needs to capture market share from competitors.
- Profits remain good, and levels of investment are low, meaning cash flow is also positive.
- Environmental analysis is important. Companies need to detect or anticipate changes in the market so that they can be ready to undertake modifications in product-market strategies to lengthen the life cycle.

8.1.4 Decline

- Eventually, products are superseded by **technically superior substitutes**.
- Sales begin to decline and there is overcapacity of production in the industry. Prices are lowered in order to try to attract business.
- Severe competition occurs, **profits fall** and some **producers leave the market**.
- The remaining producers try to prolong the product life by modifying it and searching for new (niche) market segments.
- Investment is kept to a minimum.
- Although some producers are reluctant to leave the market if they haven't found alternative industries to move into, many inevitably do because of falling profits.

8.2 Uses and criticism of the product life cycle model

Uses of the product life cycle (PLC)	Criticism
Identify appropriate strategies in relation to existing products.	Real products show much more complex behaviour (eg strategic decisions could change or extend a product's life cycle).
Identify the need for successor products.	PLC cannot be used for forecasting. Not all products go through every stage.
Ensure profit and cash flow balance within the firm's product portfolio (links in to idea of the BCG matrix – see Section 9).	The stages are of very different lengths in different industries.
	Can be difficult for managers to recognise where a product is in its life cycle.
	A product may be at different stages of its life cycle in different markets.

8.3 The industry life cycle concept

In the same way we can identify a product life cycle, it may also be possible to discern an **industry life cycle**, which will have wider implications for the nature of competition and competitive advantage.

	Introduction	Growth	Maturity	Decline
Products	Basic, no standards established	Better, more sophisticated, differentiated	Superior, standardised	Varied quality but fairly undifferentiated
Competitors	None, to few	Many entrants Little concentration in industry	Competition increases, weaker players leave	Few remain. Competition may be on price
Buyers	Early adopters, innovators	More customers attracted	Mass market, brand switching common	Enthusiasts, traditionalists, sophisticates
Profits	Negative	Increasing as sales increase rapidly	High, but beginning to decline	Falling, as sales and prices have fallen

	Introduction	Growth	Maturity	Decline
Objectives and strategy	Build product awareness Dominate market, build quality	Try to maximise market share React to competitors with marketing spend	Maximise profit while defending market share Cost reductions sought	Control costs Possibly harvest or divest

Notice the last row in the table: objectives and strategy. This is important because it highlights that the most suitable strategy for a firm to adopt is likely to depend on the stage of the industry in its life cycle.

Activity 2: Product life cycle

The following brief profiles relate to four commercial organisations, each of which operates in a different industry.

- **Company Alpha.** Established in the last year; manufactures state of the art laptop security which replaces the need for a password with computer image recognition of fingerprint patterns. It currently has few competitors.
- **Company Beta.** An ethical product manufacturer for animal feed that supports non-GM foods; has been established for three years and is gaining market share in a rapidly growing market.
- **Company Gamma.** A confectionery manufacturer, which has been established for many years and is now experiencing low sales growth but high market share in a long-established, profitable, yet competitive industry.
- **Company Zeta.** A retailing organisation which has been very profitable but is now experiencing a loss of market share with a consequent overall reduction in turnover.

Required
Identify the phase of development in which each of the industries served by the four companies is positioned.

Alpha [　　　　　▼]

Beta [　　　　　▼]

Gamma [　　　　　▼]

Zeta [　　　　　▼]

Picklist:

Introduction

Growth

Maturity

Decline

Solution

9 Portfolio planning and the Boston Consulting Group (BCG) Matrix

9.1 Portfolio planning

Portfolio planning aims to create a balance among the organisation's market offerings in order to maximise competitive advantage. Ideally, firms should have a portfolio of products at different stages in their life cycles.

Four major strategies can be pursued with respect to products or strategic business units (SBUs):

(a) **Build**. A build strategy foregoes short-term earnings and profits in order to increase market share. For a business unit, this could be achieved either through organic growth, or through external growth (acquisition, strategic alliances etc).

(b) **Hold**. A hold strategy seeks to maintain the current position, defending it from the threat of would-be 'attackers' as necessary.

(c) **Harvest**. A harvesting strategy seeks short-term earnings and profits at the expense of long-term development.

(d) **Divest**. Disposal of a poorly performing business unit or product. Divestment stems the flow of cash to a poorly performing area of the business and releases resources for use elsewhere.

9.2 The Boston Consulting Group (BCG) matrix

The BCG matrix (*Boston Consulting Group, 1970*) is another framework which can be used to assess the internal balance of an organisation's product portfolio, with the logic being that a firm should aim to have a balanced portfolio of products (or business units).

The matrix assesses a company's products in terms of potential cash generation and cash expenditure requirements, but presupposes that there are only two factors that directly influence competitive position:

- The **growth rate** of the market segment the product or SBU serves. (This is likely to slow over time due to the impact of the product life cycle); and

- The **relative market share** of the segment held by the product or SBU. (Relative share is the product's market share **compared to the market share of its largest competitor**. A relative market share of >1 indicates that a product or business unit is the market leader.)

Relative market share is assumed to be an indicator of a product's (or business unit's) capacity for growth within its market.

		Relative market share	
		High	Low
Market growth	High	Stars	Question marks/ problem children
	Low	Cash cows	Dogs

9.3 Matrix axes

Relative market share is calculated as:

$$\frac{\text{Own market share}}{\text{Market share of largest rival}}$$

By definition, therefore, any company with **'High' relative market share is the market leader**, reaping all of the associated benefits such as:

- Economies of scale
- Prestige
- Brand value

Market growth is calculated as the annual percentage change in sales volume in the industry as a whole. As a guide, 10% is often used as the dividing line between high and low growth.

The model presumes that high market growth indicates good opportunities for profitable operations.

9.4 Elements of the BCG matrix (BCG, 1970)

The four classifications of products, based on relative market share and market growth rate, are:

- **Stars** – products or services with a high relative market share in a high growth market. In the short term, they require expenditure in excess of cash generated to maintain relative market position, and to defend their position against competitors' attack strategy. However, they promise high returns in the future.
- **Cash cows** – Cash cows hold a high share of a low growth, mature market. Cash cows need little capital expenditure (because opportunities for growth are low) but they generate high levels of cash income. Because they generate a cash surplus, they can finance the growth of rising stars and question marks.
- **Question marks** – a product in a high growth market but holding a relatively low market share. Question marks have the potential to become stars if they are successfully developed, but considerable expenditure may be required to turn a question mark into a rising star. As such, they have a negative cash flow.
- **Dogs** – products with a low share of a low growth market. Dogs are not necessarily 'bad'; they just happen to be products that are not market leaders in a mature market. For instance, in the UK/USA, Pepsi Cola would fit this criteria (because Coca Cola is the market leader), yet no one would suggest that Pepsi Cola is discontinued.

Some dogs may, however, be former cash cows that have fallen on hard times, and unless the trend can be reversed (classified as a 'war horse') they should be allowed to die or be killed off.

In some cases, though, dogs can be useful to complete a product range (in which case they should be retained).

9.5 Strategies for the BCG matrix

The prescribed strategies for the BCG Matrix are:

- **Star – Build.** Continue to invest, to maintain market share and match the rivals in the industry

- **Cash cow – Hold, or Harvest if weak.** Use the cash generated by cash cows for investing in stars and question marks, and to pay out dividends
- **Question mark – Build or divest.** Building could help question marks fulfil their potential to become stars. If investing, the organisation can build market share through price reduction, promotions, acquisitions, or potentially by modifying the product. If question marks look like they could be squeezed out of the market by rival products (so their development will not be successful), then it may be more appropriate to divest, rather than investing in them.
- **Dog – Divest or hold,** depending on the returns generated and future prospects.

> ### Assessment focus point
>
> The syllabus requires you to be able to recommend how to manage the product portfolio of an organisation to support the organisation's strategic goals.
> As such, it is important to understand which strategies could be appropriate for different products (according to their market growth, and relative market share).

9.6 Uses of BCG analysis

The **uses** of the BCG Matrix are that it:

- Provides management with a visual summary of the company's diverse activities, and the different needs and potential within the company's portfolio
- Identifies the need for sufficient successor products to replace declining stars and cash cows
- Identifies the need for sufficient cash cows to permit investment in high-growth businesses (question marks and stars)
- Can be used to evaluate the competition and their product portfolios
- Evaluates risk by adjusting the portfolio to reflect the impact of hypothetical scenarios or changes in key environmental variables (eg changes in market growth rates)

9.7 Criticisms of the BCG matrix

The **uses** of the BCG Matrix are that it:

- The axes are **too simplistic.** A high market share is assumed to indicate competitive strength but this is not necessarily true. A strong brand may yield competitive strength despite a relatively low market share.
- **High market growth** is deemed to indicate an **attractive industry.** But fast-growing industries are likely to require significant investment, so they may not be attractive to a firm with limited available capital.
- The requirement that firms have a high relative market share is justified by the ability of large producers to benefit from scale economies and experience effects, and thereby to assist in surviving price pressure in late life cycle markets. However, a differentiation strategy or **a niche strategy could allow a firm to prosper even with a small relative share.**
- **Ignores linkages** between products. For example, if a firm stops producing one product (eg a 'dog'), could this have a knock-on effect on sales of other products?
- There is an assumption that the market can be easily defined, but this may not be the case.

> ### Assessment focus point
>
> The syllabus requires you to be able to recommend how to manage the product portfolio of an organisation to support the organisation's strategic goals.
> One of the uses of the BCG matrix is in highlighting the need for a balanced product portfolio. However, it is also important to think whether the balance of products fits with the organisation's strategy; eg if an organisation's objectives are based around growth, then a portfolio dominated by cash cows may not be appropriate, because – by themselves – they are unlikely to provide the growth required.

Activity 3: Using the BCG matrix

A listed conglomerate has the following subsidiaries.

Company	Our turnover	Market growth	Turnover of nearest rival
Construction	€5.4bn	2%	€3.8bn
Engineering	€3.5bn	4%	€8.7bn
Transport	€2.8bn	11%	€4.7bn
Gaming	€1.2bn	13%	€0.7bn

Required

Using the BCG Matrix, assess the portfolio of the company.

Solution

10 Benchmarking

Benchmarking involves the establishment of best practice in business-critical processes. By the adoption of identified best practice it is hoped that performance will improve in both financial and non-financial aspects of the organisation.

KEY
TERM

> **Benchmarking:** The 'establishment, through data gathering, of targets and comparators, through whose use relative levels of performance (and particularly areas of underperformance) can be identified. By the adoption of identified best practices, it is hoped that performance will improve' (*CIMA 2005*).

10.1 Types of benchmarking

Types of benchmarking include:

- **Internal.** Compares one operating unit or function with similar ones in the same organisation.
- **External – industry competitor.** Compares an organisation's performance against that of direct competitors.
- **External – industry, non-competitor.** This is particularly relevant for not-for-profit organisations (eg exam success rates in schools).
- **External – functional.** Compares functions to 'best-in-class' practitioners, regardless of their industry.

10.2 Benchmarking programmes

The stages involved in undertaking a benchmarking programme include:

(a) **Set objectives** and determine the areas to benchmark.

(b) **Establish key performance measures** or performance drivers which will be measured during the benchmarking exercise. (Priority should be given to the areas of performance which are most important to an organisation's success.)

(c) **Select organisations** to benchmark performance against.

(d) **Measure own and others' performance** using the measures identified in Step 2.

(e) **Compare results** and identify gaps between the performance of your organisation and the comparator organisations.

(f) Design and implement an **improvement programme** to close the performance gaps identified. (An important element in this step will be analysing **how** the comparator organisations achieve superior performance, then assessing whether similar processes and techniques could be introduced into your own organisation).

(g) **Monitor** improvements in performance.

 ### Illustration 2: Benchmarking

Frustrated at the varying financial performance of its trading companies, the chairman of a diversified conglomerate (comprising construction, engineering, transport and online gaming companies) has suggested undertaking some internal benchmarking analysis. However, other board members were highly sceptical of this suggestion, pointing out that little could be learnt about building office blocks from a separate group company offering online poker tournaments.

Required
Identify the advantages of undertaking an internal benchmarking exercise, and its potential drawbacks.

Solution

The correct answer is:

Advantages

- It acts as a spur to the managers of each business to innovate.
- It forces management to look beyond their own businesses/markets.
- Best practice may be identified and then shared between the group businesses.
- Improved performance should result if points 1–3 above hold true.

Disadvantages

- Overcoming initial scepticism of managers may prove difficult.
- It may divert management attention away from managing current operations.
- Information gathering and analysis will be difficult and time-consuming.
- Perhaps more can be learnt via competitor analysis for each business.

Chapter summary

Resources and capabilities

Resource audit

Does an organisation have the resources and capabilities to implement a strategy?

9Ms model

Identifies areas of strength and weakness

- Manpower
- Money
- Machinery
- Materials
- Markets
- Management
- Methods
- Make up
- MIS

- Helps to inform resource planning (eg gap analysis)

Creating value

- Threshold vs distinctive resources and capabilities

Characteristics for competitive adv:

- Value
- Rarity
- Inimitability
- Organisational support

Dynamic capabilities

Respond to needs of changing environment:

- Sensing
- Seizing
- Transforming

Business models and value drivers

- Value creation
- Value configuration
- Value capture

Need to focus on the factors or capabilities that generate competitive advantage:

- Growth (eg R&D; innovation)
- Efficiency
- Financial

Importance of intangible drivers:

- Management; brand; IP

Rappaport: Seven drivers:

- Sales
- Profit margin
- Reduce tax rate
- Investment in capital expenditure
- Duration of competitive advantage
- Reduce working capital
- Reduce cost of capital

Value chain

Value created through primary and secondary activities which need to be consistent with generic strategies

Primary:

- Inbound logistics
- Operations
- Outbound logistics
- Sales and marketing
- Service

Secondary:

- Firm infrastructure
- Technology development
- HRM
- Procurement

Potential issues with value chain:

- Ecosystems competing rather than organisations
- Increased role of IT
- Application to service businesses?

Supply chain management

Key issues in supply chain management:

- Responsiveness
- Reliability
- Relationships

Lean supply chains:

- Reduce cost
- Improve quality
- Reduce inventories
- Shorten lead times

Product life cycle

Product strategies can be planned through the stages of:
- Introduction
- Growth
- Maturity
- Decline

Life cycle model can also be applied to industries as well as products

Portfolio planning and BCG matrix

Assess products/SBUs on basis of:
- Relative market share
- Market growth

Apply different strategies according to classification:
- Star: Build
- Cash Cow: Hold, or Harvest if weak
- Question Mark: Build or divest
- Dog: Divest, or hold

Aim is to develop a balanced portfolio

Benchmarking

Compare relative levels of performance

Types:
- Internal
- Industry (competitor; non-competitor)
- Functional

Stages:
- Identify areas to benchmark
- Establish key performance measures
- Select comparators
- Measure performance
- Compare results
- Devise and implement improvements
- Monitor progress/ improvements

Key terms

Capabilities: An organisation's capabilities are the ways which enable it to use its assets effectively (*Johnson et al, 2017*).

Threshold resources and capabilities: Those needed for an organisation to meet the necessary requirements to compete in a given market and achieve parity with competitors in that market (*Johnson et al, 2017*).

Distinctive resources and capabilities: Those required to achieve competitive advantage.

Dynamic capabilities: An organisation's ability to renew and recreate its resources and capabilities to meet the needs of changing environments (*Johnson et al, 2017*).

Business model: 'A business model describes a value proposition for customers and other participants, an arrangement of activities that produces this value, and associated revenue and cost structures' (*Johnson et al, 2017, p229*).

Value drivers: The factors or capabilities that give a firm a competitive advantage over its rivals. Value drivers are often linked to the features of a product or service that enhance its perceived value for customers, and thereby create value for the producer.

Value chain: The 'sequence of business activities by which, in the perspective of the **end-user**, value is added to the products or services produced by an entity' (*CIMA, 2005*).

Benchmarking: The 'establishment, through data gathering, of targets and comparators, through whose use relative levels of performance (and particularly areas of underperformance) can be identified. By the adoption of identified best practices, it is hoped that performance will improve' (*CIMA 2005*).

Activity answers

Activity 1: ABC Ltd

The correct answer is:

Input	Area		
Lecturer recruitment	HRM	Operations	
Good pass rates	Service	Sales and marketing	
Good support facilities	Firm infrastructure	Service	
Online booking system	Technology development	Inbound logistics	
Well-qualified non-teaching staff	Firm infrastructure	HRM	Service
Improved reputation	Sales and marketing		

Activity 2: Product life cycle

The correct answer is:

Alpha **Introduction**

Beta **Growth**

Gamma **Maturity**

Zeta **Maturity**

Alpha	The product is still 'new', and the fact that there are few competitors is a key characteristic of the introduction phase.
Beta	Rapid growth and a high number of market entrants are characteristic of the growth phase.
Gamma	Although profits remain high in the maturity phase, competition increases as market growth slows (because in order to increase sales, firms need to capture market share from competitors).
Zeta	The retailing industry as a whole is most likely to be in its mature stage – it is the company that is in decline, rather than the industry.

Activity 3: Using the BCG matrix

The correct answer is:

Company	Market growth	Market share	
Construction	2% – Low	5.4 / 3.8 = 1.42 High	Cash cow
Engineering	4% – Low	3.5 / 8.7 = 0.40 Low	Dog

Company	Market growth	Market share	
Transport	11% – High	2.8 / 4.7 = 0.60 Low	Question mark
Gaming	13% – High	1.2 / 0.7 = 1.71 High	Star

Test your learning

1   **Required**

Complete the following statement.

An organisation's ability to renew and recreate its resources and capabilities to meet the needs of changing environments reflects its ☐ .

2   **Required**

Which one of the following is a primary activity in Porter's value chain?

A   Service

B   Technology development

C   Procurement

D   Human resource management

3   **Required**

What are the four main stages of the product life cycle?

4   One of the strategic business units in the FGL Group is the G&L chain of gyms and leisure centres.

G&L's share of the total market in its country is 11% but the market is quite fragmented and its largest competitor only has a market share of 9.5%.

In the last year, the overall gym and leisure market grew by 1% but G&L's revenue increased by 12% as a result of a successful marketing campaign and opening two new gyms.

Required

According to the classifications of the BCG matrix, G&L is a?

A   Star

B   Question mark

C   Cash cow

D   Dog

5   **Required**

Which of the following statements about the product life cycle is/are correct?

(i) Competition is stronger in the growth phase than the introduction phase.

(ii) Sales volumes are higher in the growth phase than in the maturity phase.

A   Neither of them

B   (i) only

C   (ii) only

D   Both of them

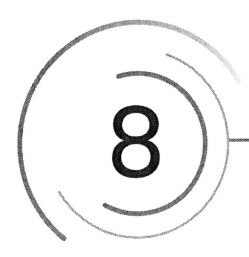

Evaluating strategic choices

Syllabus learning outcomes

Having studied this chapter you will be able to work through the following syllabus outcomes:

Syllabus Area E3: Strategic choices

1	Options
a- c	Criteria for evaluation, Options against criteria and Recommend appropriate options

Exam context

In the exam, you will be expected to demonstrate competence in the following representative task statements:

- Analyse strategic options and criteria for evaluation including the application of the suitability, acceptability, and feasibility framework
- Analyse options against criteria for strategic options
- Recommend appropriate action for strategic options

Chapter overview

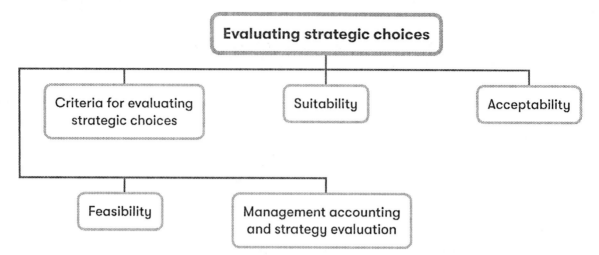

1 Introduction

In the preceding chapters, we have looked at a number of models that organisations can use to provide them with different options for strategies. However, management then have to select the strategy which they believe is most appropriate for their organisation.

This raises a key question: how do managers assess whether a particular strategy should be pursued by an organisation?

In this chapter, we will look at the way mangers can make this assessment, by looking at the three criteria of suitability, acceptability and feasibility (SAF).

As far as possible, management should only recommend a strategy if it meets all three of these criteria.

The contribution of the management accountant could be very important in the 'A' and 'F' elements of the SAF framework, as financial analysis will be a significant element of both acceptability and feasibility.

Topics covered in this chapter:

- Suitability, acceptability and feasibility framework

2 Criteria for evaluating strategic choices

Once an organisation has identified its current strategic position, and the different potential strategic options available to it, it then has to choose which of these options it wants to pursue.

The evaluation process examines strategies according to a number of different criteria. Johnson et al (2017) narrow these down to three broad categories: **suitability, acceptability** and **feasibility.**

> **Assessment focus point**
>
> The syllabus identifies that you need to be able to analyse options against criteria for strategic options. If you are asked to analyse a strategy, you should consider its suitability, acceptability and feasibility – relating these elements specifically back to the context given in the question scenario.

3 Suitability

Suitability relates to the strategic logic of a strategy: does it 'fit' with an organisation's strategic position?

> **Suitability:** Concerned with assessing which proposed strategies address the key opportunities and threats an organisation faces through an understanding of the strategic position of an organisation (*Johnson et al, 2017*, p380).

Questions to consider in relation to the suitability of a strategy:

- Does it exploit the organisation's **strengths** and **capabilities**?
- Does it rectify the organisation's **weaknesses**?
- Does it neutralise or deflect environmental **threats**?
- Does it help the organisation seize **opportunities**?
- Does it fit with the organisation's **mission** and **objectives**?
- Will new products/markets fit with existing ones? Will the strategy improve the balance of the organisation's **portfolio**?
- Will it help the organisation to **compete successfully** against its rivals (eg by providing it with a source of sustainable competitive advantage)?

3.1 SWOT analysis

In Chapter 3, we discussed SWOT analysis as a tool for assessing an organisation's strategic position (strengths, weaknesses, opportunities and threats).

Strategies should be developed to remove weaknesses or develop strengths, and to exploit opportunities and counter threats. This logic can be used to help evaluate the suitability of a strategy.

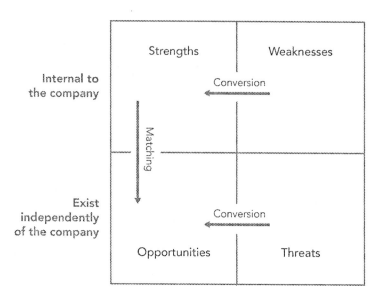

3.2 Gap analysis

Gap analysis could be used to identify the scale of the strategic initiatives that may be needed in order to close the gap between actual and desired levels of performance.

Part of the evaluation of the suitability of a potential strategy could be the extent to which it helps an organisation 'close the gap'.

 Gap analysis: Compares an entity's expected level of performance to its desired level of performance.

The aim of product-market strategies (Ansoff's matrix) is to **close the profit gap** that is found by gap analysis. A mixture of strategies may be needed to fill the gap between the current profit forecast (F_0 in the following diagram) and the target profit.

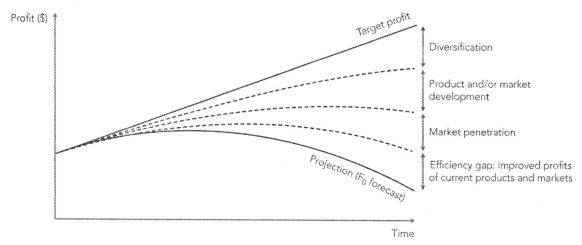

Illustration 1: Strategic models

A number of the models we have looked at in Chapters 5 and 6 of this Workbook could be useful for assessing the suitability of a strategy.

Required

Identify ways in which the following models could help assess the suitability of potential strategies.

Model	Helps with understanding
PESTEL analysis	
Porter's five forces	
Porter's generic strategies	
BCG matrix	

Solution

The correct answer is:

Model	Helps with understanding
PESTEL analysis	Key environmental drivers (opportunities and threats) – does the strategy respond to those opportunities and threats?
Porter's five forces	Competitive forces – does the strategy respond to (or is it appropriate for) competitive forces? Industry attractiveness – if a strategy proposes entering a new market, is that market attractive?
Porter's generic strategies	The 'fit' between the proposed strategy and an organisation's current strategy (eg if an organisation is currently employing a cost leadership strategy, a proposed strategy based on differentiation may not be suitable). Competitive advantage – will the strategy help to create or maintain a (sustainable) competitive advantage? (The value chain could also be used to identify similar issues. Will the activities required for the proposed strategy 'fit' with the nature of the activities in the current value chain?)
BCG matrix	The impact of any new products or business units on an organisation's portfolio. Will they improve the balance of the portfolio? Is a strategy appropriate for the stage in its life cycle that a product or industry has reached (and therefore, for example, the opportunities for growth it offers)?

4 Acceptability

Acceptability is concerned with whether the expected performance outcomes of a proposed strategy meet the expectations of stakeholders.

The acceptability of a strategy relates to **stakeholders' expectations** of it: do the expected performance outcomes of the proposed strategy meet stakeholders' expectations of it?

For example:

- **Financial considerations.** Strategies will be evaluated by considering how far they contribute to meeting the **dominant objectives** eg return on investment, profit, growth, EPS and cash flow.
- Evaluating acceptability can also involve quantitative analysis, such as **NPV calculations.**
- **Customers** may **object** to a strategy if it means **reducing service or increasing price**, but on the other hand they may have no choice.
- A **bank** may restrict a strategy if it involves **extra borrowing** or breaches loan agreements.
- **Local communities** or the wider **public** may oppose strategies which have a detrimental impact on the **environment**. (In this context, it is important to remember that the 'acceptability' of a strategy should be considered in relation to **corporate social responsibility** as well as narrower financial criteria.)

4.1 Risks and rewards

The potential **risks** and **rewards** of a strategy are also important factors which could affect its acceptability.

Different shareholders have different attitudes to risk. A strategy which changes the risk/return profile, for whatever reason, may not be acceptable.

Consideration of risk (and stakeholders' **attitudes to risk**) could also be relevant in relation to the product-market strategies identified in Ansoff's matrix. Eg a diversification strategy (new products, new markets) is likely to present a higher level of risk than a market penetration strategy, but equally it has the potential to generate higher rewards.)

4.2 Feasibility

In essence, the feasibility of a strategy relates to whether an organisation is able to implement the strategy it is considering.

The following factors could affect the feasibility of a strategy:

- **Finance** – is there **enough money** to finance the strategy? What options does the organisation have for raising finance – eg debt, equity?
- **Resources** – does the company have the **capacity** to deliver the goods/services specified in the strategy? Can it obtain the necessary resources (eg technology, materials, distribution channels) if it does not currently have them?
- **Capabilities** – does the company have the necessary people and skills, or can they be obtained?
- **Change management** – does the company have sufficient time to implement the strategy? Does it have sufficient experience of change management (eg to overcome resistance to change caused by the new strategy)?

Assessment focus point

The syllabus identifies that you need to be able to analyse strategic options and the criteria used for evaluation (including suitability, acceptability and feasibility). If an organisation is looking to make a strategic decision but isn't evaluating the options properly (eg because it is not considering the suitability of an option) you need to be able to identify this.

The syllabus also identifies that you need to be able to recommend appropriate action for strategic options. In order to make your recommendation, you first need to analyse the suitability, acceptability and feasibility of the potential options. Always assess suitability first. Little can be done if a potential strategy is unsuitable, but it may be possible to adjust the factors that suggest a strategy is not currently acceptable or feasible.

Activity 1: Evaluating strategy

Demand for a company's product has increased significantly in recent years. To meet demand, and to support its growth strategy, the company needs to increase its production capacity. The company is considering automating part of the production line to achieve this. The automation will improve the speed and quality of the manufacturing process but will result in around 30 of the existing manufacturing staff (who are all members of a trade union) being made redundant.

The automated machinery will cost around $10 million. The company does not currently have this amount of cash available, but its bank has agreed to loan the money required to buy the machine.

Required

On the basis of this information, which of the following criteria does automating the production line meet?

A   Suitable only

B   Suitable and acceptable

C   Acceptable and feasible

D   Suitable and feasible

Solution

5 Management accounting and strategy evaluation

A management accountant could play an important role in evaluating a potential strategy, particular in relation to assessing its acceptability and feasibility.

5.1 Professional scepticism

When using management accounting techniques to evaluate a strategic option, you must:

- Ascertain why management accounting information is needed, and for what purpose.
- Assess whether the information is incomplete and, if so, make relevant assumptions.
- Recognise the degree of uncertainty attached to estimated data, possibly from a dubious source.

The **minimum acceptable return** for any strategic option should equate to the cost of capital.

5.2 Financial analysis techniques

The principal techniques which could be used in the financial analysis of a potential strategic choice include:

- Cost benefit analysis
- Forecasting techniques (eg cash flow forecasts to ensure loan repayments can be met)
- Capital expenditure techniques: NPV, payback period, IRR
- Return on capital employed (ROCE), residual income (RI)
- Expected values (taking account of the probability of different outcomes occurring)
- Ratio analysis (profitability, liquidity, gearing)
- Breakeven analysis
- Sensitivity analysis
- Economic value added
- Total shareholder return

5.2.1 Real options

Quantitative analysis, such as NPV calculations, can potentially undervalue projects which involve significant future flexibility (eg through the possibility of 'follow-on' projects). Real options (which we discussed in Chapter 6) provide a way of incorporating this flexibility into a strategic NPV calculation.

Activity 2: SAF tools

Required

Match each of the techniques or frameworks listed below to the aspect of strategic evaluation (suitability, acceptability, feasibility) which it is MOST relevant to.

Input	Evaluation
Return on investment (ROI)	▼
Net present value (NPV)	▼
SWOT	▼
Mendelow's matrix	▼
Cash flow forecast	▼
PESTEL	▼

Picklist:

Suitability

Acceptability

Feasibility

Solution

Chapter summary

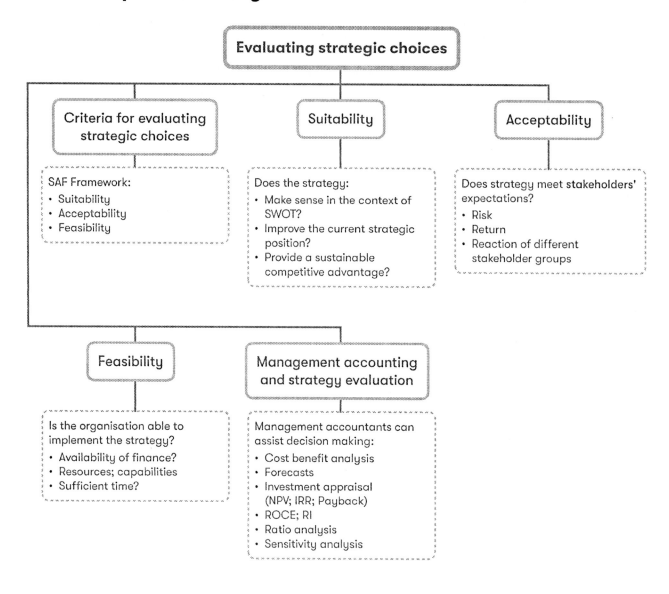

Evaluating strategic choices

Criteria for evaluating strategic choices

SAF Framework:
- Suitability
- Acceptability
- Feasibility

Suitability

Does the strategy:
- Make sense in the context of SWOT?
- Improve the current strategic position?
- Provide a sustainable competitive advantage?

Acceptability

Does strategy meet stakeholders' expectations?
- Risk
- Return
- Reaction of different stakeholder groups

Feasibility

Is the organisation able to implement the strategy?
- Availability of finance?
- Resources; capabilities
- Sufficient time?

Management accounting and strategy evaluation

Management accountants can assist decision making:
- Cost benefit analysis
- Forecasts
- Investment appraisal (NPV; IRR; Payback)
- ROCE; RI
- Ratio analysis
- Sensitivity analysis

Key terms

Suitability: Concerned with assessing which proposed strategies address the key opportunities and threats an organisation faces through an understanding of the strategic position of an organisation (*Johnson et al, 2017*, p380).

Gap analysis: Compares an entity's expected level of performance to its desired level of performance.

Activity answers

Activity 1: Evaluating strategy

The correct answer is:

Suitable and feasible

Automating the production line appears to be suitable because it supports the company's growth strategy and enables it to increase production.

The investment is feasible, because the company can raise the money required to buy the machinery (through the bank loan), even though it doesn't have the cash itself.

The automation is unlikely to be acceptable to employees, due to the redundancies it will cause. The fact that the manufacturing staff are all members of a union could increase their power to resist the redundancies.

Activity 2: SAF tools

The correct answer is:

Input	Evaluation
Return on investment (ROI)	Acceptability
Net present value (NPV)	Acceptability
SWOT	Suitability
Mendelow's matrix	Acceptability
Cash flow forecast	Feasibility
PESTEL	Suitability

- Suitable: makes strategic sense
- Acceptable: in the eyes of stakeholders
- Feasible: is possible

Test your learning

1 **Required**
   What describes whether a strategy can work in practice?

2 A company is evaluating a strategy to see whether it is appropriate for the company's current situation.

   Required
   Which of the following issues relates most specifically to the suitability of the strategy (in the context of Johnson et al's model of suitability, feasibility and acceptability)?

   A   Whether the company has enough resources to implement it

   B   The amount of return on investment the strategy will generate

   C   The level of risk involved in the strategy

   D   Whether the strategy will help to generate or sustain a competitive advantage for the company

3 **Required**
   Which of the following analysis tools would be the most useful for assessing the acceptability of a potential strategy?

   A   Porter's value chain

   B   Mendelow's matrix

   C   The cultural web

   D   Porter's five forces

4 **Required**
   Is the following statement true or false?

   In order for a strategy to be feasible, an organisation must already possess the necessary people and skills to implement the strategy.

   A   True

   B   False

5 The initial capital cost of a proposed investment project, with an expected useful economic life of three years, is $125,000. The equipment used in the project will have no residual value at the end of the project.

   The income generated by the project (and received at the end of each year) is expected to be:

   Year 1: $20,000

   Year 2: $70,000

   Year 3: $50,000

   The company considering the project uses a cost of capital of 8%.

   Required
   On the basis of the project's net present value, should the company undertake the project?

   A   Yes

   B   No

Performance management systems

Syllabus learning outcomes

Having studied this chapter you will be able to work through the following syllabus outcomes:

Syllabus Area E: Strategic control	
1	Strategic performance management system
a - d	Detailed action plans, Action plan communication, Implementation and Incentives to performance

Exam context

In the exam, you will be expected to demonstrate competence in the following representative task statements:

- Set appropriate strategic targets through the use of non-financial measures of strategic performance and their interaction with financial ones
- Evaluation of strategic targets through the development of critical success factors (CSFs)
- Link CSFs to Key Performance Indicators and corporate strategy and their use as a basis for defining an organisation's information needs
- Effective communication of strategic performance targets, including the need to drive strategic performance through stretch targets and promotion of exceptional performance

Chapter overview

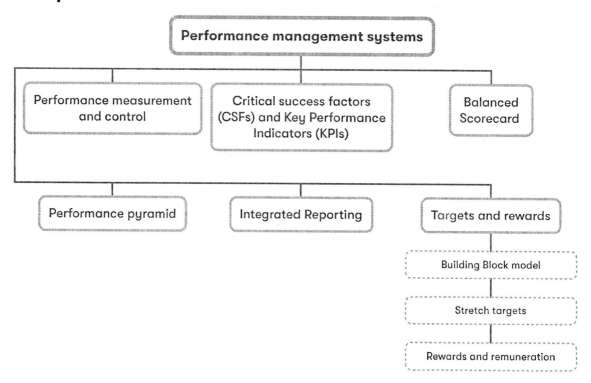

1 Introduction

Once a set of strategies is decided upon, an important control will be to measure the impact that these are having on organisational performance.

To do this, management need to identify a range of targets and performance measures which they can monitor. Setting performance measures can also be an important way of communicating targets to staff and other stakeholders, indicating which aspects of performance are important for the organisation.

A useful way of identifying performance measures is by linking them to the critical success factors (CSFs) which will enable an organisation to implement its strategy successfully. CSFs can often be non-financial, so performance measurement systems should also include indicators of non-financial performance as well as financials ones.

Models such as the balanced scorecard and the performance pyramid allow organisations to monitor performance, and strategic impact, across a range of areas that determine organisational success eg customer satisfaction and internal efficiency, to name but two. If an organisation performs well in such areas, this should increase the chances of it also being financially successful as a result.

Topics to be covered in this chapter:

- Action plans
- Target setting
- Critical success factors (CSFs)
- Key performance indicators (KPIs)

2 Performance measurement and control

Once an organisation has selected an overall strategy, it also needs to convert this into specific objectives, or performance targets. Targets are only useful if they can be measured. Therefore, performance measurement is a key part of performance management.

> **Performance measurement:** The 'process of assessing the proficiency with which a reporting entity succeeds, by the economic acquisition of resources and their efficient and effective development, in achieving its objectives. Performance measures may be based on non-financial as well as on financial information' (*CIMA, 2005*).

2.1 The purpose of performance measurement

Performance measurement has become such a familiar part of business life that we sometimes lose sight of its purpose. Neely (1998) summarised the purpose of performance measurement as the following – the four 'CPs' of performance measurement:

- **Check Position** – how well is the business doing? (This should look at both financial and non-financial factors.)
- **Communicate Position** – to stakeholders so that they know how the business is performing. This communication could be internal (eg to managers and teams) or external (eg to investors).
- **Confirm Priorities** – setting targets for the business and developing action plans to help achieve them.
- **Compel Progress** – measuring performance is a strong driver for change, especially if it is linked to reward (eg if staff are rewarded for achieving certain targets in certain areas of performance, this will give them a greater incentive to perform well in those areas).

2.2 Financial and non-financial performance

An organisation's financial performance is likely to reflect the overall impact of its operational activities and how well it is performing them. For example, its revenues will be the result of developing products or services that customers want to buy and then attracting – and retaining – customers. However, this also highlights that non-financial aspects (eg product innovation, quality, customer service, brand and reputation) could all be important elements in shaping an organisation's performance. Therefore, non-financial measures are likely to be needed to manage the 'drivers' of performance more effectively.

2.3 Importance of non-financial performance measures

Several other factors have led management to move beyond sole reliance on financial performance measures, including:

- Competitive strategies (particularly those based around differentiation) are often based on improvements in quality, innovation, customer relationships etc – not profit alone. If non-financial variables are important in a company successfully achieving its strategy, then it follows that the company should also measure its performance in relation to them.
- Financial measures tend to lag behind business performance and therefore simply measure success. However, organisations also need to monitor indicators that ensure success. Some of these indicators, which will be linked to an organisation's critical success factors (such quality and flexibility) will be non-financial in nature.
- Financial performance measurement systems often focus on annual or short-term performance (against financial targets), leading to short-term decision making. Non-financial objectives may be vital in achieving longer-term strategic goals.
- Management have tracked non-financial measures for years. Why not formalise this?

When choosing what to measure, beyond traditional financial measures, a good starting point will be the **corporate objectives**. As the objectives should be linked through to the corporate mission and vision, there will be **vertical consistency** (eg individual business unit objectives are aligned with overall corporate objectives).

However, it is also important to ensure **horizontal consistency** (eg compatibility of performance measures used in all functional areas).

> ### Assessment focus point
>
> The syllabus requires you to be able to set appropriate strategic targets through the use of non-financial measures of strategic performance and their interaction with financial ones. Although we have highlighted the importance of non-financial performance measures, this doesn't mean financial measures are no longer important. For commercial organisations, maximising profit is likely to remain one of their key goals, so they cannot ignore the financial aspects of performance. If you are asked to set performance targets for an organisation, it is important to think about the mix of financial and non-financial targets, to encourage the organisation to monitor both aspects of performance.

3 Critical success factors and key performance indicators

3.1 Critical success factors (CSFs)

Once an organisation has identified its objectives, it also needs to identify the key factors and processes that will enable it to be successful and to achieve those objectives. These are its critical success factors (CSFs).

> **Critical success factors:** Those aspects of a product or service which are particularly valued by customers (and therefore at which a business must excel in order to outperform its competitors), or which provide a significant advantage in terms of costs (*Johnson et al, 2017*).

3.1.1 CSFs and capabilities

Identifying CSFs can also be used in evaluating an organisation's resources and capabilities (as discussed in Chapter 7). Does the organisation have the resources and capabilities it needs to excel in its key performance areas?

In effect, an organisation's competencies and capabilities illustrate what it is good at; while its CSFs illustrate what it needs to be good at, to be successful.

To maximise its chances of being successful, an organisation needs to ensure its competences and capabilities are aligned to its CSFs (eg if the technical quality of its products is a CSF for an organisation, then having a production process that focuses on minimising cost rather than maximising quality would not be appropriate).

3.1.2 Sources of CSFs

CSFs can be identified by considering a company's mission and strategy. However, CSFs don't only relate to internal processes or aspects of performance. For example, for a road transport company, the availability and price of fuel are likely to be vital for operational planning and could have a significant impact on financial performance.

Rockart (1979) suggests that, in broad terms, organisations can identify four general sources of CSFs:

(a) The industry that the organisation is in; for example, in the supermarket industry, having the right product mix available in each store and having products actually available on the shelves for customers to buy will be prerequisites for an organisation's success, regardless of the detailed strategy it is pursuing.

(b) The company itself and its situation within the industry (eg market leader or small company, competitive strategy, geographical location).

(c) The external environment, for example consumer trends, the economy, and political factors of the country in which the company operates (eg from PESTEL analysis, or Porter's five forces).

(d) Temporal organisational factors, which are areas of corporate activity that are currently unacceptable and represent a cause for concern, such as high inventory levels; new laws or regulations could also be seen as temporary factors: eg if a regulator has recently fined a financial services company for mis-selling its products, then a possible CSF for the company would be to ensure that similar mis-selling does not occur again in the near future.

Assessment focus point

The syllabus requires you to be able to evaluate strategic targets through the development of CSFs. An important factor to consider when evaluating performance targets will be whether they relate to the areas in which an organisation needs to perform well in order to be successful (ie its CSFs).

3.2 Key performance indicators (KPIs)

Once an organisation has identified its CSFs, it also needs to know whether it is delivering on them. This is done by using key performance indicators (KPIs), which **measure** how well the organisation is performing against its CSFs.

Key performance indicators: The measures which are used to assess whether or not an organisation is achieving its critical success factors (CSFs). Effective KPIs focus on the processes and activities which are most important for achieving strategic objectives and performance targets.

KPIs should be designed to **address the key areas of performance identified by the CSFs**, to ensure that stepping stones to achieving corporate objectives are put in place.

KPI measures should be:

Specific

Measurable

Attainable

Relevant (ie addressing the CSFs or objectives)

Time-bound

3.3 The relationship between objectives, CSFs and KPIs

We can illustrate the relationship between objectives, CSFs and KPIs using an example of a supermarket company.

Let us assume the company has defined two of its **objectives** as follows:

- To ensure the loyalty of its customers ('to generate lifetime loyalty')
- To ensure its prices are at least 2% cheaper than the average of rival supermarkets ('to create value for customers')

The supermarket then needs to identify the **CSFs** which will help it achieve those objectives. These CSFs could be:

(a) Stocking the goods that customers most want to buy

(b) Making the shopping experience as pleasant as possible

(c) Refining internal processes to operate the business on a cost-effective basis

(d) Using economies of scale to source appropriate goods as cheaply as possible

Then in order to **measure how well it is performing against these CSFs**, the supermarket needs to set **KPIs**. Examples of KPIs could be:

- The proportion of goods taking more than a week to sell (relates to CSF A)
- Results of customer feedback surveys (relates to CSF B)
- Percentage of customers who are repeat customers (relates to CSF B)
- Market share (relates to CSF B)
- Cost measures and progress against savings targets (relates to CSF C)
- Percentage of products cheaper than competitors (relates to CSF D)
- Price of a 'basket of goods' compared to the price of the equivalent basket of goods at competitors (relates to CSF D)

Assessment focus point

The syllabus requires you to be able to link CSFs to key performance indicators and corporate strategy, and to use them as a basis for defining an organisation's information needs.
In any questions about CSFs and KPIs it is very important to remember the relationship between the two. CSFs are the areas where an organisation needs to perform well. KPIs are the measures which indicate how well an organisation is actually performing in these areas.

Activity 1: KPIs

Customer retention is very important for Ambud Co, and it has identified the effectiveness with which it responds to customer complaints as being one of its critical success factors. Complaints are dealt with by the complaints handling department.

Required
Which of the following is the most suitable key performance indicator for this critical success factor?

A   Improve the effectiveness of training given to staff in the complaints handling department.

B   Reduce the number of complaints received by 15%.

C   Reduce the average time taken to resolve complaints by 12%.

D   Increase customer satisfaction by 10%.

Solution

3.4 CSFs, KPIs and information requirements

Managers will need information about the key areas of performance (CSFs, KPIs) in order to monitor performance. This has implications for an organisation's management information systems (and, in many cases, for management accountants who are responsible for producing information):

- Can the current information systems provide the information required to measure performance in key areas (non-financial information, as well as financial)?
- What changes might be required to the information systems to ensure they can provide the information required?

> **Assessment focus point**
>
> In Chapter 11, we look at performance measurement in digital businesses. Traditional financial KPIs can often be ineffective for measuring the success of a digital business, so digital companies need to develop metrics linked to their CSFs – such as attracting and retaining customers onto their platforms.
>
> More generally, this also highlights the importance of organisations making sure their KPIs are linked to their objectives and CSFs.

4 The balanced scorecard

A key theme in this chapter has been that financial measurements alone do not capture all the strategic realities of the business. Nonetheless, it is important that financial measurements are not overlooked. A failure to attend to the 'numbers' can rapidly lead to failure of the business.

Therefore, businesses need to monitor financial **and** non-financial performance measures, linked to key areas of strategic performance.

Perhaps the most popular technique which has been developed to integrate the various features (financial and non-financial) of corporate success is the **balanced scorecard** (Kaplan and Norton, 1996a).

The balanced scorecard seeks to translate **vision** and **strategy** into **objectives** and **measures**, and focuses on **four different perspectives**. However, Kaplan and Norton also viewed the scorecard as a means of **communicating** mission and strategy, and using the measures to inform employees about the key drivers of success (*Kaplan and Norton, 1992*).

BPP LEARNING MEDIA

Financial perspective

How should we create value for our shareholders to succeed financially?

(covers traditional measures such as growth, profitability and shareholder value, with measures set through talking directly to the shareholders)

Internal business process perspective

What business processes must we excel at to achieve financial and customer objectives?

Vision and strategy

Customer perspective

To achieve our vision, how should we appear to our customers? What do new and existing customers value from us?

(cost, quality, reliability etc)

Innovation and learning perspective

How can we continue to create value and maintain the company's competitive position through improvement and change?

(acquisition of new skills; development of new products)

For each of the four perspectives, the scorecard aims to articulate the **outcomes** an organisation desires, and the **drivers** of those outcomes.

- **Financial perspective**: Successful strategies should create value for **shareholders**. Measures look at **survival** (cash flow), **success** (sales or profit) and **prosperity** (shareholder value).
- **Customer measures**: Often focus on aspects of product or service (eg quality, functionality) but could also focus on relationship (eg customer retention) or brand and reputation.
- **Internal business process measures**: For processes that are important in meeting **customer expectations** (eg quality, timeliness, reliability).
- **Innovation and learning measures**: Improving key internal processes and creating value for **customers**. Measures often focus on the amount of innovation and the success of innovation in creating value resources for the future.

4.1 Features and benefits of the scorecard

- It links performance measures to key elements of a company's **strategy**.
- It requires a **balanced consideration** of all **four perspectives**, to prevent improvements being made in one area at the expense of another.
- It considers **financial** and **non-financial** measures and goals and both **internal** and **external** factors.
- It attempts to identify the needs and concerns of customers to identify **new products and markets**.

4.2 Implementing the balanced scorecard

Kaplan and Norton (1996b) recognise that introducing the balanced scorecard could be subject to problems around balancing long-term strategic progress against the management of short-term tactical and operational imperatives. They recommend an iterative, four-stage approach to the practical problems involved:

- **Translating the vision**: the organisation's strategy must be expressed in a way that has clear operational meaning for each employee.
- **Communicating and linking**: the next stage is to link the strategy to departmental and individual objectives, including those that transcend traditional short-term financial goals. (This is one of the key features of the scorecard: that it translates strategy into day-to-day operations.)
- **Business planning**: the third stage is to integrate business plans with financial plans. In effect, the scorecard is used to prioritise objectives and allocate resources in order to make the best progress towards strategic goals.
- **Feedback and learning**: the organisation gathers feedback on performance, assesses whether the assumptions on which its strategy is based remain valid, and makes any adjustments necessary to improve its performance against all four perspectives.

4.3 Practical steps in setting up a balanced scorecard

As with any other projects or changes, if an organisation is going to implement a balanced scorecard successfully, it will need to think carefully about the steps involved:

- Identify the key outcomes critical to the success of the organisation (CSFs).
- Identify the key processes that lead to these outcomes.
- Develop KPIs for these processes.
- Develop reliable systems for capturing the data necessary to measure those KPIs.
- Develop a mechanism for communicating or reporting the indicators (eg through infographics or a dashboard).
- Develop improvement programmes to ensure that performance improves as necessary.

Activity 2: Balanced scorecard

The supermarket industry in the UK is fiercely competitive. Although four major companies dominate, accounting for about 75% of the market, their individual market shares fluctuate as shoppers have an abundance of choice and information allowing them to switch between stores. In order to maintain market share, the major stores compete on price using a variety of discounting and price cutting promotions as well as using loyalty card schemes in an attempt to reduce the impact of price pressure.

Required
The major supermarket chain you work for has determined that corporate success must be measured using a wider range of metrics, going beyond market share alone. Identify three sets of CSFs and KPIs that would be important, and suitable measures for your supermarket's balanced scorecard.

Solution

5 The performance pyramid

Another performance measurement system which looks at a range of performance measures is the performance pyramid (*Lynch and Cross, 1991*). The pyramid provides a broader template for control than the balanced scorecard, and specifically highlights the need to link an organisation's strategic vision to its day-to-day operations.

Performance Pyramid (after *Lynch and Cross, 1991, p65*)

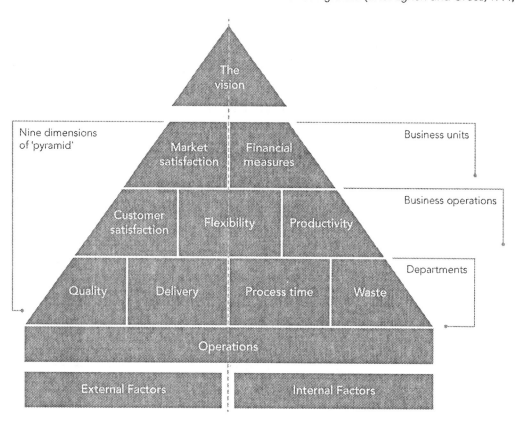

At the top of the pyramid, **vision** is about how long-term corporate success is to be achieved.

Market and financial **objectives** then need to be set for strategic business units in accordance with an organisation's vision. Supporting this, an organisation needs to ensure its internal systems and processes enable it to perform well in areas which will help it achieve its market and financial objectives:

- Meeting customer expectations (**customer satisfaction**) and the responsiveness of the systems and processes (**flexibility**) help to achieve **market objectives**.

- **Flexibility** (responsiveness of systems and processes) and **productivity** (management of resources, such as labour and time) enable **financial objectives** to be achieved.

In turn, strategies then need to be developed for the day-to-day operations in departments and work centres, to support the higher-level strategies, and performance needs to be measured to assess how effectively they are doing this:

- **Quality** of the product or service, consistency of product and fit for the purpose.

- **Delivery** of the product or service ie the method of distribution, its speed and ease of management. Aspects of quality and delivery contribute to customer satisfaction.
- **Cycle time** of all processes from cash collection to order processing to recruitment. Delivery and cycle time provide flexibility. (Cycle time is sometimes also called process time.)
- **Waste** meaning the elimination of all non-value-added activities. Improving cycle time and reducing waste should ensure rising productivity.

5.1 Features of the pyramid

- **Highlights linkages between measures and objectives** – linking operational performance to strategic objectives should help to ensure goal congruence. Objectives come from the top down, performance measures and information flow upwards.
- **The model ensures that internal and external aspects of performance are both considered** – the right-hand side of the pyramid focuses on internal efficiency; the left-hand side focuses on external effectiveness.
- **Focuses on value creation** – business activities need to focus on customer requirements (to achieve customer and market satisfaction).

Activity 3: Performance policy

Required

Match each of the following elements to the correct level of the performance pyramid.

Elements	Level of the performance pyramid
Waste	▼
Delivery	▼
Financial objectives	▼
Productivity	▼
Quality	▼
Market satisfaction	▼

Picklist:

Business units

Operating systems

Departmental level

Solution

5.2 Drawbacks of the performance pyramid and the balanced scorecard

Critics have pointed to many problems that apply to both the performance pyramid and the balanced scorecard.

The common problems associated with these techniques include:

- **Costly** systems to develop and maintain – new information systems may be needed as traditional management accounting systems cannot deal with qualitative data. Can an organisation's information systems capture the data necessary to measure the key indicators selected?
- **Indicator overload** – you may be measuring too much and are at risk of 'clouding the issue'. Indicators should only be included because they add value, not because they are easy to measure.
- Measures could **conflict** (eg potential trade-offs between quality and cost). This could demotivate managers if they feel caught in a 'no win' situation.
- Can **slow** the decision-making process – 'paralysis by analysis'.
- They concentrate on two main groups of stakeholders: customers and shareholders (financial performance). But organisations may also need measures which reflect the interests of other stakeholders (eg **staff**). Also, neither takes account of **corporate social responsibility**.

6 Integrated reporting

Another framework which encourages organisations to look beyond narrow financial performance in the context of their performance management is **integrated reporting**.

Integrated reporting (**IR**) aims to explain an organisation's ability to **create** and **sustain value**. In doing so, it also highlights the importance of **long-term business sustainability** within an organisation.

Rather than focusing on narrow financial performance objectives, IR should encourage management to focus on creating and sustaining value over the longer term.

> **Integrated report:** 'A concise communication about how an organisation's strategy, governance, performance and prospects, in its commercial, social and environmental context, leads to the creation and enhancement of value over the short, medium and long term' (International Integrated Reporting Council (IIRC), 2013).

6.1 Elements of an integrated report

The IIRC (2013) has suggested that, in general terms, an integrated report should answer the following questions:

- **Organisational overview** – what does an organisation do, and what are the circumstances under which it operates?
- **Governance** – how does the organisation's governance structure support its ability to create value in the short, medium and long term?

- **Opportunities and risk** – what are the specific opportunities and risks which affect the organisation's ability to create value over the short, medium and long term; and how is the organisation dealing with them?
- **Strategy and resource allocation** – where does the organisation want to go, and how does it intend to get there?
- **Business model** – what is the organisation's business model, and to what extent is it resilient?
- **Performance** – to what extent has the organisation achieved its strategic objectives and what are the outcomes in terms of effects on the capitals?
- **Future outlook** – what challenges and uncertainties is the organisation likely to encounter in pursuing its strategy, and what are the potential implications for its business model and its future performance?

6.2 Integrated reporting and non-financial information

One of the main potential benefits of IR is that it helps organisations identify more clearly the links between financial and non-financial performance. Therefore, one of the main consequences of IR is likely to be the increased use of non-financial data to gain a clearer picture of an organisation and its performance.

IR should also encourage greater attention being paid to non-financial data in strategic decision making. For example, investment appraisals may need to include non-financial costs and benefits (and sustainability information) as well as traditional financial costs and benefits.

6.3 Six capitals

The International Integrated Reporting Council's (IIRC's) International Integrated Reporting Framework (*IIRC, 2013*) encourages organisations to report on six categories of capital:

(a) **Financial** – the funds available, obtained through financing or generated from operations

(b) **Manufactured** – manufactured physical objects used in production or service provision including buildings, equipment and infrastructure

(c) **Human** – alignment and support for an organisation's governance framework and ethical values, ability to understand and implement an organisation's strategies

(d) **Intellectual** – intangible assets, providing competitive advantage (patents, brands etc)

(e) **Natural** – areas where an organisation's activities have an impact on the natural environment: including water, land, minerals and forests

(f) **Social** – key stakeholder relationships, willingness to engage with stakeholders

6.4 Impact of integrated reporting on information requirements

Integrated reports describe an organisation's performance in relation to the six different capitals – in contrast to 'traditional' annual reporting which focuses primarily on financial performance.

This means an organisation needs information about its performance in relation to each of the different capitals; therefore it will need to record non-financial (eg social, environmental) performance in a way that provides it with suitable information to include in an integrated report.

7 Targets and rewards

Targets and rewards are tools that can be used to motivate employees to achieve corporate goals.

By definition, objectives and targets have to be set before performance can be measured against them. Equally, targets must be communicated across an organisation, so that managers and staff know what they are trying to achieve.

It is very important that targets and reward schemes encourage managers and staff in a way that **supports the organisation's strategy** and is **ethical**.

Staff are most likely to pay attention to the aspects of performance that are measured most closely, so if the 'wrong' performance measures of targets are set, this could lead to staff **behaviour being different to that originally intended,** and adversely affecting performance as a result (eg prior to the global financial crisis of 2008 to 2009, the structure of investment bankers'

annual bonuses encouraged short-term, risky behaviour that maximised profit in the short term, but could be loss-making in the longer term (and therefore contributed to the crisis).

Illustration 1: Performance measures

Organisations must take care when setting targets and performance measures to avoid any potential negative consequences arising from the performance measures they set.

A company has decided to measure a salesperson's performance purely on the number of sales the salesperson achieves in a month.

Required

What are the possible negative consequences of using number of sales as the primary performance measure?

Solution

The correct answer is:

You may have thought of others, but some potential consequences are as follows:

- The salesperson might offer potential customers large discounts in order to make the sale (but with the effect that the company makes a loss on the sale).
- The salesperson is concerned solely with the immediate sale, which may lead to poor after-sales service, low customer satisfaction levels and poor customer retention.
- The salesperson might use expensive promotions that actually generate less in sales value than they cost, but which allow the salesperson to register a number of sales.
- Once a salesperson has reached their target figure for the month, they might look to defer future sales into the next period.

It may be better to use a balanced mix of targets – for example, setting customer care and customer profitability targets as well as the number of sales made.

7.1 Reward and corporate strategy

Reward is encapsulated within the **building block model** developed by **Fitzgerald and Moon** (1996), which was initially devised as a solution to problems with performance management in service industries but can be used more generally to help design effective performance management systems in any industry.

Fitzgerald and Moon (1996) identify three key building blocks: **dimensions**, **standards** and **rewards**.

Building block model (after *Fitzgerald and Moon, 1996*)

Dimensions

Results
- Competitive performance
- Financial performance

Determinants
- Quality
- Flexibility
- Resource utilisation
- Innovation

Standards
- Ownership
- Achievability
- Fairness

Rewards
- Clarity
- Motivation
- Controllability

7.2 Dimensions

The six dimensions are split into results and determinants. The **'results'** are:

(a) **Financial performance** eg profitability

(b) **Competitive performance** eg sales growth, market share

However, these results are determined by the other four dimensions (the **'determinants'**):

(a) **Quality** – reliability, competence, courtesy (of staff). (Remember, the model was originally designed for service businesses.)

(b) **Flexibility** – the ability to deliver at the right time in response to customer needs, eg speed of delivery, responding to different customer requirements, coping with fluctuating levels of demand

(c) **Resource utilisation** – how efficiently resources are being used to create outputs (eg productivity of staff)

(d) **Innovation** – developing new products or services to find new, more effective ways of satisfying customers' needs

As well as identifying the dimensions over which performance should be measured, the model identifies the standards against which performance should be measured, and the rewards associated with achieving these standards.

7.2.1 Standards

The standards are the actual measures used. Fitzgerald and Moon (1996) stressed that to be successful, these standards must be viewed as fair and achievable by employees.

- **Ownership:** employees need to participate in the creation of standards to take ownership of them, and to feel more motivated to achieve them.
- **Achievement:** the standards set must be challenging but achievable. If staff perceive standards to be set so high that they are unachievable, this is likely to demotivate them.
- **Equity (fairness)** each division or department in an organisation must have appropriate standards set for it in order to ensure fairness in measurement.

7.2.2 Rewards

To ensure employees remain motivated, the standards set must be clear and controllable.

- **Clarity** – the objectives of the organisation need to be clearly understood by those whose performance is being assessed; they need to know what targets they are working towards.
- **Motivation** – individuals need to be motivated to achieve the objectives. Goal clarity and participation in target setting can contribute to higher levels of motivation to achieve targets.
- **Controllability** – managers and staff should not be held responsible for aspects of performance over which they have no control (eg managers should not be held responsible for costs they do not control).

Activity 4: Building block model

Morale among the managers in the residential lettings division of a nationwide estate agent firm has been falling in recent years, although morale in the house sales division has remained high.

The HR director has been trying to find out why this is, and he has identified that one of the main reasons is that virtually all the managers in the house sales divisions achieve their annual performance targets and therefore receive a bonus, while less than 5% of the managers in the lettings division achieve their targets.

Required
Which of the characteristics of effective performance standards that Fitzgerald and Moon identify in the 'building block' model does the estate agency need to improve?

A   Achievability

B   Fairness and Achievability

C   Ownership and Fairness

D   Fairness

Solution

7.3 Stretch targets

Although we have identified the importance of targets being perceived as achievable, it is equally important that targets remain challenging and so cannot be achieved too easily. In this context, the notion of setting 'stretch targets' could be useful in helping to improve performance in organisations.

A stretch target is one that an organisation cannot achieve simply by working a little harder or a little more efficiently. To achieve a stretch target, people have to devise **new strategies** and **new ways** of operating.

Real life example – Jack Welch

Jack Welch is credited with introducing the concept of stretch targets while he was president of General Electric (GE). His logic was that if people strive for what might initially appear to be impossible, even if they don't achieve it they end up doing much better than they otherwise would have done if they had simply been aiming for routine targets.

Welch used the development of bullet trains in Japan to illustrate his point. He argued that if the goal in developing them had simply been to achieve a modest improvement in speed or operating efficiency, the designers and engineers would have (possibly unintentionally) limited their thinking to relative minor alterations. However, by aiming for levels of performance that were significantly beyond what was previously being achieved, they were forced to 'think outside the box' and, as a result, they improved performance to an extent that they hadn't thought was possible (*Kerr and Landauer, 2004*).

7.4 Dangers with stretch targets

However, a danger with setting targets which appear to be unachievable is that people will treat them as such and will therefore not bother trying to achieve them. Therefore, instead of energising an organisation, poorly conceived stretch targets could actually serve to demotivate staff.

When setting stretch targets, the following issues need to be considered:

*   **Resources required** – staff, or departments more generally, need to be given sufficient resources to be able to fulfil the targets set.

- **Targets need to be linked to reward** – if staff attain the targets which are set for them but are not recognised and rewarded for doing so (not necessarily with financial rewards), then they may be less motivated to try to achieve similar targets set for them in future.
- **Unethical behaviour** – overly stretching targets may encourage some people to resort to unethical behaviour in order to achieve them.

> ### Assessment focus point
> The syllabus requires you to be able to analyse how effectively performance targets are communicated, and the way performance is driven through stretch targets. In any such analysis, make sure you think about the implications of the targets on employees – for example, might they have any unintended consequences on employees' behaviour?

7.5 Rewards and remuneration

Rewards are the tools used to motivate employees towards the achievement of corporate targets. By setting attractive and attainable rewards, employees should be motivated to work in line with the company's goals.

Rewards can take the form of a combination of the following:

- Monetary awards
- Pleasure gained from work-based achievements
- Power and status in the workplace

It is important to remember that there is only a limited degree of correlation between pay levels and performance and motivation. Salary is often a 'hygiene' factor, rather than a 'motivating' factor (*Herzberg, 2003*). By contrast, non-financial factors (eg a sense of achievement, opportunities for advancement and growth, recognition, or increased responsibility) may be more effective in motivating employees.

To be effective, a financial reward scheme should transparently link outputs to the rewards available. This can be done via:

- Profit related pay
- Profit sharing schemes
- Group incentives (eg commissions for sales staff)

There are arguments against linking pay directly to performance, and these include:

- Short-term behaviours
- The ability to accurately measure employee performance (eg how far does performance reflect an individual's efforts, or the effort (or lack of effort) from other members of their team?)
- Dysfunctional behaviour eg slowing down once targets are achieved
- Encourages gaming eg manipulating data to earn rewards

Chapter summary

Performance management systems

Performance measurement and control

Strategies need to be converted into specific objectives and targets

Purpose of performance measurement:
- Check position
- Communicate position
- Confirm priorities
- Compel progress

Importance of non-financial measures:
- Non-financial factors (quality; innovation; CRM) = vital to strategies
- Financial measures lag behind performance
- Financial measures can lead to short-term decisions

Critical success factors (CSFs) and Key Performance Indicators (KPIs)

CSFs:
- Areas where an organisation needs to excel in order to be successful and to achieve objectives
- Alignment between CSFs and competences?

KPIs:
- Measured used to assess whether or not an organisation is achieving its CSFs
- Can be financial and non-financial
- Should be 'SMART'

Balanced Scorecard

Four perspectives:
- Financial
- Customer
- Internal business
- Innovation and learning

Setting up a Balanced Scorecard:
- Identify CSFs
- Identify key processes behind CSFs
- Develop KPIs for key processes
- Develop data capture methods
- Develop methods to report data
- Enact improvement programmes

Performance pyramid

- Look at linkages in performance across different levels
- Three levels; plus split between external effectiveness and internal efficiency
- Corporate level
  - Market satisfaction
  - Financial measures
- SBU level
  - Customer satisfaction
  - Flexibility
  - Productivity
- Operational level
  - Quality
  - Delivery
  - Process time
  - Waste

Integrated Reporting

- Look at organisation's ability to create and sustain value in long term

Monitor six types of capital:

- Financial
- Manufactured
- Human
- Intellectual
- Natural
- Social

Targets and rewards

- Used to motivate employees to achieve goals
- But dangers of using measures that encourage unintended behaviour

Building Block model

- Results:
  Financial; competitive
- Determinants:
  Quality; Flexibility; Resource utilisation; Innovation
- Standards:
  Ownership; Achievability; Fairness
- Rewards
  Clarity; Motivation; Controllability

Stretch targets

- Can only be achieved by devising new strategies and new ways of operating
- But danger of seeming unachievable?

Rewards and remuneration

- Rewards can be:
  Monetary; pleasure gained; power based
- To be effective, there must be transparent links between reward and performance
- Dangers of linking pay to performance:
  - Short-termism
  - Difficulties of accurate measurement
  - Dysfunctional behaviour
  - Gaming

Key terms

Performance measurement: The 'process of assessing the proficiency with which a reporting entity succeeds, by the economic acquisition of resources and their efficient and effective development, in achieving its objectives. Performance measures may be based on non-financial as well as on financial information' (*CIMA, 2005*).

Critical success factors: Those aspects of a product or service which are particularly valued by customers (and therefore at which a business must excel in order to outperform its competitors), or which provide a significant advantage in terms of costs (*Johnson et al, 2017*).

Key performance indicators: The measures which are used to assess whether or not an organisation is achieving its critical success factors (CSFs). Effective KPIs focus on the processes and activities which are most important for achieving strategic objectives and performance targets.

Integrated report: 'A concise communication about how an organisation's strategy, governance, performance and prospects, in its commercial, social and environmental context, leads to the creation and enhancement of value over the short, medium and long term' (*International Integrated Reporting Council (IIRC), 2013*).

Activity answers

Activity 1: KPIs

The correct answer is:

Reduce the average time taken to resolve complaints by 12%.

Options 1 and 4, while being desirable, would be difficult to measure, and so would not be suitable KPIs. Option 2 is not specifically linked to the handling of complaints, and so would not be a suitable KPI for this CSF. Option 3 is measurable and links directly to the complaints handling process.

Activity 2: Balanced scorecard

The correct answer is:

Financial perspective

(a) Generate acceptable returns to shareholders – dividend yield + ROCE

(b) Achieve increased annual growth – sales growth % + market share %

(c) Increase profitability – gross profit % + net profit %

Customer perspective

(a) High levels of customer satisfaction – repeat business % + customer survey results

(b) Convenient store locations – % population within five miles of a store

(c) Supermarket of choice / brand loyalty – customer survey results

Internal business perspective

(a) Lean purchasing operation – % food wasted

(b) Process customers quickly – average time taken to serve customers at tills

(c) High staff utilisation – £ turnover per staff member

Innovation and learning perspective

(a) New products and services – % turnover generated by new products/services

(b) Invest in staff training – hours' training per staff member per year

(c) Grow internet sales – % turnover from internet sales

Activity 3: Performance policy

The correct answer is:

Elements	Level of the performance pyramid
Waste	Departmental level
Delivery	Departmental level
Financial objectives	Business units
Productivity	Operating systems
Quality	Departmental level
Market satisfaction	Business units

Refer to Cross and Lynch's performance pyramid.

Activity 4: Building block model

The correct answer is:

Fairness and Achievability

Fairness – the disparity in the proportion of managers receiving a bonus suggests that it is easier for managers in the house sales division to achieve their targets than for their colleagues in the lettings division. In order to be fair, the targets for both divisions should be equally challenging.

Achievability – the most effective targets are ones which are challenging yet achievable. If the targets are too difficult to achieve (as they seem to be in the house sales division) the managers' inability to achieve the targets is likely to demotivate them, and they may stop trying to achieve them.

Test your learning

1 **Required**
   What does the following describe?

   Those aspects of a product or service which are particularly valued by customers, and therefore at which a business must excel in order to outperform its competitors.

   A   Mission

   B   Objectives

   C   Critical success factors

   D   Key performance indicators

2 The four statements below represent a selection of objectives, CSFs, and KPIs.

   Required
   Which one of them is a CSF?

   A   To ensure prices are at least 1% lower than the average prices of rival companies

   B   Percentage of customers who would recommend the company to friends

   C   Using economies of scale to procure high-quality goods as cheaply as possible

   D   Number of products which are more expensive than equivalent products sold by competitors

3 **Required**
   Which of the following statements is true?

   (a) Financial indicators tend to be leading indicators, which can point to future performance problems or successes.

   (b) A problem with financial performance measurement systems is that they often focus on annual (short-term) performance, and so may not be directly linked to longer-term organisational objectives.

   A   Both of them

   B   (a) only

   C   (b) only

   D   Neither of them

4 **Required**
   What are the four perspectives of Kaplan and Norton's balanced scorecard?

5 **Required**
   Which one of the following is NOT one of the aspects of performance at the operational level (departments and work centres) in Lynch and Cross's performance pyramid?

   A   Flexibility

   B   Cycle time

   C   Delivery

   D   Quality

6 **Required**
   In Fitzgerald and Moon's 'building block' model, which of the following are classified as determinants of performance?

   (i)   Innovation

   (ii)   Quality

   (iii)   Motivation

   A   (i) and (ii) only

   B   (i) and (iii) only

   C   (ii) and (iii) only

D   (i), (ii) and (iii)

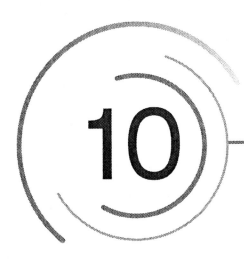

10 Change management

Syllabus learning outcomes

Having studied this chapter you will be able to work through the following syllabus outcomes:

Syllabus Area E3: Strategic choices

3   Change management techniques and methodologies

a - c   Impact of strategy on organisation, change management strategies and the role of the leader in managing change

Exam context

In the exam, you will be expected to demonstrate competence in the following representative task statements:

- Understand the importance of managing critical periods of adaptive, evolutionary, reconstructive, and revolutionary change
- Analyse the impact of change on organisational culture (including the cultural web and McKinsey's 7s model)
- Evaluate the role of leadership in managing the change process and building and managing effective teams
- Evaluate the approaches and styles of change management and managing the resistance to change

Chapter overview

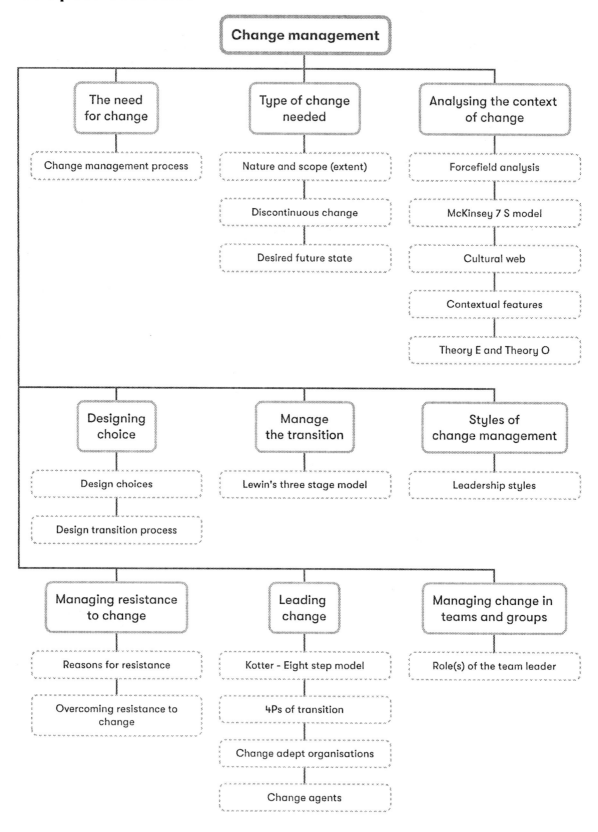

1 Introduction

Once an organisation has developed its strategies, it then has to implement them. Implementing new strategies will often require some organisational change, and change management is an integral part of strategic management. In this chapter we will look at some of the key issues relating to this change, and how change is managed. It is important for managers to identify the type of change required in any given situation, because this will affect the way change is managed.

It is also important to recognise that although some stakeholders will support a change, others are likely to resist it. Force field analysis provides a way of assessing the driving and resisting forces for change. However, in order to implement change successfully, an organisation will have to overcome any resistance to it. Appreciating the different ways to overcome resistance to change is another important topic covered in this chapter.

Any significant alterations will impact upon the existing culture of an organisation. Indeed, part of the change may be to explicitly alter the culture itself. In any case, a good point for managing cultural change will be to document the existing culture, and consider the impact that wider changes will have upon this. This analysis can be performed with the aid of the cultural web and the McKinsey 7S models.

Leadership is a key factor affecting the success of change programmes. Leaders need to have the vision to identify changes and be able to deliver them. Effective communication is also crucial in enabling change to be implemented successfully.

Topics to be covered:

- Types of change
- Impact of change on organisational culture
- Resistance to change
- Approaches and styles of change management
- Role of change leader in communication

2 The need for change

Implementing new strategies, or modifying existing strategies if they have not worked as well as had been intended, represents changes for an organisation. As such, organisations need to understand how change can be achieved, and how resistance to change can be overcome.

> ### Assessment focus point
>
> Change management is often an integral part of strategy implication. It is important to be able to recognise the factors in a scenario that highlight the need for change, but also influence the ways in which it should be managed.

In Chapter 3 we identified how events in the external environment can act as **drivers for change** in an organisation. Any organisation that ignores change does so at its own peril, because its inactivity is likely to weaken the organisation's ability to respond effectively to the opportunities and threats it faces.

As such, 'strategy' and 'change management' are inherently linked, as organisations need to select strategies which allow them to compete effectively, and then organise their resources and capabilities in a way which enables them to implement those strategies. For example, in order to implement a strategy successfully, an organisation may need to change its **structure** or its **systems**.

> **Change management:** The continuous process of aligning an organisation with its marketplace and doing it more responsively and effectively than competitors (*Berger, 1994*).

2.1 Drivers of change

Although in Chapter 3 we focused on external drivers of change (eg PEST factors, competitors), a change process could be prompted by either **internal** or **external** drivers of change (or a combination of both).

Internal drivers of change could include:

- Restructuring (through downsizing or cost-cutting)
- Introduction of a new product or service
- Expansion into new markets
- Introduction of new business processes (eg just-in-time (JIT) or total quality management (TQM))
- Change in senior management (eg a new CEO)

Activity 1: Change triggers

Falling incomes for a national heart disease charity, HFU, have resulted in the decision to hire a new Chief Executive Officer with extensive commercial experience in business turnaround. The new CEO has been tasked with taking whatever steps are necessary to increase the amount of money HFU spends on medical research.

Required

Indicate which of the following are external changes that may have triggered the recent changes within HFU.

Select ALL that apply.

A Staff unrest

B Changes in charity legislation

C Falling household incomes

D Ageing population

E Rising administration costs

F Increasing incomes at other medical charities

Solution

2.2 The change management process

In a similar way that choosing a strategy encourages an organisation to assess its current position, evaluate its strategic choices, and then decide upon a course of action, we can also view change management as a sequence of stages.

Balogun and Hope Hailey (2008) summarise the process of change management in the flow chart presented below:

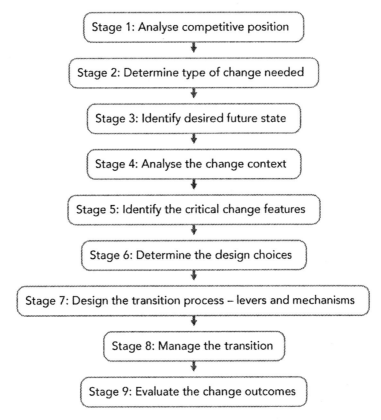

Stages 1 and 2 can be summarised as the '**why and what**' of change, while Stages 3 to 9 can be summarised as the '**how**' of change: how the change is actually implemented.

2.3 Analyse competitive position

While assessing the external drivers of change, organisations will typically analyse their competitive position within their industry.

Models such as PESTEL analysis, competitor analysis and Porter's five forces could all be useful here.

3 Identifying the type of change needed

Identifying the type of change required is important, because it will affect the leadership styles required to implement change effectively. This is Stage 2 in Balogun and Hope Hailey's change management process.

3.1 Nature and scope (extent) of change

The type of change will be dictated by its **nature** and **extent** (*Balogun et al, 2016*).

Nature of change relates to the speed of change required. **Incremental** change builds on existing skills and routines and allows for learning as the change proceeds, enabling adjustments to be made in the experience. However, if an organisation is facing a crisis, or needs to make a rapid change, then a '**big bang**' approach might be needed, where everything is attempted all at once.

The **extent** (or **scope**) of the change relates to the end result of the change. A change that occurs in line with an organisation's existing business model is **realignment** of strategy, whereas a more extensive change – eg changing the existing business model or culture – is **transformational**.

Johnson et al (2017) quoting Balogun et al (2016) define four basic types of change:

Types of change (after *Balogun et al, 2016*)

		Extent (scope) of change	
		Realignment	Transformation
Nature of change	Incremental	Adaptation	Evolution
	'Big bang'	Reconstruction (or turnaround)	Revolution

3.1.1 Adaptation

Adaptation is the most common type of change. Change is gradual, building on what the organisation has done in the past, and in line with the existing business model and organisational culture. Changes in product design or methods of production, or launches of new products could be examples of adaptation.

3.1.2 Reconstruction

Reconstruction is a more rapid and extensive change response than adaptation but remaining within the existing business model. Reconstruction is often required as a result of significant performance decline, eg cost-cutting programmes in response to falling profits.

3.1.3 Evolution

Evolution characterises an incremental process that results in the development of a new business model or culture. It may arise from careful analysis and planning or may be the result of learning processes. The transformational nature of the change may not be obvious while it is taking place. Evolution is arguably the most challenging type of strategic change, since it involves building on existing strategic capabilities while also developing new capabilities for the new business model (*Johnson et al, 2017*).

3.1.4 Revolution

Revolution is characterised by fast-paced and wide-ranging change, often to ensure an organisation's survival in response to extreme environmental changes. Revolution can often be necessary following a period of strategic drift, in which an organisation has previously failed to respond to environmental or competitive pressures. Revolution can be challenging to manage because it is likely to not only require rapid change, but also culture change.

Assessment focus point

The syllabus requires you to understand the importance of managing critical periods of adaptive, evolutionary, reconstructive, and revolutionary change.

However, the way change is managed will depend on the type of change required. It is important that you can identify the extent (scope) and nature of change required in different scenarios, and consequently the type of change which is appropriate.

Activity 2: Change types

Matthew plc operates in a fiercely competitive environment where change is an almost daily requirement. Being a small company, operations can alter radically on a weekly basis, with the company's business model being very fluid.

Mark Co is aware of subtle changes within its marketplace but feels that any change should be gradual so as not to unwind the existing cultural model which it believes will continue to serve it well.

Luke plc operates in the same industry as Mark Co and also appreciates that change is inevitable. However, its view is that a transformational cultural change is required in its business if it is to adapt and thrive.

John Co is an established company with an unwieldy and bureaucratic structure making the change process painful, slow and expensive. Management have reluctantly accepted that radical changes are needed to its processes, and need to be made quickly if John Co is to remain competitive, although the overall business model will remain largely unaltered.

Required
Match the most appropriate change type to each of the organisations described.

Matthew [▼]

Mark [▼]

Luke [▼]

John [▼]

Picklist:

Adaptation

Reconstruction

Evolution

Revolution

Solution

3.2 Discontinuous change

Adaptation is an example of a response to **continuous change**, and the ability to deal with this is a crucial skill for a change manager.

Equally important, however, is the ability to deal with **discontinuous change**. This tends to be caused by sudden changes in either the organisation's environment or operations and is also known as 'frame-breaking' as it results in a new paradigm.

The distinct characteristics of discontinuous change include:

- **Strategic vision** is reshaped.
- **Multiple aspects** of the organisation change ie strategy, structure and systems.
- The **future state** is initially unclear.
- **Leadership** of change cannot be delegated; it requires executive input.
- The **speed of change** is rapid.

3.3 Stage 3 – identify desired future state

In order to ensure that change occurs in an orderly and planned way, an organisation must identify at the outset where it wishes to be at the end of the process.

Kotter (1996) identified that having clear vision of the change required is a vital component in leading change. This vision provides a sense of direction for the change and acts as a bridge between the current and future state.

As Kotter (1996) notes, it is also very important to communicate the vision to people involved in a change project, if they are to understand and commit to the changes.

4 Analysing the context of change

A key issue element in designing change programmes is identifying the elements which support or resist change.

4.1 Forcefield analysis

Forcefield analysis involves identifying those stakeholders who support change, those who oppose it, and those who are more or less neutral. The key task for change leaders is to persuade those who are neutral, or who oppose the change, to support it.

For example, key issues might include:

- What aspects of the current proposal are causing people to resist change, and how might these be overcome?
- What needs to be introduced or improved to add to the forces supporting change?

The relative number and weight of the forces supporting – or resisting – change (illustrated by the relative sizes of the arrows in the diagram below) also help management estimate the effort needed to achieve change.

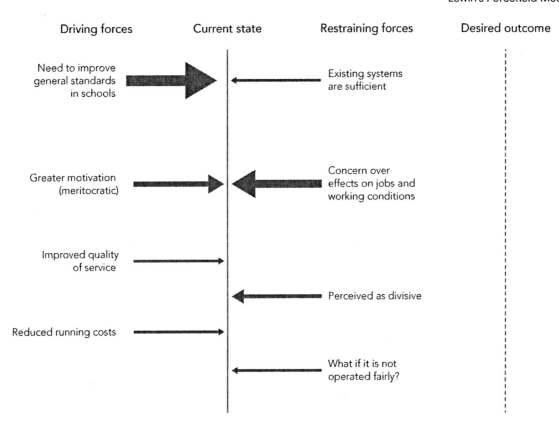

Assessment focus point

Note the possible link between force field analysis and **stakeholder analysis**. Stakeholder mapping (Mendelow's matrix) could help to identify different stakeholders with an interest in a change project, and the power of those different groups in promoting or resisting change.

4.2 Organisational infrastructure and culture

The existing infrastructure and culture of an organisation can also be factors which promote or resist change. The following example illustrates how the need to desire to change culture acted as a driving force for change in an organisation:

Real life example – Ryanair

The budget airline Ryanair has historically made a virtue of its zero-tolerance attitude towards customer service and customer complaints. The company's flamboyant CEO Michael O'Leary took almost every negative story about poor customer service as an opportunity to highlight that Ryanair took extraordinary cost-cutting measures, without which the company would not be able to offer cheap fares. However, after two profits warnings in 2013 O'Leary took the decision to re-engineer the company to be 'nicer', resulting in the launch of the 'Always Getting Better' campaign launch in 2014. (*The Irish Times, 2018*)

In order to facilitate the necessary change in culture, a high-level management reshuffle was undertaken and a number of small but significant changes were instituted, including:

- The website was overhauled to make it more user-friendly (the number of clicks to book were reduced from 17 to 5).
- Excess baggage fees were reduced by half.
- Fines for not printing boarding passes were reduced from €60 to €15.

- Seat allocations were introduced.
- Check-in staff were instructed to smile more often.
- A reward scheme was created: 'My Ryanair Club'.

4.3 McKinsey 7S model

The **McKinsey 7S model** (*Peters and Waterman, 1982*) provides a useful way of analysing the infrastructure in an organisation. The impact that a potential change has on the different elements (or how well it fits with them) could affect the extent to which the change is promoted or resisted.

Equally, by analysing infrastructure and culture, management can gain a better understanding about which elements might need to be changed in order to support the overall changes an organisation is seeking to implement.

McKinsey 7S model (after *Peters and Waterman, 1982*)

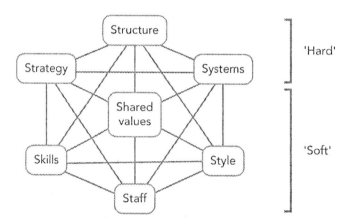

'Hard' elements deal with facts and rules, and are relatively easily quantified or defined.

'Soft' elements can be harder to define, but are equally important in shaping an organisation.

All elements (hard and soft) must be aligned for an organisation to be effective.

- **Structure**: how the organisation is structured (eg functional, divisional, networked) and who reports to whom
- **Strategy**: how the organisation plans to gain and maintain competitive advantage over its competitors
- **Systems**: the processes and procedures employees use to get work done; also including accounting, HR and management information systems
- **Shared values**: the norms and standards that guide employee behaviour and reinforce its purpose/mission
- **Style**: the way the company is managed, style of leadership, and the attitudes of senior management (eg what they focus on, how they conduct themselves)
- **Staff**: the type of employee recruited, and how they are trained and motivated
- **Skills**: the things an organisation does well (in particular, the skills and competences of its staff)

4.4 Cultural web

An alternative or complementary model for understanding an organisation's culture is the **cultural web** (*Johnson et al, 2017*).

The cultural web analyses the paradigm (assumptions) in an organisation's culture, together with the physical manifestations of that culture (*Johnson et al, 2017*).

The cultural web (after *Johnson et al, 2017, p175*)

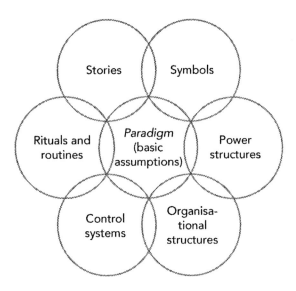

The elements of the cultural web can be defined as follows:

- **Control systems** – what is measured and rewarded in the organisation; eg people may be rewarded based on volume of sales rather than customer service.
- **Routines** – the way members of an organisation behave to each other and to those outside the organisation; and **Rituals** – events that are important to the organisation, whether formal (eg recruitment and induction processes) or informal (eg drinks after work).
- **Organisation structure** – this will determine formal and informal relationships and what is important; eg a hierarchical structure suggests a 'top-down' approach.
- **Symbols** – this can include logos, office layouts, titles and uniforms, often in the form of 'status symbols'.
- **Power structures** – people holding power in the organisation. This may not just be based on seniority, eg in professional firms, technical experts may hold significant power.
- **Stories and myths** – stories told to each other, outsiders and new recruits such as the organisation's foundation or key decisions.
- **Paradigm** – the shared assumptions of the organisation, including beliefs, that are taken for granted and represent a collective experience.

4.4.1 The cultural web and strategy

The importance of the cultural web for business strategy is that it provides a means of looking at cultural assumptions and practices, to make sure that organisational elements are aligned with one another, and with an organisation's strategy.

If an organisation is not delivering the results its management want, management can use the web to help diagnose whether the organisation's culture is contributing to the underperformance.

Equally, management can use the web to help them understand what the organisation's culture needs to look like, in order to deliver a future strategy successfully.

> **Assessment focus point**
>
> The syllabus requires you to be able to analyse the impact of change on organisational culture, including the cultural web and McKinsey 7S model.
> You need to be able to identify how a potential change might affect different elements of the cultural web or the 7S model. However, equally, as part of an 'analysis' you might also need to consider what implications this has for the scope of the change required. For example, what level of changes might be required to the culture of an organisation (illustrated by the cultural web or the 7S model) in order to implement a strategy?

Activity 3: Change models

Required

Match each of the following terms to the correct change model:

Controls [▼]

Desired outcome [▼]

Staff [▼]

Symbols [▼]

Systems [▼]

Picklist:

Cultural web

McKinsey 7S

Forcefield analysis

Solution

4.5 Contextual features

A common reason for failures in change management is the failure to understand the context in which change is happening. Context refers to the organisational setting in which change is occurring and Balogun and Hope Hailey (2008) highlighted the following eight aspects of context which a change agent needs to consider during implementation, and which can support or resist change.

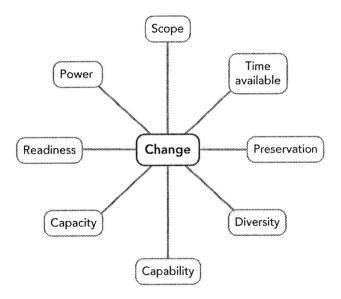

Aspects of context

- **Time available:** This could depend on the trigger for change; eg there may be little time to make changes if responding to competitive or regulatory pressure. Less can be achieved in shorter time horizons.
- **Preservation:** Some particular characteristics may need to be preserved eg quality, innovation, customer service.
- **Diversity:** A range of general experience, views and opinions within an organisation is likely to help the change process. An organisational culture which encourages the sharing of ideas and challenging of existing ways of working may prove useful when implementing a change programme.
- **Capability:** The organisation must have the skills/resources needed to implement planned changes (eg managers or staff with past experience of change projects).
- **Capacity:** To undertake change depends on the availability of resources, particularly finance, IS/IT, and management time and skill, but it is important to note that unrealisable or out-dated systems could become a blockage in the change process.
- **Readiness:** The degree to which the workforce appreciates the need for change and are ready for change will affect the success of a change programme; eg are staff ready for change or will they resist it?
- **Power:** Does the change leader have the authority to make the changes required?
- **Scope:** This relates to the extent of the change required (as we have already noted when looking at types of change).

Assessment focus point

Analysing the contextual features can be very useful in helping to identify the appropriate leadership style(s) for different change situations. For example, in situations where there is little time and low workforce readiness for change a top-down, directional style may be necessary. However, if workforce readiness is higher and employees have previous experience of change programmes ('capability') a more collaborative style could be appropriate.

Once the context of change has been analysed, **Stage 5** in Balogun and Hope Hailey's change process can then be completed – **Identify the critical change features** – by identifying the key issues arising from the first four stages.

4.6 Theory E and Theory O

Beer and Nohria (2000) suggest that although every organisation's change is unique, each change is ultimately a variant of two underlying approaches which Beer and Nohria call Theory E and Theory O.

Theory E starts from the premise that the purpose of change is to increase economic value, often expressed as shareholder value. The features of Theory E include:

- The focus of change is on formal structure and systems.
- Change is seen as a top-down process, often with extensive help from external consultants.
- Changes are planned and programmatic, and often involve the use of economic incentives, drastic layoffs, downsizing and restructuring.

Theory O is concerned with developing an organisation's capabilities to implement strategy and to develop corporate culture through organisational learning.

- The focus of change is on culture and cultural adjustment, rather than structure and systems.
- The process is participative (rather than being top-down).
- Change is emergent rather than planned and programmatic, with an emphasis on feedback and reflection.

Activity 4: Theory E&O

Bellti's is a high street electronics retailer that is struggling to remain profitable in the face of rising online completion. The new CEO is looking at a range of options to restore the company's fortunes.

Required

According to Beer and Nohria, which of the following initiatives would be consistent with a Theory E approach to change management?

A   Reducing in-store staff numbers

B   Stocking higher priced and margin products

C   Closing unprofitable stores

D   Boosting investment in staff sales training

E   Changing the staff culture, to give increased focus on customer service

Solution

5 Designing change

5.1 Determining the design choices

Once the context of change has been considered, the change agent may then consider the six design choices available which affect implementation:

- **Change path** – the nature and scope as referred to in Section 3
- **Start point** – will change be driven by a bottom-up or top-down approach?
- **Change style** – covering the range from collaborative to coercive – see Section 7
- **Change target** – at what level of the organisation is change aimed?
- **Change interventions** – the levers and mechanisms to be deployed – see Section 5.2
- **Change roles** – deciding who leads and directs the change

5.2 Design the transition process

Balogun and Hope Hailey (2008) identify four types of mechanism and lever used to physically drive change:

- Technical changes – alteration to structures and systems
- Political interventions – directions from senior management
- Cultural interventions – changing the culture in an organisation (see Section 4)
- Interpersonal interventions – communication to staff, education (about the benefits of a change) and training (to provide them with the skills needed for a new strategy) (see Section 8.3)

> **Assessment focus point**
>
> The reference to 'communication' in interpersonal interventions highlights the importance of leadership in the change process – with change leaders communicating to stakeholders the need and benefits of change. This point is reinforced later when we look at the steps (identified by Kotter, 1996) that leaders can take to help to ensure the success of change projects.

6 Manage the transition

Having designed a change programme, in order to gain the benefits from that programme an organisation then has to implement it successfully. We will now look at the issues involved in implementing and managing the change process itself.

6.1 Lewin's three-stage model

Lewin (1958) recommends a three-stage process as illustrated in his diagram below:

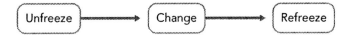

6.1.1 Unfreeze

This involves breaking up the current state of affairs and preparing an organisation for change. An important aspect of this is creating a **readiness to change** among stakeholders (especially staff).

More generally, a key part of the unfreeze stage is **weakening** the forces that resist change and **strengthening** the driving forces that are promoting change (forcefield analysis).

6.1.2 Change (or 'move')

The next step is to move towards the desired state. This will require **staff participation** in order to ensure that they 'buy into' the new status quo.

Two important elements which encourage change are:

- **Identification:** encouraging individuals to identify with role models from whom they can learn new patterns of behaviour
- **Internalisation:** placing individuals in a situation in which new behaviours are required for success, so they **have** to develop coping behaviours

6.1.3 Refreeze (or 'freeze')

The new state is **embedded**, via a combination of coercive measures (eg setting policies which require new behaviours, establishing new standards) and positive reinforcement (eg bonuses dependent on staff adopting new methodology).

Activity 5: Lewin's forcefield model

Required

Match each of the following actions to the relevant stage of Lewin's model.

Removing individuals from current posts and routines [▼]

Habituation – staff become accustomed to the new state [▼]

Negative reinforcement as non-compliance is punished [▼]

New systems implemented [▼]

Consulting individuals on proposals for change [▼]

Confronting individuals' perceptions about change [▼]

Creating a positive agenda supporting change [▼]

Positive reinforcement as compliance is rewarded [▼]

Picklist:

Unfreeze

Change

Refreeze

Solution

6.2 Evaluation of Lewin's ideas

Although the three-stage model provides a useful outline of the change process, it is not a planning tool for the process.

There is a danger that some managers may view 'unfreeze' as a planning session, before using 'change' as implementation and 'refreeze' as a post-implementation review.

Unfortunately, such an approach ignores the fundamental issue that **people will only change if they feel and appreciate the need to do so.** If this need is not properly communicated, the change process will not harness the energy of key players effectively and will not tackle any potential resistance within an organisation.

7 Styles of change management

Communicating appropriately and effectively to staff is very important in managing change. However, it is also important that the style in which change is managed is appropriate to the context.

7.1 Leadership style and contextual features

Johnson et al (2017) identify that the appropriate leadership style will vary according to the contextual features of change (time, readiness, capability etc).

They identify that readiness and capability are particularly important in determining the appropriate style, and recommend four possible styles:

- **Persuasion** – involving education, training and coaching. Likely to be appropriate where there is high readiness for change, but low capability.
- **Collaboration** – involving extensive consultation and teamwork in defining the change. Likely to be appropriate where both readiness for change and capability for change are high.
- **Participation** – allowing staff to participate in the change process may help to gain employee support. This is likely to be appropriate where capability is high, but readiness for change is low.
- **Direction** – if readiness for change and capability are both low, then top-down direction (imposing the change) may be the most appropriate style. This could be particularly the case if change is urgent.

Styles of change leadership (*Johnson et al, 2017, p476*)

| | | Readiness | |
		Low	High
Capability	High	Participation	Collaboration
	Low	Direction if urgent; participation if time available	Persuasion

7.2 Leadership style inventory

Reardon et al also highlight that leaders need to adapt their styles for different circumstances, although they identify four basic styles which leaders adopt:

- Commanding
- Logical
- Inspirational
- Supporting

The characteristics of these styles can be summarised as follows (*Reardon et al, 1998*):

	Focuses on	Persuades by	Makes changes	Learns by
Commanding	Results	Directing	Rapidly	Doing
Logical	Innovation	Explaining	Carefully	Studying
Inspirational	Opportunities	Creating trust	Radically	Questioning
Supportive	Facilitating work	Involvement	Slowly	Listening

8 Managing resistance to change

One of the greatest challenges for a change manager is staff resistance, or resistance from other stakeholders (eg suppliers, distributors, customers).

People typically feel comfortable with what they know but fear the unknown and the uncertainty that goes with it. Consequently, they feel uncomfortable with change.

8.1 Reasons people resist change

Kotter and Schlesinger (1979) identify four main reasons why people will resist organisational change:

- **Parochial self-interest** – they think they will lose something of value to them as a result of the change. They focus on their own interests rather than the organisation as a whole.
- **Misunderstanding and lack of trust** – this can be the case if people do not understand the implications of the change and think that the disadvantages will outweigh the advantages. This can often arise due to poor communication. However, this resistance can also occur if there is a lack of trust between employees and management.
- **Different assessment of the situation** – management may believe a change is beneficial but employees may identify practical problems with a proposed change that managers had not foreseen. In this case, resistance could be beneficial if it allows the organisation to avoid problems which would otherwise have arisen if the original change had been implemented.
- **Low tolerance of change** – people fear they will not be able to develop the new skills and behaviours that will be required of them. Other people might simply resist change because it means they have to move outside their 'comfort zone'.

 Illustration 1: Resistance to change

ABC Air, which is based in Wayland, has completed the research, design and planning phase of a business process re-engineering (BPR) project designed to streamline its procurement and inventory management operations. The agreed solution involves the merger of these departments into a single 'inventory management' department to be located in Essland. This change has been facilitated by the emergence of a new integrated software program, allowing these activities to be seamlessly managed by a single entity.

The main driver behind the choice of location was cost, which is much lower in Essland due to cheaper labour and land costs along with a more flexible employment framework. Implementing these plans will necessitate the closure of existing facilities in both the Wayland and Essland resulting in hundreds of compulsory redundancies.

Required

Identify why staff within ABC will be resistant to change and advise the management on how to lessen this resistance.

Solution

The correct answer is:

You may have thought of additional points, but the following could all be relevant here:

Reasons for resistance

- Inertia, staff generally do not like change as a function of human nature.
- Fear of losing jobs
- If staff are unionised, this will galvanise and focus resistance.
- Jealousy on behalf of Wayland staff seeing jobs transferred to Essland
- Changes will feel like a criticism of existing performance.

Lessening resistance

- Communicate clearly the need and rationale behind the changes.
- Consult with staff and try to take on board their ideas.
- If the workforce is unionised, work with unions to reduce the threat of strike action.
- Take legal advice to ensure redundancies are handled fairly.
- Provide money for redundant staff to retrain or re-skill.

As we saw earlier in the chapter, forcefield analysis illustrates the importance of removing the forces that oppose change rather than focusing solely on the drivers of change themselves.

8.2 Groups

Group resistance poses a particular challenge to change agents. Some of the specific problems that groups may pose during a period of change include:

- Group members may respond in different ways, making a single approach to change management hard to formulate.
- Influential group members who oppose change may harden the attitudes of more neutral members.
- Groups provide a focal point for more organised resistance to change.

8.3 Overcoming resistance to change

Kotter and Schlesinger (1979) identified six approaches to overcoming staff resistance:

(a) **Education and communication** – assumes resistance is caused by a lack of understanding about the reasons or benefits of the change. Change must therefore be 'sold' to staff eg by highlighting the potential benefits.

(b) **Participation and involvement** – staff involvement in the design of processes lessens resistance. Involvement may alleviate fears about how staff will cope with change.

(c) **Facilitation and support** – staff should be offered support eg counselling or managers being available for staff to talk about their concerns with them. Training should also be offered for new aspects of jobs. If employees have to be made redundant, they should be offered support eg through career support to help them find an alternative job.

(d) **Negotiation and agreement** – negotiation may often be necessary where union influence is strong eg to resolve areas of dispute about the changes. Incentives to accept change may be required eg additional payments.

(e) **Manipulation and co-optation** – resistance is undermined in covert ways, such as manipulation of information. However, this is a risky strategy as manipulation may increase resistance. It may also raise ethical issues – how ethical is it to manipulate people to accept change?

(f) **Coercion, implicit and explicit** – a suitable approach where management are powerful and staff are weak (eg threatening individuals with redundancy if they do not accept change). It may be necessary if **rapid change** is required, although staff resentment may be high.

Assessment focus point

The syllabus requires you to be able to evaluate the approaches and styles of change management and managing the resistance to change. One of the key things you may need to do here is to evaluate whether the style of management currently being used in a situation is appropriate.

9 Leading change

Although there is often a presumption that staff and other stakeholders will oppose change, in many cases staff will **accept change** when they can see it could be **beneficial to them**, or that it is **necessary for the organisation**. Nonetheless, resistance to change can often be caused where the reasons why change is required have not been properly communicated.

This again highlights the importance of **communication as a change lever**, and the fact that effective communication is likely to be crucial in change management.

Assessment focus point

Although communication is often directed towards employees, effective communication could equally improve relationships with other key stakeholder groups eg customers and suppliers. How will the changes affect them? What benefits will the changes bring them?

However, leading change can be one of the key demonstrations of leadership because it requires a range of **leadership capabilities**:

- Challenging the status quo
- Communicating and inspiring people to future visions
- Motivating and inspiring people
- Influencing and handling conflict

9.1 Kotter – eight step model

Effective leadership is essential during times of change; **Kotter** (1996) suggests eight key steps a leader can undertake to ensure success.

Step	Comment
Establish a sense of urgency	Discuss the current competitive position and look at potential future scenarios. Increase the perceived need for change (ie promote the driving forces for change).
Form a guiding coalition	Assemble a powerful group of people who can work well together to promote the change.
Create a vision	Build a vision to guide the change effort, together with strategies for achieving it.
Communicate the vision	Effective communication (eg of the vision and accompanying strategies and behaviour) is crucial.
Empower others to act on the vision	This includes removing obstacles to change, such as unhelpful structures or systems. People need to be allowed to experiment (to find out what works and what doesn't).

Step	Comment
Plan for, and create, short-term wins	Identifying (and communicating) visible, short-term improvements will help to sustain the driving forces for change.
Consolidate improvements and produce still more change	Promote and reward those who are able to further advance and work towards the vision. Maintain the energy behind the change process by introducing new projects, resources and change agents.
Institutionalise new approaches	Ensure that everyone understands that the new behaviours and systems will lead to corporate success.

Assessment focus point

The syllabus requires you to be able to evaluate the role of leadership in managing the change process and building and managing effective teams. An important element of the leader's role in the course of managing change is effective communication. So, for example, has a leader communicated their vision of change to other people? More generally, Kotter's Eight step model could be a useful framework for assessing how effectively a leader is managing the change process (for example, have the steps been followed, or have some been omitted?).

9.2 The 4 Ps of transition

Bridges and Mitchell (2000) highlight that periods of change can be stressful for staff and recommend that leaders and managers should acknowledge this in their communication with staff affected by change.

Bridges and Mitchell suggest that leaders can assist people through the change process by communicating the 4 Ps of transition:

- **Purpose** – why change is necessary
- **Picture** – where the change will lead, and what the future position will look and feel like when it is reached
- **Plan** – steps to be taken to reach the future goal; how the organisation can get there
- **Part** – what each person needs to do to contribute to achieving the future goal

The 'part' aspect could have particularly important implications for the communications required in relation to change. Most employees will be interested in the operational features of change, and how it will affect them. Therefore, it is important to include these points – and what the benefits of a change will be for individuals – rather than only focusing on strategic issues or benefits.

9.3 Change adept organisations

Organisations that are able to anticipate, create and respond effectively to change were deemed by **Kanter** (1999) to be 'change adept'.

Kanter (1999) suggested that these change adept organisations shared three key attributes, each of which have implications for leaders:

(a) **The imagination to innovate** – effective leaders help to develop new concepts, models and applications of technology that enable an organisation to maintain a competitive advantage over its rivals.

(b) **The professionalism to perform** – leaders ensure staff receive the training and development they need, supported by infrastructure and systems, to use their skills to a very high operational standard in order to deliver value to increasingly demanding customers.

(c) **An openness to collaborate** – leaders develop relationships with partners who can extend the organisation's reach, enhance its product or service offerings, or energise its practices.

BPP
LEARNING
MEDIA

> **Link to earlier topic**
>
> In Chapter 4, we highlighted customer empowerment as one of the drivers for change in business ecosystems and the organisational environment. This reinforces the importance (within 'Professionalism to perform') of delivering value to increasingly demanding customers.

9.3.1 Leadership skills in change adept organisations

In order to create change adept organisations, Kanter (1999) suggested that the leaders need to demonstrate the following skills:

- **Tuning in to the environment** – listen and learn from your environment eg understanding what key stakeholders (customers, suppliers) want or need from an organisation.
- **Challenging the prevailing wisdom** – look at issues from different perspectives; the current ways of working may not be the best ones.
- **Communicating a compelling aspiration** – leaders need a clear vision of what they want to achieve, and to 'sell' this to other people (to overcome potential resistance to it).
- **Building coalitions** – building broad support for change. Leaders need the support and involvement of people with the resources, knowledge and influence to make change happen.
- **Transferring ownership to the work team** – leaders cannot introduce change by themselves; they need members of their coalition (resource owners, influencers) to enlist other people to implement changes.
- **Learning to persevere** – things will inevitably go wrong, but leaders must persevere in order to reap the rewards in the end.
- **Making everyone a hero** – recognising and rewarding achievement (which will help boost employee motivation and support for any future change programmes).

Part of managing change is enabling employees to perform once the desired changes have been implemented. Whilst formal training is useful management may also consider a process of mentoring and coaching to support their staff.

9.3.2 Mentoring

This refers to the process of a senior manager helping, guiding and supporting the learning and development of another staff member. The key features of mentoring include:

- **No specific time period** – mentoring can be indefinite
- **No formal process** – there is no rigid agenda, the process may evolve to meet the needs of either party
- **Aims to build wisdom** – the mentee is being equipped with new skills and experience to aid them at work

9.3.3 Coaching

This refers to developing a person's skills and knowledge so that an employee's job performance improves. The key features of coaching include:

- **One-to-one** – the coach works directly with the employee
- **Specific purpose** – a specific programme is typically being followed, tailored to the needs of the employee

Whilst there are differences between mentoring and coaching there are also noticeable similarities:

- Neither is about telling someone what to do – both techniques aim to help the employee find solutions to their own problems
- Both are flexible – even though coaching follows a programme, this in itself may evolve over time
- Both require similar skills from the mentor/coach – the 'leader' in each case aims to facilitate, acting as a 'critical friend' rather than a traditional teacher

9.4 Change agents

Leadership in the context of change is often provided by a dedicated manager, the 'change agent'.

> **Change agent:** An individual or group that helps to being about strategic change in an organisation.

Although a change agent can be selected internally, many organisations choose to use external consultants as change agents. In many cases, this may be because the organisation doesn't have the capabilities required internally, but there are also benefits from using an external change agent:

- **Best practice** – an external change agent can recommend 'best practice' approaches, drawing on their experience from working with other organisations.
- **Fresh perspectives** – the agent can take an independent view of the change required. This may enable them to see things that people familiar with the organisation had stopped noticing or chose to ignore due to internal politics within the organisation.

9.4.1 Skills of change agents

Kanter (1999) identified seven 'power skills' that a change agent needs to help them overcome apathy or resistance to change:

(a) Ability to collaborate effectively

(b) Ability to work independently, and without relying on senior management to provide visible support

(c) Developing relationships founded on trust, with high ethical standards

(d) Self-confidence, coupled with humility

(e) Being able to work across different business units

(f) Being respectful of the process of change, not just the desired outcomes

(g) A willingness to invest a personal stake in the process eg linking pay to performance

9.4.2 Managing decline

In reality, not all businesses can be 'saved' or 'turned around'. In such situations the change agent may find themselves having to manage decline rather than growth. In such circumstances this may involve:

- **Retrenchment** – trying to carry on with 'business as usual' whilst drastically cutting costs
- **Turnaround** – an attempt is made to regain competitive advantage by repositioning within the market
- **Divestment** – seeking a trade sale, or closing down part of a business
- **Liquidation** – closing down and selling assets

10 Managing change in teams and groups

Change programmes can often lead to changes in the composition of work teams, so change programmes may result in the need to establish new work teams, and to ensure they operate as effectively as possible.

For this process, some of the theories you have studied in previous papers (eg E2) will be of relevance, including **Tuckman's** group formation stages (*Tuckman, 1965*) and **Belbin's** group roles theory (*Belbin, 1996*).

Illustration 2: Team formation

Tuckman described five stages in group formation.

Required

Describe the following stages of group formation:

Forming

Norming

Storming

Performing

Dorming

Solution

The correct answer is:

Forming - Putting people together; team members find out about each other.

Norming - Relationships formed and conflict occurs.

Storming - Rules established

Performing - Group achieves more than the sum of its parts.

Dorming - Sub-optimal outputs occur where a group becomes complacent.

 ## Illustration 3: Team roles

Belbin described the roles that must be performed in an effective team.

Required

Describe the following team roles:

Plant

Monitor evaluator

Resource investigator

Team worker

Completer-finisher

Implementer

Specialist/expert

Solution

The correct answer is:

Plant - Creative and unorthodox ideas generator

Monitor evaluator - Fair and logical, evaluates ideas

Resource investigator - Co-ordinates activities

Team worker - Supportive, understanding, diplomatic

Completer-finisher - Task focused individual

Implementer - Conscientious individual who is driven by delivering on time

Specialist/expert - Provides knowledge and skills in rare supply

10.1 Role(s) of the team leader

Adair's model of **action-centred leadership** (*Adair, 1973*) provides a framework for the leadership and management of any team or organisation. It identifies three core management responsibilities:

- Achieving the task
- Managing the team
- Managing individuals

Although Adair's model was developed to describe the complexity of the leadership context in general, it is particularly relevant here – since it identifies the challenge for a leader in addressing the needs of team members as individuals (eg salary, sense of purpose and achievement), as well as the needs of the team as a whole. However, the nature of the model – comprising three interrelated variables – means the needs of the team and its members cannot be detached from the requirement to perform (ie to achieve the task at hand).

Adair's action-centred leadership.

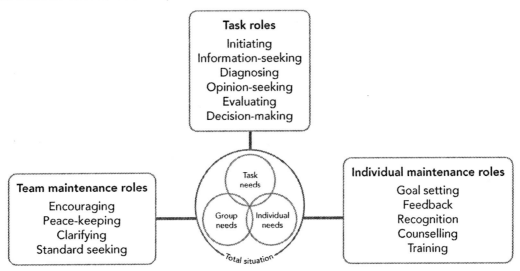

In addition to the management responsibilities, Adair (1973) also highlights eight basic rules of motivation for leaders. These include:

(a) Be motivated yourself.

(b) Select motivated people.

(c) Treat each person as an individual.

(d) Set realistic but challenging targets.

(e) Understand that progress itself motivates.

(f) Create a motivating environment.

(g) Provide relevant rewards.

(h) Recognise success.

Chapter summary

Change management

The need for change

Organisation may need to change in order to implement strategy
- eg: structure; systems

Drivers for change:
- Can be internal or external

External:
- PESTEL factors; competitors

Internal: (for example):
- New products/markets
- New processes
- New management

Change management process
- Analyse competitive position
- Determine type of change needed
- Identify desired future state
- Analyse change context
- Identify critical change features
- Determine design choices
- Design transition process
- Manage the transition
- Evaluate the change outcomes

Type of change needed

Nature and scope (extent)
- Nature:
  incremental or big bang
- Scope:
  realignment; transformation

Types of change:
- Adaptation
  (incremental; realignment)
- Reconstruction
  (big bang; realignment)
- Evolution
  (incremental; transformation)
- Revolution
  (big bang; transformation)

Discontinuous change
- Caused by sudden changes
- Results in a new paradigm

Desired future state

Need a vision for change, to help ensure change proceeds in an ordered way

Analysing the context of change

Forcefield analysis
- Driving forces
- Restraining forces

To get to desired future state, need to remove/weaken restraining forces

McKinsey 7 S model
- Helps define infrastructure and culture
- What elements may need to change to support a strategy?
- 'Hard' elements:
  Structure; Strategy; Systems
- 'Soft' elements:
  Shared values; Skills; Staff; Style

Cultural web
- Used to analyse culture
- Elements:
  Stories; symbols; power; routines; controls; structures; paradigm

Contextual features
- Change leader needs to consider factors which can help to support or resist change
- Time available; preservation; diversity; capability; capacity; readiness; power; scope

Theory E and Theory O
- Theory E: top down; focus on economic value
- Theory O: participative; focus on organisational learning

Designing choice

Design choices

- Path: nature and scope of change
- Start point: top down; bottom up?
- Change style
- Change target – levels of organisation affect
- Change interventions – tools used
- Change roles

Design transition process

Four levers to drive change:

- Technical changes – new systems
- Political interventions – senior management input
- Cultural invention – new culture
- Interpersonal intervention – impact of change team

Manage the transition

Lewin's three stage model

- Unfreeze: create readiness for change; weaken resisting forces
- Change (move): implement planned changes; need staff participation
- Refreeze: embed new state
- But... does model overlook the fact that people will only change if they recognise the need to?

Styles of change management

Leadership styles

Johnson et al:

- Appropriate style will vary according to contextual features of change
- Four possible styles: Persuasion; Collaboration; Participation; Direction

Reardon et al:

- Four basic styles: Commanding; Logical; Inspirational; Supporting

Managing resistance to change

Reasons for resistance

- Parochial self-interest
- Misunderstanding and lack of trust
- Different assessment of the situation
- Low tolerance of change

Overcoming resistance to change

Kotter & Schlesinger: Six methods

- Education and communication
- Participation and involvement
- Facilitation and support
- Negotiation and agreement
- Manipulation and co-optation
- Coercion

Choice of method needs to be guided by context

Leading change

Leadership capabilities required in leading change:
- Challenging the status quo
- Communicating future vision
- Motivating and inspiring people
- Influencing and handling conflict

Kotter - Eight step model
- Establish sense of urgency
- Form a guiding coalition
- Create a vision
- Communicate the vision
- Empower others to act
- Generate short-term wins
- Consolidate improvements
- Institutionalise new approaches

4Ps of transition
- Purpose; picture; plan; part

Change adept organisations
Characteristics:
- Imagination to innovate
- Professionalism to perform
- Openness to collaborate

Leadership skills in change adept organisations:
- Tune in to the environment
- Challenge prevailing wisdom
- Communicate a compelling aspiration
- Build coalitions
- Transfer ownership to the work team
- Learn to persevere (things will go wrong)
- Make everyone a hero

Change agents
Skills of change agents:
- Ability to collaborate effectively
- Ability to work independently
- Developing relationships, with high ethical standard
- Self-confidence + humility
- Work across different business units
- Respect the process of change
- Invest in the process

Managing change in teams and groups

Tuckman: Team formation:
- Forming; Storming; Norming; Performing; Dorming

Belbin: Team roles:
- Plant; Monitor evaluator Co-ordinator; Resource investigator; Shaper; Team worker; Completer-finisher; Implementer; Specialist / Expert

Role(s) of the team leader
- Adair: Action-centred leadership
- Three core responsibilities:
  - Achieving the task
  - Managing the team
  - Managing individuals

Key terms

Change management: The continuous process of aligning an organisation with its marketplace and doing it more responsively and effectively than competitors (*Berger, 1994*).

Change agent: An individual or group that helps to being about strategic change in an organisation.

Activity answers

Activity 1: Change triggers

The correct answers are:

- Changes in charity legislation
- Falling household incomes
- Ageing population
- Increasing incomes at other medical charities

Activity 2: Change types

The correct answer is:

Response option	Explanation
Adaptation	Subtle change in a relatively steady environment
Reconstruction	Rapid change is required, but the business model remains unchanged
Evolution	Transformational change in a relatively steady environment
Revolution	Radical and constant change

Matthew **Revolution**

Mark **Adaptation**

Luke **Evolution**

John **Reconstruction**

Activity 3: Change models

The correct answer is:

Controls **Cultural web**

Desired outcome **Forcefield analysis**

Staff **McKinsey 7S**

Symbols **Cultural web**

Systems **McKinsey 7S**

By definition, refer to the Forcefield, 7S and Cultural Web models.

Activity 4: Theory E&O

The correct answers are:

- Reducing in-store staff numbers
- Stocking higher priced and margin products
- Closing unprofitable stores

The correct options relate to cost-/profit-related initiatives, consistent with Theory E.

The other two options are more focused on employees and culture, and so are more characteristic of Theory O.

Activity 5: Lewin's forcefield model

The correct answer is:

Removing individuals from current posts and routines **Unfreeze**

Habituation – staff become accustomed to the new state **Refreeze**

Negative reinforcement as non-compliance is punished **Refreeze**

New systems implemented **Change**

Consulting individuals on proposals for change **Unfreeze**

Confronting individuals' perceptions about change **Unfreeze**

Creating a positive agenda supporting change **Unfreeze**

Positive reinforcement as compliance is rewarded **Refreeze**

- Unfreeze: steps to prepare the entity for change
- Change: steps taken to effect desired changes
- Refreeze: positive and negative reinforcement to entrench changes made

Test your learning

1 **Required**

According to Lewin's three-stage model, which one of the following activities is part of the 'unfreezing' stage?

A Publicising success stories of divisions which have embraced a change

B Creating new performance management and reward schemes

C Explaining the need for change

D Training staff in new ways of working

2 Depending on the speed and extent of the change required, organisational change can be classified as adaptation, reconstruction, evolution or revolution.

Required

Which of the following describes an organisational change which can be introduced incrementally, and which realigns – rather than transforms – an organisation's existing processes and culture?

A Evolution

B Adaptation

C Reconstruction

D Revolution

3 **Required**

Which one of the following is NOT one of the aspects of the cultural web?

A Capability

B Control systems

C Organisational structure

D Symbols

4 **Required**

What are the six approaches for dealing with resistance to change which Kotter and Schlesinger identify?

5 In a message to staff, a leader has communicated: where a change will lead the organisation and what the future position will look like once it is reached; the steps which need to be taken to reach the future goal; and what each person needs to do to help achieve that goal.

Required

According to Bridges' and Mitchell's model – 4 Ps of transition – which 'P' has the leader failed to communicate?

A Part

B Picture

C Plan

D Purpose

6 **Required**

Which of the following best describes a change agent?

A An external consultant who analyses an organisation and recommends the changes that need to take place in it

B A senior manager who knows all the parts of the organisation and therefore understands what needs to change

C A senior manager who proposes a strategic change in an organisation

D A person, or group of people, who takes on the role of promoting strategic change within an organisation

Building and implementing digital strategy

Syllabus learning outcomes

Having studied this chapter you will be able to work through the following syllabus outcomes:

Syllabus Area F: Digital strategy	
1	The governance of digital transformation
a	The roles and responsibilities of the board and executive leadership in digital strategy
3	Elements of digital strategies
a - e	Economics of digitisation, Digital ecosystems, Digital consumption, Data and metrics and Leadership and culture

Exam context

In the exam, you will be expected to demonstrate competence in the following representative task statements:

- Analyse the board's and senior leadership's role in an organisation's digital strategy including defining value and charting, articulating, and overseeing the execution of digital strategy and transformation

- Advise management on how digital transformations and the creation of vast, interconnected ecosystems driven by business to business can disrupt and reshape industries

- Advise management on how the participants in an ecosystem impact an organisation's strategy, including the participant's role within the environment, reach through the environment, and capability or key value proposition

- Advise management on how technology and experience with new platform technologies and business models have transformed customer expectations to integrated and customized experiences

- Analyse digital traction metrics including scale, active usage, and engagement to assist management in measuring the success of a digital business

- Advise management on leadership's role in building a digital workforce including attracting and retaining talent, becoming an employer of choice, creating a workforce with digital skills, brining leadership to the digital age, and fostering a digital culture

Chapter overview

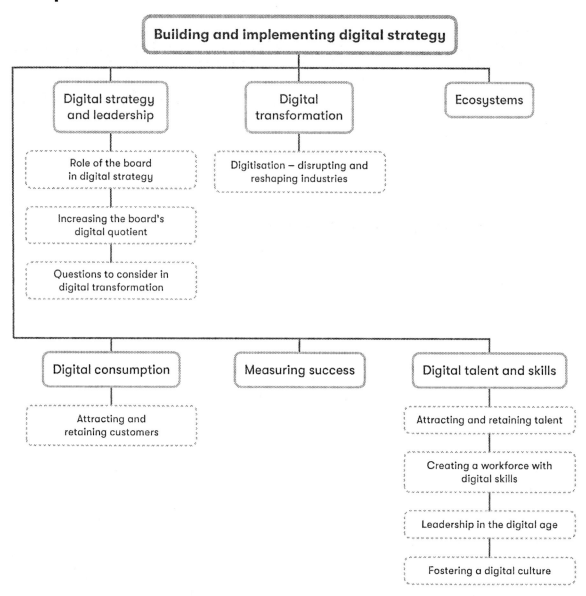

1 Introduction

In the previous chapter we discussed issues around change, and digitisation is one of the most significant factors (if not, *the* most significant factor) shaping strategies and driving change in modern business. As a result, digital transformation is likely to be a key strategic issue for many boards, with the board members being responsible for overseeing a company's digital vision.

Strategically, digitisation is enabling companies to create new business models, and – potentially – to disrupt existing industries. We have already seen some of the changes associated with digitisation in Chapter 4 where we discussed the development of business ecosystems, based around digital platforms.

Digitisation enables companies to reach customers in new ways and gather increased amounts of data about customers. However, customers also have changing expectations of companies, meaning companies need to adapt their strategies to meet these expectations.

Speed and agility are important features in the digital environment, but while technology can provide some elements of this (eg through automation), companies also need employees with the appropriate skills to help them implement their digital strategies successfully.

Topics covered in this chapter:

- Role of board and senior leadership in digital strategy
- Business case for digital transformation
- Participants, interactions and dynamics of ecosystems and impact on strategy
- Trends in consumption (eg hyper-personalisation, move from products and services to experience
- New metrics (scale, active usage and engagement metrics)
- Leadership in digital transformation

2 Digital strategy and leadership

Faced with increasing disruption from new digital entrants, many existing companies will need to transform themselves into digital enterprises to compete successfully and thrive.

This transformation needs to involve much more than simply investing in the latest digital technologies. A digital enterprise's competitive advantage comes from its **culture, strategy,** and **way of operating.**

Successful digital transformation requires a culture that **promotes innovation, encourages risk taking, and empowers employees** at all levels of an organisation (*World Economic Forum (WEF), January 2016*).

> **Digital strategy:** The use of digital technology and digital assets to challenge existing ways of doing things, and to restructure accordingly, in particular in relation to the way a business interacts with its customers.

Two key features of a digital enterprise (*WEF, 2016*) are that they:

- Constantly strive to implement new, and leaner, operating models underpinned by agile business processes, connected platforms, analytics and collaboration capabilities that enhance the productivity of the firm
- Continuously search for, identify, and develop new digital business models, ensuring that customers and employees are at the centre of what the enterprise does

The World Economic Forum (WEF) has carried out extensive research into digital transformation and they have identified five key enablers of digital strategy, with the first of these relating to leadership (*WEF, 2018*):

- **Agile and digital-savvy leadership** – the strategic vision, purpose, skills, intent and alignment across management levels ensure a nimble decision-making process for innovation
- **Forward-looking skills agenda** – developing a digital mindset in the workforce, by making innovation the focus of training and hiring programmes

- **Ecosystem thinking** – collaborating within the value chain eg with suppliers and distributors
- **Data access and management** – ensuring a strong data infrastructure and data warehouse capability, combined with the right analytics and communication tools to drive competitiveness
- **Technology infrastructure readiness** – building the required technology infrastructure to ensure strong capabilities in relation to cloud, cybersecurity and interoperability

2.1 The role of the board in digital strategy

As with any other strategy, **digital strategy needs effective leadership**. Some companies have hired a chief digital officer (CDO) to drive through the changes that are needed to become a digital enterprise. But installing a CDO does not guarantee success.

The board, led by the CEO, ultimately remain responsible for setting the digital vision and strategy of a company.

Although 'digital' is not only about technology, boards must make sure that the technology agenda is properly integrated into strategy development.

Key questions for boards to consider, in relation to digital strategy and digital transformation, include:

- What is the company's current digital position? To what extent is it digitised?
- How can existing legacy systems be modernised to meet customer and employee needs?
- What factors might impact strategy (eg the potential impact of emerging technologies)?
- What capabilities and resources will the company need for a successful digital transformation?
- Is technology aligned with the company's purpose and supporting business and customer goals?

2.2 Leading digital transformation

Implementing a digital strategy could involve a number of change management issues for an organisation. A structured process such as the one below may help address these:

(a) Understand the current position (including existing competencies) and how the digital transformation supports the overall corporate strategy.

(b) Have a vision of what the digital future looks like and what benefits can be expected eg enhancing the customer experience and streamlining internal operations.

(c) Look for ideas from all stakeholders, formally and informally.

(d) Build a framework for change, including a methodology and a change team.

(e) Communicate clearly and effectively – digital transformation may mean different ways of working which may lead to fear. Once the vision has been set, it should be shared across the whole organisation.

(f) Anticipate costs, to include not just equipment but recruiting or retraining staff, redesigning processes, and staff time.

(g) Measure success – establish whether initial goals have been met.

2.2.1 Allocating funds

Another important decision in a digital transformation will be how funds are allocated. Senior managers need to ensure that resources get to the right places to enable the transformation.

Expenditure needs to be carefully targeted – withdrawing funding from projects that fail to meet expectations and investing more in those that do well. Similarly, transformation projects can often require funding to be withdrawn from legacy operations to make more funds available to invest in new projects.

The budgeting process typically also needs speeding up during transformation projects. In large companies, the budgeting process tends to follow an annual cycle, but during a transformation project this should shift to a quarterly or even monthly cycle, to ensure that funds are being allocated to the optimal place *(Dahlstrom et al, 2017)*.

2.3 Increasing the board's digital quotient

In order to operate effectively in the digital age, board members need an understanding about the technology environment, its potential impact on different parts of an organisation and its value chain, and how digital could disrupt existing strategies and stimulate the need for new ones.

The far-reaching nature of digital disruption means that boards need to view themselves as being responsible for digital transformation efforts.

McKinsey (*Sarrazin and Willmott, 2016*) has suggested that, in order to achieve this successfully, boards need to raise their digital quotient.

(Based on: Sarrazin and Willmott, 2016)

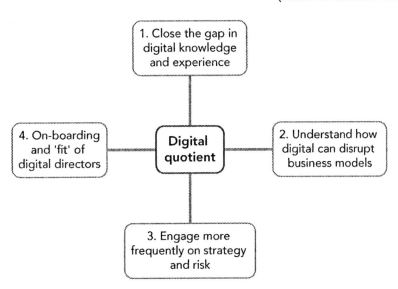

(a) **Close the gap in knowledge and experience** – boards need sufficient technological insight to recognise and respond to digital initiatives, as well as potential security or data risks. Typically, directors may not have sufficient digital expertise to have meaningful discussion with senior management. A company needs to assess whether it needs to recruit new board members with suitable digital experience and skills for its circumstances.

(b) **Understand how digital can disrupt business models** – board members need to understand the threats to an organisation's business model, and the factors which are critical to its success.

(c) **Engage more frequently** – the pace of disruption and change in the environment means that it is no longer appropriate for boards to meet once or twice a year to discuss strategy.

(d) **On-boarding** – new digital directors must be able to influence change within the culture of the board. Many 'digital' directors will be younger than traditional board members and may have little previous board level experience. The on-boarding process should help to ensure these new directors can participate effectively in discussions, and therefore the company benefits from their insights.

2.4 Key questions for leaders

The World Economic Forum (2016) identifies some key recommendations and questions for board members and senior managers to consider in order to help them with their digital transformation:

- **Examine every aspect of operations** – is 'digital' included in strategic plans across business functions? (eg does the operating model support ecosystem partnerships, either by creating a platform, or allowing the organisation to participate in other platforms?)

- **Automation** – have you identified areas in the business where automation is most relevant? Is the company making efficient use of automation?

- **Investment in security** – is ensuring the security of data and systems an important board-level issue? Has the company increased its investment in security (cyber security) sufficiently to support its move to a digital business model?

- **Digital workforce** – does the company have a digitally literate leadership team? Are there appropriate training schemes to overcome digital skills gaps among employees?
- **Digital metrics** – has the company established appropriate KPIs to measure the traction of its digital business model? Is real-time data capture possible?
- **Investors** – what steps have been taken to convince investors about the company's digital vision, and the long-term value-creation impact of its digital transformation?

Board members also need to consider the way their organisation is using data and innovation:

- Is the organisation using data and analytics to uncover business insights, and to develop products, services and experiences tailored to customers' needs?
- Is the company using emerging technologies, such as machine learning and artificial intelligence, to create innovative products and services that help to build competitive advantage?

Assessment focus point

The syllabus requires you to be able to analyse the board and senior leadership's role in an organisation's strategy, including overseeing the execution of digital strategy and transformation. In this section we have looked at a number of issues leadership teams need to consider in the context of digital transformation, and an important part of your analysis could be considering the extent to which leaders have considered these issues effectively in the context of executing a digital strategy.

3 Digital transformation

Advances in digital technology are re-shaping industries. Cheaper, and better, technology is revolutionizing business and society; a top of the range smartphone cost $499 in 2007, but a model with similar specifications in 2015 cost $10 (*World Economic Forum, 2016*). However, the falling costs of technology mean the world is becoming ever more connected.

Mobile technologies, 'cloud', artificial intelligence, sensors (IoT), data analytics, robotics/automation are all key elements of progress (and we will discuss these in more detail in Chapter 12). However, the rapid pace of technological advances means that existing organisations need to transform themselves into digital enterprises in order to compete effectively.

Digital transformation is much more significant than simply investing in the latest digital technologies. Instead companies will need to:

- Search for new **business models** (eg in the context of business ecosystems – see Chapter 4).
- Rethink their **operating models** (see Chapter 12).
- Revise how they **measure the success** of their business (see Section 6).
- Reconsider how they attract and nurture **digital talent** (ie staff – see Section 7).

Note. Although industries are being disrupted by digital enterprises, this does not mean existing companies cannot survive. Established companies have significant resources (tangible assets, brands, know-how and IP, distribution networks, customer relationships, data) which they can harness. However, they do need digital capabilities if they are to compete effectively and maintain their margins.

Illustration 1: Digital transformation

High street retailers are facing increasing competition and disruption from online retailers, such as Amazon.

Although existing companies can survive digital disruption, it is likely they will need to make significant transformations in order to do so.

Required

What factors might the senior management team at a 'traditional' high street retailer need to overcome when attempting to change their business model to respond to industry disruption?

Solution

The correct answer is:

You may have thought of others, but some possible factors could be:

- **Resistance to change** – reluctance among key stakeholders, such as employees, to change existing ways of working. There may also be a belief that the 'digital era' is a 'fad' and that staying the course may be a viable strategy.

- **Culture** – the resistance to change may also be linked to a wider need to change the organisational culture to support new business models (eg becoming more 'agile').

- **Lack of vision** – to maximise the chances of the transformation being successful, management will need a clear understanding of how digital transformation will be implemented in their organisation. However, given their 'traditional' background, management may not have a clear vision for what they want the 'digital' customer journey to look like, and how that will fit with the existing business.

- **Knowledge** – lack of individuals within the organisation with technical knowledge and skills to implement new business models.

- **Technology** – the company's current technology infrastructure and processes may not have the capacity to support the new business model.

- **Data management capability** – one of the key factors which influences the success of digital businesses is their ability to gather and analyse customer data. Non-digital-natives often gather lots of data about customer interactions, but they can often be stores across a number of different 'siloed' systems. One of the challenges the business is likely to face is deciding how to manage and use its data (eg integrated systems) in a way that enables it to increase the value it provides to its customers.

3.1 Digitisation – disrupting and reshaping industries

Digital technologies are creating new profit pools by transforming customer expectations and how companies can address them.

McKinsey's report 'The economic essentials of digital strategy' (Dawson et al, 2016b) identifies six main ways that 'digital' can disrupt and reshape industries:

- **Unconstrain supply** – as transaction costs are reduced, firms can now provide products/services that were previously uneconomic to supply.

- **Remove distortions in demand** – unbundling aspects of products and services that were previously combined, by necessity or convenience eg buying single songs rather than whole albums. Alternatively digitisation could lead to the re-bundling of products or services that were previously kept separate (eg booking flights and hotels through a travel website, like Expedia, rather than having to deal separately with airline companies and hotels).

- **Make new markets** – digitisation facilitates cheaper and easier ways to connect supply and demand eg AirBnb and Uber.

- **Create new and enhanced value propositions** – customers' expectations are increasing, and companies need to meet these with new value propositions; eg Google Nest enables people to control home thermostats from their phones.

- **Reimagine business systems** – new entrants can surprise incumbents by introducing completely different ways to make money eg cloud computing replacing local storage.

- Hyperscale platforms **(ecosystems)** – by offering a range of different products and services, platforms are able to offer customers a unified value proposition which is much broader than they could previously obtain from one supplier eg Amazon, Alibaba as retail ecosystems, or internet comparison sites offering deals on a wide range of insurance contracts. The scale of their operations also enables platforms to gather more information about customers (which in turn helps to inform their decisions about the products and services they provide).

Activity 1: Digital disruption

Required

Which of the following best describes the way hyperscale digital platforms (ecosystems) can disrupt and reshape markets?

A   They enable the unbundling of products and services that were previously combined.

B   They offer customers a much broader range of products and services than they could otherwise obtain from one supplier.

C   They reduce transaction costs, meaning that firms are able to provide services which were previously uneconomic to supply.

D   They enable firms to provide new products and services by removing supply constraints.

Solution

Assessment focus point

The syllabus requires you to be able to advise management on how digital transformations and the creation of vast, interconnected ecosystems driven by business to business can disrupt and reshape industries. We have already looked at the characteristics of ecosystems in Chapter 4, but a key issue here is the impact they can have on existing firms and industries. For example, what impact are ecosystems (like Amazon) having on physical 'bricks and mortar' retailers?

4 Ecosystems

We have already discussed, in Chapter 4, the significance of ecosystems in the digital economy.

In relation to developing a digital strategy, in the context of ecosystems, a key factor for an organisation to consider is what role it could play in an ecosystem.

As a reminder, four key roles an organisation could play in an ecosystem are:

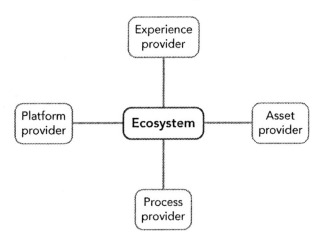

To be a valuable participant in the ecosystem, an organisation needs to ensure its capabilities allow it to perform one, or more, of these roles.

To assess its ability to do this successfully, an organisation needs to assess what its capability or key value proposition is:

- What is the organisation contributing to the ecosystem?
- What range of activities is the organisation able to undertake in the ecosystem?

Equally, however, as well as considering its own capabilities, an organisation needs to consider what other organisations there might be in the ecosystem that can act as **complementors** and add value to its products or services. For example, an electronics firm (like Sony) can create accessories (eg speakers) that work with a central platform business's products (eg Apple's).

Depending on the other participants in an ecosystem, an organisation can also play more than one role within that ecosystem.

Real life example – Ticketmaster

Ticketmaster's business has historically involved working with concert venues and promoters to sell tickets through its website.

However, Ticketmaster has now also opened its website to allow individuals to resell tickets, via 'fan-to-fan resale.'

Ticketmaster has adjusted its revenue model to receive a transaction fee for each ticket re-sold on the site. As such, Ticketmaster is now pursuing a hybrid strategy in which it acts as both a vendor and a platform-based business, enabling transactions between others.

Assessment focus point

The syllabus requires you to advise management on how the participants in an ecosystem impact an organisation's strategy. Possible issues you may need to consider here could be: what role could an organisation play in an ecosystem, or what value can it add to the ecosystem? Does it have the capability to perform that role successfully?

5 Digital consumption

Businesses have always faced the challenge of keeping up with changing customer expectations, but the pace of technological advances in the 21st century has transformed these expectations, while also providing companies with the tools to create the experiences that are needed to satisfy customers.

5.1 Customer expectations

A factor determining companies' success is how effectively they compete in the race to deliver what 'on-demand customers' want (*World Economic Forum (WEF), 2016c*):

- **On demand consumption** – increasing penetration of the internet and smartphones means consumers are increasingly becoming used to a world in which they have access to products, services and experiences at any time, and on-demand.

- **Customer experience** – customers (both in a B2B and a B2C context) form expectations about speed, convenience and ease of use from their perceived leaders in customer experience.

- **Demographics** – the increasing share of millennials, and post-millennials, in the population has had a significant effect on customer expectations. They are digital natives, so have different expectations from customers of previous generations.

5.2 Attracting and retaining customers in a digital world

Three areas are becoming increasingly important in the battle to attract and retain customers in a digital world (*WEF, 2016c*):

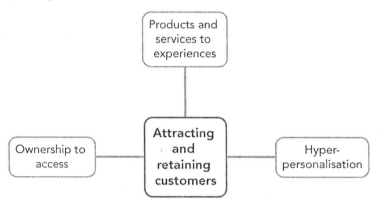

- **From 'products and services' to 'experiences'** – the quality of the goods and services a company offers, on its own, is often no longer a sufficient basis to differentiate the company from its competitors. Companies increasingly use digital technologies to offer customers unique experiences. The importance of 'experiences' is illustrated by the popularity of social media – focusing on videos and stories about what people are doing and experiencing, rather than simply what they own.

- **Hyper-personalisation** – marketers have been using the concept of targeted marketing for some time now, but the idea of hyper-personalisation takes this further.

  WEF (2016c) suggests there are two main forms of hyper-personalisation:

  - Giving customers control to customise their own product/experience (eg NIKEiD allows customers to design customised shoes)

  - Providing more relevant interactions by analysing customer data (eg BeatsMusic tailors playlists, in real time, to listeners' mood and location) and by harnessing the power of data analytics.

- **From 'ownership' to 'access'** – digital connectivity has increased access to products and services through peer-to-peer markets and matching platforms (eg Uber, AirBnB and WeWork). Alongside this, users' ability to leave reviews on social media helps to build trust in peer-to-peer transactions.

 ### Real life example – BMW

The car manufacturer, BMW, has responded to the collaborative economy – the shift from 'ownership' to 'access' – by setting up its own car-sharing service: DriveNow.

DriveNow, which is available in a number of European cities, gives users on-demand access to BMW electric cars, based on a principle of 'pick up anywhere, drop off anywhere'. Customers are billed by the minute, with fuel costs and parking charges in public car parks included in the bill.

Although the DriveNow service could potentially cannibalise sales of new BMWs, the company feels the scheme is a necessary strategic move to meet customers' preference for access over ownership, and it also has the potential to expand the company's customer base (eg people who use DriveNow but who would not buy a BMW) (*World Economic Forum, 2016b*).

Assessment focus point

The syllabus requires you to be able to advise management how technology, and experience with new platform technologies and business models, have transformed customer expectations in relation to integrated and customer experiences. It is important that you understand the key trends in consumption (eg hyper-personalisation) so that you could assess how an organisation might apply them in order to meet the needs of its customers more effectively.

6 Measuring success in the digital age

We have already discussed performance measures in Chapter 9 and highlighted the importance of using non-financial measures of corporate performance alongside financial ones. The issue of monitoring appropriate non-financial indicators is particularly important for digital businesses.

Traditional financial key performance indicators (KPIs) can often prove ineffective for measuring the success of a digital business. Instead, companies should focus on digital traction metrics to measure the success of their digital transformation.

Digital traction metrics: Indicators looking at the popularity and the momentum in market adoption of a product or service, for example frequency of use, number of users and customer engagement (*WEF, 2016*).

6.1 Digital traction metrics

There are three 'elements' of digital traction metrics:

Digital traction = Scale × Active usage × Engagement

Potential metrics for each element (*WEF, 2016*):

Elements	Potential metrics
Scale	Number of unique visitors Number of registered users Month-on-month growth in registrations
Active usage	Daily active users Monthly active users Conversion rate (% of visitors who take a desired action – eg subscribing for a newsletter) Abandonment rate (% of visitors who don't complete a transaction)
Engagement	Average time spent on site Net promoter score (NPS) – see below Customer satisfaction index Bounce rate (% of visitors who enter a site but then leave without visiting any other pages) Churn/exit rate (% of customers who stop using the company) Number of 'likes' and 'shares'

Net promoter score (NPS): measures customer loyalty on a scale from -100 to +100.

A score of -100 means everyone is a detractor of the company; +100 means everyone is a promoter.

A positive NPS is considered good.

A high NPS means the company's cost of marketing falls, because customers promote the company for it.

6.1.1 Using digital traction metrics

As with any performance indicators, it is necessary to consider industry context; eg the appropriate metrics for an online retailer will differ from those for a software-as-a-service company.

Equally, the figures themselves vary with context; eg gaining one new active user a month may be a reasonable result for a specialist B2B service, but not for a social media platform (eg Facebook).

6.2 Other metrics

The following metrics can also be used to analyse the financial impact of acquiring and monetising customers:

- **Cost to acquire a typical customer (CAC):** sales and marketing expenses/number of new customers added
- **Lifetime value of a typical customer (LTV):** average monthly recurring revenue × customer lifetime. [Customer lifetime = 1/churn rate]

The ratio between LTV and CAC is an important guide for profitability and cash flow. If LTV isn't greater than CAC, this means the cost of acquiring new customers is actually greater than the benefit from acquiring them.

Activity 2: Digital traction

Inspe Co's management accountant has reported that, in the last week:

- The number of unique users on the website has increased.
- The number of repeat users has increased.
- The abandon rate has decreased.
- The churn rate has increased.

Required

Indicate what impact these results have on the elements of Inspe Co's digital traction score, assuming all other measures remain the same.

Scale [▼]

Active usage [▼]

Engagement [▼]

A   Improved

B   No change

C   Worsened

Solution

Number of unique users is a measure of scale: increasing the number of unique users will have a positive impact on scale.

The number of repeat users and the abandon rate are both measures of active usage. A fall in the abandon rate will be beneficial for Inspe Co, so its performance in relation to active usage has improved.

Churn/exit rate is a measure of engagement. However, an increase in churn rate will be detrimental to Inspe Co, because it indicates an increased proportion of customers have stopped using its website.

> ### Assessment focus point
>
> The syllabus requires you to be able to analyse digital traction metrics to assist in measuring the success of a digital business, and it specifically mentions the three elements of scale, active usage and engagement. It is important not only that you understand what each of the elements is, but also that you can interpret what changes in the metrics could indicate about a company's performance and/or the success of a strategy. For example, if a company redesigns its website and the metrics subsequently deteriorate, what does this suggest about the success of the website redesign?

7 Digital talent and skills

In order to implement a digital strategy successfully, a company needs to attract and retain digital talent, and also to create a culture in which employees, on-demand workers and robots can work together effectively (WEF, 2016d).

7.1 Attracting and retaining talent

The World Economic Forum's research into digital talent and skills (WEF, 2016d) has identified some key factors which could affect an organisation's ability to attract and retain the talent it needs to successfully implement a digital strategy.

7.1.1 Becoming an employer of choice for millennials

Millennials are likely to be a major source of talent who have the skills needed, so companies need to be able to recruit them effectively. The following are often important in helping to **attract** millennials:

- Career advancement
- Company culture
- Training/developing opportunities

Empowering and **incentivising** the workforce is also important for **retaining** talent.

7.1.2 Listen to what employees are saying

Social media platforms mean that potential recruits have greater **insights** into an organisation (eg peer-to-peer reviews expose the inner workings of an organisation). This means it is important for companies to listen to what their existing employees are saying about them, because employees' comments could influence potential recruits.

WEF (2016d) has identified that employees attracted through referrals often perform better than others, so companies should incentivise their staff to use online networks to refer potential employees.

7.2 Creating a work force with digital skills

Despite the transformation to digital business models, there is a shortage of workers with digital skills, making it harder to recruit staff with the necessary skills.

Faced with this shortage, companies need to develop the skills and capabilities they need in-house. Training should be a critical part of their talent management strategy.

Key ways in which companies can train and develop the workforce:

- Develop required competencies within the workforce. (The digital competency framework – see diagram below – can be used to help identify skills needed in future, and how these compare to employees' current skills).

- Mine the company for hidden talent, by assessing employees' competencies and matching those with in-demand skills (eg data scientists).

- Bring new skills into the company by hiring digital leaders and digital natives (young adults who have grown up using digital technologies all their lives and are therefore inherently familiar with them).

As well as developing the competencies of existing staff, an organisation could also look to acquire talent, through merger/acquisition with a 'digital' company.

(Adapted from: WEF, 2016)

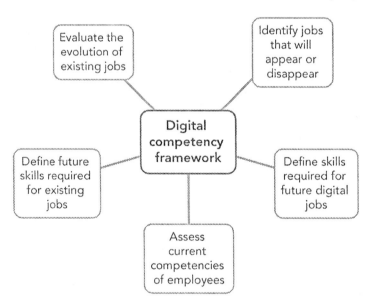

7.2.1 On-demand workers

Building a digital workforce doesn't only involve full-time employees. Companies can also tap the gig economy, for skilled on-demand workers. This can speed up the process of finding new talent and avoids employee costs such as taxes and pensions.

Using on-demand as well as employed staff can increase the talent pool available to a company. However, on-demand workers may not be suitable for some roles (eg high-risk, or business-critical roles).

7.3 Bringing leadership into the digital age

Creating a workplace that attracts high-quality digital workers, requires a progressive organisational culture. The impetus to set this culture must come from leadership.

The traditional characteristics of leadership (eg motivating, influencing others, leading change) remain relevant, but contemporary leaders also need to be familiar with digital and how it could affect their business.

In order to bring about a cultural shift across an organisation, leaders need to hire people with digital mindsets, and a willingness to challenge the status quo. To ensure real change, these people need to be placed across all levels of a company. (WEF, 2016)

7.3.1 Agility and 'failing fast'

Another area where a cultural change may be required is in relation to failure. In a complex, rapidly changing business environment, speed of execution is more important than perfect execution. Companies need to move away from a risk-averse mindset, in which they try to find a perfect solution or product – because by the time they've perfected it, the environment may already have changed, making the solution obsolete.

Instead, companies should encourage employees to take higher amounts of risk in developing new products and services and aim for a solution that is 'good enough' to launch (rather than 'perfect'). Once launched, the product can then be improved, based on market feedback. It is important that the company accepts feedback – even if it is critical – because it provides an opportunity for iterative learning.

7.4 Fostering a digital culture

Having a strong sense of purpose, and a diverse, high-quotient digital workforce, helps to identify a digital company's culture. Culture can be an important factor in supporting a company's long-term competitive advantage because it is very difficult to copy.

The following are areas senior management should focus on to introduce a digital culture (WEF, 2016):

- **Communication:** consider using digital channels (eg social media, blogs, webcasts) as well as face-to-face conversations. But make sure communication remains open and honest.
- **Across the organisation:** change needs to reach all levels of the organisation. Leaders need to encourage employees' creativity. Changes need to be supported by ensuring HR policies and rules reinforce the behaviours and culture required.
- **Visibility:** make the changes visible for employees eg by creating reference guides or charts illustrating the change journey for them.
- **Monitoring:** monitor change continuously eg through culture/feedback surveys. Ensure that the new digital culture becomes embedded in the organisation.

7.5 Humans and robots working together

Another important element of digital transformation can be the role of robots and automation. However, the increased use of robots could have an impact on human jobs (as we discussed in an earlier chapter).

Therefore, building a digital workforce could also involve creating an environment where humans and robots can work successfully together.

If jobs are threatened by automation, employers will need to assess whether it is possible to reskill workers, either to work alongside robots, or to take on new roles.

However, companies need to remember their social responsibilities to their workers (eg to retrain them if possible).

Real life example – Rio Tinto

Rio Tinto is a leading mining and metals company with operations in over 40 countries, including a strong presence in Australia and North America.

To make its mining operations more efficient, Rio Tinto created its 'Mine of the Future' programme to identify the size, location and quality of ore it is mining, by aggregating the data it collects in real time. The company collects this data from the trucks and from the drills it uses in its mines all around the world. In addition, it collects information from process surveillance cameras, control systems and maintenance system logs.

This information is then processed at its Processing Excellence Centre (PEC) in Brisbane, Australia, with 20 different analytical systems. The 'Mine of the Future' programme has generated millions of dollars by increasing productivity and reducing inefficiencies and energy consumption across Rio Tinto's global operations. It has also reduced environmental impact, and improved safety.

The 'Mine of the Future' programme relies on people and computers working together, complementing each other, rather than viewing human and machine as mutually exclusive sources of knowledge. The workers are empowered to operate more effectively on the ground, by the software that interprets complex data sets and creates a user-friendly, 3-dimensional display of the mine that is quickly and easily understood by the workforce.

Assessment focus point

The syllabus requires you to be able to advise management on leadership's role in digital transformation. In this context you could be asked to recommend ways in which leaders could make an organisation more attractive for digital talent, and how they could foster a digital culture in an organisation. Equally, you might be asked to comment on the way leadership is currently managing the workforce, and the extent to which the leadership's role is helping – or hindering – the digital transformation.

Chapter summary

Building and implementing digital strategy

Digital strategy and leadership

Enablers of successful digital strategy:
- Agile, digital-savvy leadership
- Forward-looking skills agenda
- Ecosystem thinking (see Ch 4)
- Data access and management
- Technology infrastructure readiness

Role of the board in digital strategy

Digital transformation is likely to involve a number of change management issues:
- Understand current position
- Develop vision for digital future
- Look for initiatives that can help to achieve vision
- Build a framework for change
- Communicate the vision clear
- Anticipate costs, and allocate budgets necessary for transformation
- Monitor success

Increasing the board's digital quotient

Top operate effectively in the digital era, boards need an understanding of the technological environment

Potential ways to do this:
- Need to 'close the gap' in digital knowledge and experience
- Understand how digital can disrupt business models
- Engage more frequently on strategy and risk
- On-boarding and 'fit' of digital directors

Questions to consider in digital transformation
- Is 'digital' included in strategic plans across all business functions?
- Use of automation?
- Investment in cyber security?
- Digital workforce?
- Digital performance metrics?

Digital transformation

Digital transformation is not solely about new technologies

Other elements:
- Search for new business models
- Rethink operating models
- Revise how to measure success
- Consider how to attract and retain digital talent

Digitisation – disrupting and reshaping industries

Ways digital can reshape industries:
- Unconstrain supply
- Remove distortions in demand
- Make new markets
- Create new and enhanced value propositions
- Reimagine business systems
- Hyperscale platforms (ecosystems)

Ecosystems

Potential roles in an ecosystem:
- Experience provider
- Asset provider
- Process provider
- Platform provider

Does an organisation have the capabilities to play one of these roles successfully?

BPP LEARNING MEDIA

Digital consumption

Successful companies respond to customer expectations:
- Consumption 'on demand'
- Speed, convenience, ease of use

Attracting and retaining customers

Three key areas in battle to attract and retain customers:
- Offer 'experiences' not just products and services
- Hyper-personalisation
- Offer 'access' not just 'ownership'

Measuring success

Importance of digital traction metrics:
- Monitoring popularity and momentum in market adoption of a product or service

Three elements of digital traction metrics:
- Scale
- Active usage
- Engagement

Also important to analyse the impact of acquiring and monetising customers:
- Costs of acquiring customers
- Lifetime value of typical customer

Digital talent and skills

Attracting and retaining talent
- Need to become an employer of choice for millenials (eg company culture; career advancement; empowerment)
- Listen to what employees are saying

Creating a workforce with digital skills
- Develop required competencies within the existing workforce
- Mine the company for hidden talent
- Introduce new skills from outside by hiring digital natives
- Make use of 'on demand' workers, as well as full-time employees

Leadership in the digital age

Need a progressive organisational culture in order to attract and retain high quality digital workers
- Agility
- 'Failing fast'

Fostering a digital culture

Issues when introducing a digital culture:
- Importance of communication
- Change must extend across all areas of the organisation
- Make changes visible
- Continue to monitor change

Key terms

Digital strategy: The use of digital technology and digital assets to challenge existing ways of doing things, and to restructure accordingly, in particular in relation to the way a business interacts with its customers.

Digital traction metrics: Indicators looking at the popularity and the momentum in market adoption of a product or service, for example frequency of use, number of users and customer engagement (*WEF, 2016*).

Activity answers

Activity 1: Digital disruption

The correct answer is:

They offer customers a much broader range of products and services than they could otherwise obtain from one supplier.

One of the key characteristics of hyperscale platforms (like Amazon, Alibaba) is that they offer customers a much broader range of products and services than could otherwise be obtained from one supplier.

Activity 2: Digital traction

The correct answer is:

Scale **Improved**

Active usage **Improved**

Engagement **Worsened**

- Number of unique users is a measure of scale: increasing the number of unique users will have a positive impact on scale.
- The number of repeat users and the abandon rate are both measures of active usage. A fall in the abandon rate will be beneficial for Inspe Co, so its performance in relation to active usage has improved.
- Churn/exit rate is a measure of engagement. However, an increase in churn rate will be detrimental to Inspe Co, because it indicates an increased proportion of customers have stopped using its website.

Test your learning

1 **Required**

Indicate which of the following statements are true.

A Successful digital transformation requires organisations to reduce the risks they are prepared to take

B Agile business processes are a key feature which underpins successful digital enterprises.

2 Viewers can now binge-watch television shows on digital subscription services, like Netflix and Hulu, rather than having to wait a week for the next instalment as they would historically have had to do.

Required

With reference to McKinsey's six ways in which 'digital' can disrupt and reshape industries, which of the following best describes the impact of subscription services?

A Make new markets

B Remove distortions in demand

C Unconstrain supply

D Hyperscaling platforms

3 The World Economic Forum identified three key areas which are becoming increasingly important in the battle to attract and retain customers in a digital world. One of these three key areas is hyper-personalisation.

Required

What are the other two key areas?

4 **Required**

The performance indicators 'bounce rate' and 'net promoter score' can best be used to measure which element of digital traction metrics?

A Active usage

B Engagement

C Scale

D Churn rate

5 Micsen Co encourages employees to launch new products or solutions once they are 'good enough' to do so, rather than trying to make them perfect. Micsen Co's managers argue that feedback about the new products will be invaluable in helping it to improve the products.

Required

Which aspect of digital 'culture' is Micsen Co's managers encouraging here?

A Failing fast

B Incentivisation

C Engagement

D Customer experience

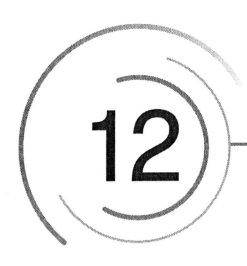

12

Digital technologies

Syllabus learning outcomes

Having studied this chapter you will be able to work through the following syllabus outcomes:

Syllabus Area F: Digital strategy
2   Digital transformation
a - b   Digital technologies and Digital enterprise

Exam context

In the exam, you will be expected to demonstrate competence in the following representative task statements:

- Analyse an organisation's use, or potential use of, digital technologies including cloud computing, big data analytics, process automation, AI, data visualisation, blockchain, internet of things, mobile, and 3-D printing

- Advise management how to survive digital disruption and thrive in a digital age by rethinking their traditional business model and incorporating digital business and operating models

Chapter overview

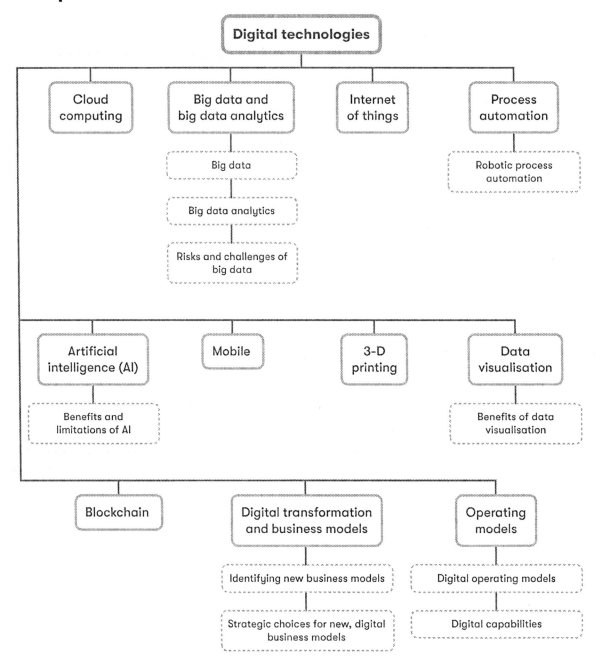

1 Introduction

One of the key themes in the E3 syllabus is the impact that 'digital' is having on the contemporary business environment, and the way organisations are responding to it.

We have looked at the issues around leading and managing digital strategy in Chapter 11. In this chapter, we will now look at the ways companies can transform their operating processes – and their business models – in response to the opportunities and threats which digital technologies present to them.

The syllabus identifies a number of elements of digital technology which help to enable digitisation and can act as drivers of change supporting digital strategies. We will begin the chapter by looking at these elements, before moving on to look, more generally, at the way digital transformation can affect companies' strategies.

Topics covered in this chapter:

- Cloud computing
- Big data analytics
- Process automation
- Artificial intelligence
- Data visualisation
- Blockchain
- Internet of things
- Mobile
- 3-D printing

> **Assessment focus point**
>
> The syllabus requires you to be able to analyse an organisation's use, or potential use, of the different digital technologies we discuss in this chapter. An important part of your analysis could be identifying the potential benefits which different organisations could gain from using the different technologies. As such, it is important that you understand the key features of the different technologies, but also try to think about real-world examples of how organisations have made use of them.

2 Cloud computing

> **Cloud computing:** The delivery of on-demand computing resources – everything from applications to data centres – over the internet on a pay-for-use basis (*IBM, no date*).

Cloud computing technologies have changed the ways in which organisations store and manage their data. An increasing amount of organisational data is now held in servers operated by cloud-based service providers, accessed over the internet.

Cloud computing involves an organisation **buying in services** (eg for storing content) rather than **owning physical assets**, such as servers.

One of the key benefits cloud computing can provide an organisation is **improved access to data**, because data becomes **accessible from anywhere around the world where there is internet connectivity**.

As we noted in Chapter 3, this increased connectedness (facilitated by cloud computing) has been a key element in the emergence of business ecosystems.

Cloud computing also means organisations' data resources become **more elastic** and can be quickly and easily scaled up (or down) to meet changing demand.

2.1 Benefits and risks of cloud computing

As with almost any technologies, there are risks associated with cloud computing as well as benefits. The main benefits and risks are as follows:

Benefits

- **Accessibility** – data stored in the cloud can be accessed at any time, and from anywhere an internet connection is available.
- **Scalability** – as an organisation grows, it can buy additional storage space as required.
- **Cost effectiveness** – there are no start-up costs (eg buying servers) or upgrade costs.
- **Greater flexibility** – there are lots of service providers to choose from. And cloud-based data storage can be set up more quickly than installing the necessary technology in-house.
- **Availability** – cloud computing is available to small entities as well as large ones.

Risks

- **Loss of control** – data security etc is outsourced to the cloud provider. If its staff interfere with the data, an organisation cannot stop/control this.
- **Reliance on data holder** – if the service provider loses the data (or the data gets corrupted), an organisation cannot retrieve it.
- **Fixed cost** – services will be stopped (and data potentially lost) if an organisation fails to keep up its payments to the service provider.

2.2 Cloud computing vs owned technology

Building upon the benefits and risks outlined above, in this section we explore the dilemma currently facing the senior management within many organisations: should the organisation pursue a cloud-based approach to data management or instead manage data using owned hardware and software in-house?

Real life example – GFI Software

A report published by IT solutions firm GFI Software™ (no date) compared some of the main considerations when choosing between in-house IT data storage solutions and adopting a cloud-based approach. Some of the key findings have been summarised below.

The final column in the table outlines the most appropriate outcome following the comparison of the two options:

Topic	In-house	Cloud	Outcome
Expertise	Employing top IT staff with niche skills can be very expensive.	Cloud-based service providers provide staff with the expertise.	Cloud
Support	Employing staff to monitor IT/ IS infrastructures 24 hours a day is expensive.	Cloud-based service providers monitor 24/7; however, they may not monitor the data regarded as being most important to the organisation.	In-house
Customisation	Data held internally can be customised to fit the organisation's needs.	Although cloud-based service providers offer lots of choices around how data is configured and held, this will be limited.	In-house
Service level agreements (SLAs)	When there is an outage it is the responsibility of the in-house IT team to make the IT/IS infrastructure operational again.	SLAs put the onus on cloud-based service providers to restore systems. The organisation may benefit from financial penalty payments for any downtime.	Cloud

The level of significance given to each area of consideration outlined above will vary from organisation to organisation and will therefore influence the end decision.

3 Big data

Big data is a term given to extremely large collections of data ('data sets') that are available to organisations to analyse.

The internet, smartphones, social media, sensors and other digital technologies are all helping to fuel a data revolution.

In the 'internet of things' (see Section 4), **sensors** embedded in physical objects, such as mobile phones, motor vehicles, smart energy meters, RFID tags, tracking devices and traffic flow monitors, all **create and communicate data** which is shared across wired and wireless networks that function in a similar way to the internet.

A frequently used definition of big data is that given by the technology research firm, Gartner:

KEY TERM

> **Big data:** 'High-volume, high-velocity and/or high-variety information assets that demand cost-effective, innovative forms of information processing that enable enhanced insight, decision making, and process automation' (*Gartner, 2018*).

Gartner's definition **highlights three key** characteristics of big data:

(a) **Volume:** there are very large amounts of data to analyse.

(b) **Velocity:** the speed with which data is generated, captured and analysed

(c) **Variety:** the different types of data to analyse eg text, audio, video etc

Data comes from a wide variety of sources, with much of it being **unstructured** (ie not in a database). For example, key words from conversations people have on social media about a product or service could be a source of unstructured data.

A fourth 'V' is often also added to the definition:

Veracity: organisations need to exercise caution when dealing with externally generated data. In the era of 'fake news', can we trust all the data we receive as being reliable?

3.1 Big data analytics

The process of collecting, organising and analysing large data sets is known as big data analytics.

Analytical tools and techniques can be applied to data to:

- Identify **relationships, outliers and exceptions** (eg if a product is selling particularly well to a specific market segment)
- Build **predictive models** (eg having bought one product, what other products might a consumer be interested in buying?)

> **Data analytics:** The process of collecting and examining data in order to extract meaningful business insights, which can be used to inform decision making and improve performance.

Big data analytics could result in performance improvements in the following areas:

- **Better understanding of customer behaviour** – by analysing current market conditions and customers' purchasing behaviour, a company can identify the products that are selling most and produce products according to this trend. Meeting customers' requirements more effectively than competitors do could be a source of competitive advantage.

- **Targeted marketing messages** – promotions and advertising can be targeted in much greater detail than previously (almost to an individual customer level); eg Netflix makes suggestions to subscribers for the next movie they should watch, based on their previous searches and viewing choices.

- **Faster decision making** – the speed of analytics software ('velocity') helps businesses analyse data immediately and make data-driven decisions based on the results of that analysis (eg retailers can use social media data, web search trends and weather forecasts to help manage inventories).

- **Managing reputation** – by monitoring customers' comments (so called 'sentiment analysis') a firm can get feedback about what people like about it (and its products/services) and what they don't. The firm can then look to address areas of weakness and build on areas of strength.

- **New products and services** – by understanding customer needs, firms can create new products according to the requirements of those customers.

3.2 Potential risks and challenges of big data

Although big data can help to improve performance, there could still be potential risks and challenges associated with using it:

- **Quality of data** – there can be a misconception that increasing the amount of data available automatically provides manages with better information for decision making. However, in order to be useful, data has to be relevant and reliable.

- **Veracity** – in order to be valuable, data also needs to be reliable. Using big data requires organisations to maintain strong governance over data quality.

- **Cost** – it could be expensive to establish the hardware and analytical software needed and to comply with data protection regulations which vary from country to country.

- **Skills** – do organisations have staff with the necessary analytical skills to process and interpret the data? The scale and complexity of data sets may require a data scientist's level of analytical skills for data mining, deriving algorithms and predictive analytics.

- **Loss and theft of data** – companies could face legal action if the source data was stolen. More generally, when collecting and storing data they need to consider data protection and privacy issues, and ensure they comply with current legislation in these areas (eg having appropriate controls in place to prevent breaches of data security).

3.3 Big data and the role of the management accountant

Big data systems will have the following impacts on businesses, and consequent implications for their management accountants.

- **Data management** – data integrity ('veracity') is essential, so businesses need to ensure their systems capture relevant data correctly, first time, and store it accessibly. The management accountant will need to maintain a good understanding of their business's information systems to ensure their reports are accurate.

- **Data culture** – to benefit from developments in data and analytics, a business must develop a culture where decisions are based on data and evidence, and the business is managed in the interests of stakeholders. Management accountants already provide professional objectivity, making them ideal champions of evidence-based decision making, able to ensure that decisions are properly informed and considered on the basis of the value to stakeholders.

- **Value creation** – translating analytical insights into commercial action requires collaboration between IT professionals, data scientists, finance professionals and business managers. As their roles bring them into contact with all aspects of the business, management accountants are well positioned to partner with business managers, IT professionals and data experts to support value creation.

(Based on: *CIMA, 2014*)

Activity 1: Big data analytics

Which of the following statements are true?

(i) Big data analytics can enable businesses to analyse and reveal insights from data which they have previously been unable to analyse.

(ii) In order for organisations to analyse big data and to gain insights from it, the source data needs to be structured within a financial software package.

(iii) One of the key characteristics of big data is the speed with which data flows into an organisation, and with which it is processed.

A   (i) and (ii) only

B   (i) and (iii) only

C   (ii) and (iii) only

D   (i), (ii) and (iii)

Solution

4 Internet of things

KEY TERM

> **Internet of things:** Devices connected to each other, and to other applications, over the internet.

The internet of things is made up of devices which are connected together across networks.

The software and **sensors** and electronics embedded in physical devices all create and communicate data, which is shared across interconnected networks that function in a similar way to the internet, creating a more 'connected' world.

This data transmitted and collected by sensors also contributes to 'big data'.

Illustration 1: The internet of things

It has been estimated that in 2016, there were around 11 billion devices connected to the internet, with that figure expected to increase to 30 billion by 2020 and then to 80 billion by 2025 (Kanellos, 2016).

Required
What devices make up the internet of things?

Solution

The correct answer is:

The following examples already exist as mainstream technology:

- Automated speakers which engage verbally with the user (Siri, Alexa)
- Home equipment which can be operated remotely via the internet (locks, central heating, lighting, fridges, plug sockets, air conditioners, water sprinklers, burglar alarms)
- Business equipment (many of the home items above plus functionality such as room monitoring/booking, building security)
- Health monitors (Fit Bits, watches, smartphones)
- Transport that can be tracked online (taxis, planes, trains)
- Traffic control (traffic lights, train signals, traffic jams)
- Weather monitors (both domestic and scientific)
- Infrastructure repair monitors (monitoring buildings, water pipes and gas pipes for wear and tear)

4.1 Using data from the internet of things

By combining connected devices with automated systems, it is possible to gather information, analyse it and create an action to perform a task, or to learn from a process.

The internet of things provides businesses with more data about the products or services, thereby improving their ability to make changes.

The following are some of the potential applications of the internet of things:

- **Sensors on products** (or components) transmit data about how that product is performing. This can help a company identify if a product, or component, is likely to fail, meaning it can carry out preventative maintenance before the failure causes any damage.
- **Real-time data** generated by sensors on products can be used to make supply chains more efficient, for example by being able to track the location of freight which is being delivered. (RFID – radio frequency identification – can also be useful in inventory and supply chain management, allowing organisations to keep track of assets by tagging them.)

- **Sensors monitoring traffic flows** can provide information about the best routes for delivery drivers to take.
- **Sensors in smart buildings** can adjust temperature automatically – for example, turning on air conditioning if sensors detect a conference room is full, or turning the heating in a building down once everyone has gone home.

4.2 Machine to machine communication

The idea of connected sensors in the internet of things also reflects the concept of machine to machine communication.

For example, a vending machine can send an automated message to the distributor's network (machine) when a particular item is running low, to identify the need for a refill.

Similarly, sensors transmitting data about the need for preventative maintenance could be an example of machine to machine communication.

5 Process automation

> ### Link to earlier topic
>
> We have already discussed automation as one of the drivers for change in the business environment (in Chapter 4), noting that new technologies have the potential to change the nature of work across industries, and – in some cases – could become substitutes for human labour. However, in the context of the syllabus areas covered in this chapter, you also need to be prepared to analyse how organisations could use automation to help them improve their business processes in the course of digital transformation.

KEY TERM

> **Process automation:** The use of digital technology to perform a business process or function.
>
> **Robotic process automation (RPA):** The use of software (a 'robot') that is programmed to perform high-volume, rules-based, repetitive tasks.

The use of robots to perform pre-programmed production activities is already standard practice in many manufacturing industries (eg car manufacturing).

However, process automation is now becoming increasingly widespread in service industries or service functions.

5.1 Robotic process automation

Robotic process automation is a way to **automate repetitive** and **rules-based processes** (eg transactional processes like accounts payable processing or bank reconciliations which might typically be located in a shared service centre). Software, acting as a 'robot', captures and interprets existing IT applications to enable transaction processing and data manipulation.

Multiple 'robots' can act as a virtual workforce, removing (or significantly reducing) the need for human resources to perform repetitive tasks.

The key benefits to organisations from using robotic process automation are:

- **Faster handling time** – higher volumes of transactions can be processed. Also, robots can work 24/7, which can increase processing efficiency and reduce processing time.
- **Reduced errors** – processes are no longer subject to 'human error', so benefit from improved quality and accuracy. In turn, this can also help to improve customer service (as can faster handling time which will allow customer enquiries to be processed more quickly).
- **Reduced costs** – the number of staff companies need to employ may be reduced if processes are performed by robots instead of humans. (RPA can also provide an alternative to offshoring or outsourcing, meaning that data can be kept in-house.)
- **Staff focus on value-adding work** – humans can focus on more complex, value-adding tasks, once rules-based processes have been automated.

Automation may still be appropriate in situations where the complexity of the work involved is greater but in these situations automation might typically augment human knowledge rather than replacing it (eg expert systems for medical diagnosis). As the complexity of the tasks being performed increases, the work being performed by computers increasingly displays artificial intelligence.

6 Artificial intelligence

Whereas robotic process automation (RPA) is typically suitable for repetitive, rules-based tasks, artificial intelligence (AI) relates to machines' ability to make decisions and solve problems.

> **Artificial intelligence:** 'The ability of a machine to perform cognitive functions we associate with human minds, such as perceiving, reasoning, learning and problem solving' and acting in a way that we would consider to be 'smart' (*McKinsey and Co, no date*).

Most of the recent advances in AI have been achieved by applying machine learning to very large data sets. Machine learning is a branch of AI in which systems or machines can learn from data, identify patterns and make decisions with minimal human intervention.

> **Machine learning:** Machine learning algorithms detect patterns and learn how to make predictions and recommendations, by processing data and experiences rather than by receiving explicit instructions. The algorithms also adapt in response to new data and experiences to improve their efficacy over time (*McKinsey and Co, no date*).

A machine's learning algorithm enables it to identify patterns in observed data, and to build models that explain these patterns or predict things. One of the key aspects of machine learning is that it is **iterative**: as models are exposed to new data they are able to adapt independently. They change the underlying algorithm based on what they learn from the data.

AI enables computers to learn from data to accurately perform new tasks and to produce reliable decisions and results. As such, AI (based on machine learning) enables organisations to make decisions without human intervention.

Machine learning can take the following forms:

- **Supervised learning** – training data and feedback from humans is used to learn the relationships between inputs and outputs. This requires:
  - Human labelling of input data and definition of output data;
  - The algorithm learns to connect inputs and outputs; then
  - When finished the algorithm is applied to new data.
- **Unsupervised learning** – an algorithm interrogated input data without being given any explicit output variables. This requires:
  - Algorithm receives unlabelled data;
  - Algorithm infers some sort of data structure; then
  - The algorithm identifies other groups of behaviour with similar behaviours.
- **Reinforcement learning** – an algorithm learns to perform a task whereby it aims to maximise its rewards for the actions that it takes. This requires:
  - The algorithm takes an action;
  - The algorithm receives a reward if its action takes it closer to its objective; then
  - The algorithm optimises for the best series of actions by correcting itself over time.

Machine learning decisions are based on two important aspects of analytics:

- **Prediction** ('predictive analytics'): anticipating what will happen, based on the data and patterns in the data
- **Prescription** ('prescriptive analytics'): providing recommendations for what to do in order to achieve goals or objectives

Illustration 2: Machine learning

Which forms of machine learning would be most suited to?

(a) Identifying customer purchase habits from a sales database

(b) Developing an automated trading platform for a stockbroker

(c) A system that predicts house prices based upon economic data

A   Supervised learning

B   Unsupervised learning

C   Reinforcement learning

Solution

The correct answer is:

A supervised learning system would work well when building a system to predict house prices. Data linking house prices with employment rates, interest rates could be used to link inputs (economic data) with outputs (predicted house prices)

Unsupervised learning could be applied to a mass of customer purchasing records. The algorithm could look for customer purchase habits that could be exploited for cross-selling and up-selling opportunities.

Reinforcement learning could be applied to electronic trading platforms. If the systems receives a 'dividend' every time it makes a 'winning' investment (and vice versa) the automated trading should soon learn how to make smart investments.

6.1 Applications of AI

The following are some of the ways AI and machine learning can be applied:

- **Transportation** – autonomous vehicles (self-driving cars) could potentially transform the way people move around.

- **Route optimisation** – analysing real-time information to identify potential problems and traffic jams, and to suggest alternative routes, can very important for transport and delivery companies.

- **Personalised recommendations** – websites recommend items a customer might want to buy based on buying history (eg Amazon), or Netflix recommends programmes to watch based on previous viewing.

- **Healthcare** – machines can record and process vast amounts of patient data and can analyse it using sophisticated AI algorithms. As such, technology can be used to diagnose illnesses and create personalised medicines based on a deep knowledge of a person's genetics to help clinicians do their jobs more effectively. AI can also help to predict people who are at risk from certain diseases and target them for early intervention, thereby reducing the cost of future treatments which would otherwise be required.

- **Portfolio management** – 'robo-advisors' (eg Betterment or Wealthfront) use algorithms to tailor investment portfolios to the goals and risk appetite of the investor, and to adjust these for real-time changes in the market.

- **Fraud detection** – detecting anomalies in patterns of payments or receipts

- **Cyber security** – AI makes decisions very quickly. One of the problems that cyber defence teams faces is that they get so many alerts it is difficult to know how to prioritise them. AI can detect anomalies, and so can alert defence teams to the specific data they need to look at.

Note. In many of these cases, the volume of data available enables algorithms to find patterns and trends. In effect, AI is being used to analyse 'big data' – so it is important to note the links between these two aspects of digital technology.

6.2 Benefits and limitations of AI

6.2.1 Benefits

The key **business benefits** of AI and machine learning include machines' ability to:

- Process large amounts of structured and unstructured data, providing fast, accurate and reliable outputs
- Identify complex patterns in data
- Make consistent decisions. Machines do not suffer tiredness like humans do, and technology does not have cognitive biases like humans do.

Also, crucially, machines' capacity for learning means they are able to process data and identify patterns **without the need for human monitoring**. (This is an important feature that distinguishes AI from big data analytics. Patterns and trends in data are also identified in big data analytics, but in AI the machines identify the trends and issues themselves without being prompted to do so by people.)

6.2.2 Limitations

Despite its potential benefits, it is also important to be aware of the potential limitations of AI:

- Although machine learning enables machines to adapt algorithms, the technology is only as good as the data it receives. (Maintaining high-quality data is crucial to a successful AI platform.)
- Machines 'learn' from the data they are given, but if there are gaps or biases in the initial 'training' data, then the models the machines learn could be incomplete or inaccurate.
- Machine learning models can lack flexibility; they can learn to carry out specific tasks but cannot reproduce the level of multifaceted analysis carried out by the human brain. (eg the technology in an autonomous vehicle enables it to drive a car, but it can only perform tasks related to driving the car.)

The growth of AI also raises some wider potential concerns:

- **Security** – although technology has a number of benefits, it could also cause significant damage if used maliciously. This reinforces the importance of cyber security in systems which rely on AI or machine learning.
- **Mistakes** – although the training phase is intended to let machines 'learn' how to detect the right patterns, the training phase cannot cover all potential situations a system may need to deal with in the real world. In one of these situations, a system could be 'fooled' in ways that humans wouldn't be. This raises two important questions:
  - How can we guard against mistakes (or unintended consequences) when using AI or machine learning? For example, an AI system might be asked to eradicate cancer in the world. After a lot of computing, the system could determine a formula to eradicate cancer – by killing everyone on the planet. The AI solution will achieve the goal of eradicating cancer, but not in the way humans intended or in a way which is acceptable to us.
  - Who is responsible for errors caused by an AI system? (eg the organisation using the system? the organisation which created the system?)

 Illustration 3: Implications of AI

In the United Kingdom, the National Health Service's 'GP At Hand' app has been championed by the Health Secretary as a means of patients receiving medical advice electronically.

Required
Machine learning algorithms (ie ones that learn through experience) are being used to diagnose medical conditions. What are the implications and risks of this?

Solution

The correct answer is:

AI can 'learn' to identify patterns in data it has been given. Given large volumes of patient data, it can therefore learn how to diagnose an illness or condition.

AI technology has already been shown to be as effective as humans in diagnosing some medical conditions (eg Finnegan, 2018).

However, the sheer volume of data that has been studied by the AI means that it is difficult (sometimes impossible) to understand the logic that has been used. This creates a risk that the diagnosis is based on inappropriate criteria. For example, an AI trained to classify potentially cancerous lesions had an impressive track record until it was discovered that its diagnosis was based on whether a ruler was present in the scan picture (an indication that the human scanning the patient was already concerned).

Furthermore, an effective diagnostic AI requires huge volumes of data. This raises questions of privacy about how many patients would be prepared to release all of their personal medical records to be included in such analysis.

7 Mobile

KEY TERM

Mobile technology: Mobile technology is concerned with technology that is portable. Mobile technology devices include: laptops, tablet computers, smartphones, GPS technologies. Mobile devices enable users to communicate with one another in different ways, some of which may make use of the internet. Communicative features of mobile technologies include: Wi-Fi connectivity, Bluetooth and 4G technologies.

The widespread use of mobile technology can change the way employees within an organisation communicate (eg sending/reading emails on their phones), but perhaps more fundamentally it has changed the way customers engage with organisations.

Mobile phones are no longer used simply for communication, but as an ordering device for almost anything. Consumers can order food and shopping through their phones, book travel, and even holidays.

This has been a key element in the digital disruption of existing markets. The way Uber has changed the way we order taxis is perhaps the best example of this but change extends across a wide range of products (eg instead of phoning up a broker to buy shares from them, investors can now buy shares themselves in a matter of minutes, using apps such as EFTmatic or Nutmeg).

More generally, as we noted in Chapter 11, mobile technology has been a key driver behind **on-demand consumption** – consumers expect to be able to have access to products and services at any time, at their convenience.

8 3-D printing

3-D printing consists of creating a physical object by printing layer on layer of material from a digital 3-dimensional drawing or model.

3-D printing (sometimes also called 'additive manufacturing') is the opposite of traditional ('subtractive') manufacturing, in which layers are removed from a piece of material until the desired shape is obtained.

8.1 Potential benefits of 3-D printing

- By contrast with mass-produced manufactured goods, 3D-printed products can be easily customised. (This could be important as customers want increasingly customised products.)
- It has the potential to create complex products, or parts, without complex equipment.
- It enables new ways of prototyping – speeding up product development.
- There are reduced procurement and inventory costs (because companies no longer need to order 'parts' but 'print' their own as required). This could also lead to reduced repair costs.

Illustration 4: 3-D printing

Despite the potential benefits of 3-D printing; there could also be negative impacts.

Required
Identify THREE potential negative impacts of 3-D printing.

Solution

The correct answer is:

Suggested solutions:

(a) Product control and regulation: 3-D printing provides opportunities for people to 'print' objects with high levels of abuse (eg guns).

(b) Impact on existing supply and logistics chains: As increasing numbers of products are printed, this will disrupt existing supply chains; falling demand will lead to job losses in the supply chain.

(c) Protecting intellectual property/piracy: 3-D printing could make it cheaper and easier to copy designs and produce 'knock-off' copies of products.

9 Data visualisation

 KEY TERM

Data visualisation: 'The presentation of data in a pictorial or graphical format. It enables decision makers to see analytics presented visually, so they can grasp difficult concepts or identify new patterns' (SAS, no date).

Interactive visualisation takes data visualisation a step further than simple data visualisation and uses technology to drill down into charts and graphs for more detail. (SAS, no date)

9.1 Uses of data visualisation

Using graphs or charts to visualise large amounts of data can make it easier to analyse the data than looking at spreadsheets or written reports. Data visualisation could be useful for:

- Identifying areas that need attention or improvement
- Highlighting the factors which influence customer behaviour
- Predicting sales volumes or costs (by looking at trends in data)
- Illustrating how sales vary in different markets (by combining business data with geographic data)

Users can also illustrate the impact of different scenarios by making adjustments to the data.

Being able to draw quick and accurate conclusions from data could be an important element in developing or maintaining an organisation's competitive advantage. SAS (SAS, no date) highlights three ways in which data visualisation can benefit organisations and their managers:

- **Understand data/information quickly** – it is quicker to analyse information in graphical format than having to analyse information in spreadsheets.
- **Pinpoint trends** – visualisation also makes it easy to identify trends and spot outliers, so the cause of these can then be investigated.
- **Identify relationships** – identifying the relationships between different factors can help organisations focus on the areas which are most likely to influence their key goals.

10 Blockchain

The digital revolution is also changing the way individuals and institutions record transactions, and blockchain is an illustration of this.

 KEY TERM

 BPP LEARNING MEDIA

> **Blockchain:** 'A secure protocol where a network of computers collectively verifies a transaction before it can be recorded and approved' (*Schwab, 2016, p19*).

Blockchain is often described as a distributed ledger, effectively a form of collective bookkeeping.

10.1 Features of blockchain

The following are important features of blockchain:

- **Shared** – unlike traditional bookkeeping records (which are owned and controlled by a single business), blockchain is a shared ledger, which can be inspected by everyone connected to the network. All transactions between participants are recorded in identical records (ledgers) held by each user throughout the network. When a transaction takes place (eg selling and purchasing items), the details of the transaction are logged in all of the blockchain ledgers simultaneously – recording the time, date, value of the deal, and the details of the participants.

- **Verified** – blockchain records are only updated when all the parties in the network have reviewed and verified that the transaction details are correct. This verification process is carried out by the computers which make up the network. Because blockchain uses a system of consensus and verification, it means there is a **single, agreed-upon version of the truth**.

- **Permanent** – all transactions and records are permanent; they cannot be changed or removed once they have been entered onto the ledger:
  - When a 'block' is added to the chain, it doesn't only contain details of the approved transactions; it also contains the block's timestamp and the unique cryptographic signature of the previous block. These references mean the block's position in the chain is unambiguous, and any attempt to change a block would be obvious (because the references will no longer match).
  - Consequently, it is not possible to change something in a blockchain after a record has been entered.

Real life example – EY Ops Chain

In 2017, EY launched EY Ops Chain, a smart supply chain, using blockchain technology, which aims to simplify supply chain management and to integrate digital contracts, shared inventory and logistics information, pricing, invoicing, and payments.

Ops Chain's aim is to improve forecast accuracy and fulfilment performance, and thereby also to reduce working capital requirements.

A spokesperson for EY said: 'Finance is embedded in every phase of business operations, and simplifying the payments, financing and insurance processes ultimately drives business performance. Using blockchain technology to improve these operations can result in business advantages. For example, cargo in transit can insure and finance itself automatically, and tariffs, taxes and duties can be paid instantly upon arrival at a port.' (*EY, 2017*)

10.2 Blockchain and security

The need for a single, agreed-upon version of the truth is important in protecting blockchain from **cyber risk**.

Any attempt by a participant to interfere with a transaction, for example by attempting to post incorrect details to the ledger, will be rejected by the network parties assigned to verify the transaction.

Failure to achieve consensus will lead to the transaction not being recorded in the ledger in the blockchain. (The unique **cryptographic signatures** of the blocks in the chain are key in making it cryptographically secure.)

However, although blockchain technology aims to remove problems relating to the storage and security of digital data, blockchains themselves are not immune from being hacked. So, organisations should not assume that blockchains can automatically secure their data without fail.

11 Digital transformation and business models

The scale and extent of digital disruption mean that companies may need to amend their business models in order to compete effectively in a disrupted ecosystem.

> **Digital transformation:** The profound transformation of business and organisational activities, processes, competencies and models to fully leverage the changes and opportunities of a mix of digital technologies and their accelerating impact across society (*i-Scoop, no date*).

Companies may also need to rethink their approach to strategy development in order to respond effectively to digital disruption. Many companies still have five-year strategic planning horizons (ie five-year plans). However, in a disruptive and uncertain market environment, this approach may not be appropriate, and a shorter planning cycle could be beneficial (eg one year).

'Companies can't afford to spend months at a single long-term strategy. To stay ahead, they need to constantly start new strategic initiatives, building and exploiting many transient competitive advantages at once.' (*McGrath, cited in WEF, 2016 p21*)

Related to this, companies may need to move to a more experiment-oriented culture: being prepared to try new initiatives, using real-time data to provide feedback about the effectiveness of those initiatives.

When thinking about how to deal with digital disruption there are five trends that business leaders are encouraged to focus on:

- **The internet of me** – users must be placed at the centre of a personalised digital experience
- **Outcome economy** – customers are attracted to outcomes, not just products
- **The platform (r)evolution** – the evolution of platforms is speeding up all of the time, offering opportunities for innovation and faster service delivery
- **The intelligent enterprise** – organisations should harness data to increase innovation and efficiency
- **Workforce reimagined** – as AI grows, human resource should be deployed in different ways, not removed altogether

11.1 Rethinking business models

Although analogue (existing) companies can successfully adapt their business models to cope in a digital era, companies looking to rethink their business models and incorporate digital business models face two main challenges:

(a) The business model that has worked successfully for them in the past has been disrupted by digital innovation and no longer works as required.

(b) Attempts to create a new business model, appropriate for the digital era, will fail unless the company is willing to disrupt itself.

Christensen (1997) highlighted a general issue with disruptive innovation, which is that companies do not respond effectively to new technologies focused on different markets, because they are attached to their current business model as well as their relationships with existing customers. They are reluctant to 'cannibalise' their existing business by introducing new. However, this attachment to the processes and business model that make them successful at their existing business actually makes them uncompetitive in the disruption.

Incumbents also face the following challenges:

- **They often have a risk-averse culture** that focuses on the present rather than the future.
- **Managers are often very successful at running their existing business units,** but do not have the creativity to identify radically different business models or are not willing to commit resources to experiment.

- **Companies focus too much on the 'traditional' approach to generating revenue** (ie revenue = price × volume). This narrow focus means they fail to consider how other frameworks (eg networks, customer engagement) could create value for their business. Also, companies could monetise the data they have collected about their customers.

11.2 Identifying new business models

Companies can adopt different methodologies for developing new business models.

Methodologies for developing new business models (WEF, 2016)

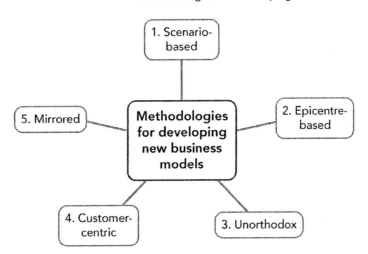

The key features of the different methodologies are as follows (WEF, 2016):

- **Scenario-based:** The company creates future business models in response to trends disrupting the industry.
- **Epicentre-based:** The company uses the strengths and weaknesses of its existing business model to generate ideas for its future business model.
- **Unorthodox:** The company forms its business model by challenging existing industry logic and company clichés.
- **Customer-centric:** The company builds a business model from a customer's perspective, based on the question: Does it solve their problems or meet their needs?
- **Mirrored:** The logic here is that the vast majority of 'new' business models are not actually new, so the company will look to creatively imitate business models from other industries.

11.3 New business ventures

In Chapter 5 we looked at the growth strategies available to companies, for example whether to expand organically or by means of acquisition.

In traditional business models, companies' approaches to growth can often just be viewed in terms of acquisition versus organic growth. However, in the context of digital transformation, existing companies (ie non-digital-natives) need to explore additional ways of developing new business ventures: for example investing in, or partnering with, start-ups. Analog companies often have large asset bases, so they can use their retained cash to help finance these ventures.

Corporate venturing can be an important strategy for large enterprises. It can help them:

- Acquire innovation (and stay on top of the latest innovations)
- Protect against disruption
- Find the right talent they need to succeed in the digital environment

11.4 Strategic choices for new, digital business models

Existing (analogue) companies have a choice of approaches for how to develop a digital business model. WEF (2016) identifies five main approaches:

- **Build** – use your own staff and resources to develop digital business capabilities.
- **Buy** – acquire a company (eg a digital start-up) with the skills that you require.

- **Partner** – find a digital native you can work with to plug your digital skills gaps.
- **Invest** – find a digital start-up you can invest in to develop the competencies you need. This is a relatively long-term and risky approach.
- **Incubate/accelerate** – this is a similar approach to 'investing' but with a closer relationship between the funding company and the start-up. The funding company provides more than cash eg infrastructure and capabilities.

 ## Illustration 5: Developing digital strategies

As with any growth strategy, an organisation needs to select an approach which is appropriate for it and its context.

Required

Identify the main factors which an organisation needs to consider in relation to each of the five main approaches when deciding how to develop a digital business model.

Approach	Considerations
Build	
Buy (ie acquire a digital start-up)	
Partner	
Invest (in a digital start-up)	

Approach	Considerations
Incubate/accelerate	

Solution

The correct answer is:

Approach	Considerations
Build	• May be the best approach if the digital opportunity is related to the company's core business • Company needs sufficient time to react to changes • Company must be able to hire the necessary talent
Buy (ie acquire a digital start-up)	• Often appropriate if there is a need to 'own' a market • May be necessary if a rapid response is needed to market change • May be necessary if it is not possible to hire the right talent • May be appropriate if the new opportunity has few links to the company's current business model • But potential issues (time, effort, cost) in trying to integrate acquisition operations into the existing company • May be more appropriate to retain the entrepreneurial culture of the innovative company, rather than trying to integrate
Partner	• Partnering with a digital native can help an incumbent learn more about the market and the partner's model • Can be appropriate if there is no immediate need to 'own' a market, and there is time to identify emerging opportunities • Can be a stepping-stone to deeper partnerships or acquisitions in future
Invest (in a digital start-up)	• Incumbent can connect with the skills and capabilities of the start-up • Start-up retains its agility, entrepreneurial nature, and attractiveness to young talent (Contrast with acquisition) • But corporate venture capital (CVC) activity can be risky. CVCs should look to aim to develop a good portfolio of investments

Approach	Considerations
Incubate/accelerate	• Similar to investing ('invest'), but with a closer relationship between the funding company and the start-up
	• Funding company may provide capabilities, infrastructure and resources to the start-up
	• Enables intrapreneurship (behaving like an entrepreneur, while working within a large organisation)
	• Incumbent needs to commit capital and leadership (including leaders with entrepreneurial experience)
	• Incumbent needs a commitment to risk

Assessment focus point

The syllabus requires you to be able to advise management on how to survive digital disruption and thrive in a digital age by rethinking their traditional business model and incorporating digital business and operating models. When considering different strategies, it is important to ensure they are appropriate for the particular circumstances in which an organisation finds itself. In the same way that 'traditional' growth strategies (eg organic, acquisition, franchising etc) have advantages and disadvantages which could affect their suitability for different circumstances, so do these strategies for developing 'digital' business models. Make sure you appreciate the characteristics of the different strategies which could shape their suitability for different contexts.

Activity 2: Klarg Co

Klarg Co, a non-digital-native company, is evaluating different ways to develop a digital business model.

Klarg's board are keen for the company to work with digital natives to learn more about the markets they serve, the products and services they provide, and the technologies they use. However, Klarg's board do not want to acquire a digital native at this stage, nor to commit capital and leadership to it.

Required

What approach to developing a digital business model is most suitable for Klarg?

A   Buy

B   Partner

C   Invest

D   Incubate

Solution

12 Operating models

To keep pace with digital natives, incumbents may need to change not only their business model, but the way they deliver that model. This means they need to re-examine the way their operations are structured.

Capital-intensive industries are suffering a decline in margins while asset-light, idea-intensive industries based on intangibles such as brands and software are enjoying higher margins.

Benefits for 'asset-light' operating models (such as platforms – as discussed in Chapter 3):

- **Greater flexibility** – asset-light models respond more quickly to changing demand, new market opportunities, supply chain disruption or advances in technology.
- **Lower profit volatility** – firms with high fixed costs have a high level of business risk. Fixed costs make profit more volatile, because operating profit becomes more vulnerable to downturns in business volume. Reducing the extent of fixed costs reduces this volatility.
- **Lower capital requirement** – asset-light models reduce the amount of capital required in order to achieve scale.

12.1 Digital operating models

The World Economic Forum (2016) has suggested five broad types of digital operating model:

- **Customer-centric** – focuses on making customers' lives easier, with an emphasis on front-office processes
- **Extra-frugal** – optimises manufacturing, supply and support processes to provide a high-quality service at a low cost. Based on a culture of 'less is more'
- **Data-powered** – built around capabilities in analytics and software intelligence (eg Google, Netflix), with an agile culture, focused on innovation through empirical experimentation
- **Skynet** – makes intensive use of machines to increase productivity and flexibility in production, with an engineer-led culture, dedicated to automation
- **Open and liquid** – looks outwards to try to create an ecosystem that enriches the customer proposition. All processes are characterised by a dialogue with the outside world (eg Facebook, PayPal).

(WEF, 2016)

12.2 Digital capabilities

The following capabilities are also vital to creating digital operating models and efficiencies:

- **Sense and interpret disruption.** Don't focus solely on your own industry but look for wider developments which could disrupt your industry.
- **Focus on customer problems.** Instead of looking at innovation as a product-led process, look to solve customer problems instead. Develop platforms which support experiments to solve these problems.
- **Focus on user experience.** IT architecture must be driven by user experience, not vice versa.
- **Understand and leverage data.** This doesn't just mean 'big data' but highlights the need to consider different types of data and find ways to monetise data. Use real-time data to give instant feedback about strategic initiatives. (Creating an analytics team could be key.)

BPP
LEARNING
MEDIA

- **Build and maintain a digital team** (discussed in Chapter 11). Organisations must assess how digitally smart their workforces are. It may be necessary to reskill employees.
- **Partner and invest for non-core activities.** Organisations need to appreciate that they don't need to do everything themselves. **Ecosystem partnerships** can provide operational efficiencies, scalability, innovation and a better customer experience. Collaboration and partnership can also be particularly important in helping create technologies faster than a company could build them independently.
- **Embed lean start-up principles.** Two key principles here: (i) eliminate all expenses that don't create value for the customer; (ii) fail fast, fail often.

The notion of 'failing fast' also highlights the importance of being able to spot emerging opportunities. By spotting new opportunities, and cutting their losses in obsolescent ones, companies are able to earn greater profits and revenue growth (*McKinsey, 2019*).

Real life example – Minimum viable products

A fundamental aspect within lean start-up principles is that of building minimum viable products (MVP), ie creating the simplest possible product that can be brought to market. Once that initial product has been launched, a company can then collect feedback from users, and incorporate that into the next round of development. The early websites of Facebook and LinkedIn, for example, were difficult to navigate, but the companies used feedback to understand key user requirements and improved the websites accordingly.

(*WEF, 2016*)

Assessment focus point

The syllabus requires you to advise management on how to survive digital disruption by rethinking their traditional business models and incorporating digital operating models. In preparing your advice, it could be useful to think about the extent to which an organisation currently has the capabilities identified in Section 12.2 – and which elements of its operating model it might need to modify in order to develop them.

Chapter summary

Digital technologies

Cloud computing

Provision of computing resources, on demand, over the internet

Benefits:
- Accessibility
- Scalability
- Cost effective
- Flexibility

Risks:
- Loss of control
- Loss or corruption of data
- Loss of access to data

Choice: use cloud or owned (in-house) technology?

Big data and big data analytics

Big data
- Volume
- Velocity
- Variety
- Also: Veracity

Big data analytics
- Use data to inform decision-making and improve performance
- Identify relationships, outliers and exceptions
- Build predictive models

Risks and challenges of big data
- Quality of data?
- Veracity?
- Costs?
- Skills needed (data scientists?)
- Loss and theft of data

Internet of things

- Devices connected to each other, and to other applications, over the internet
- Data from IoT (eg sensors) contributes to big data
- Potential benefits:
  - Real time information / real time decision making
  - Preventative action (eg preventative maintenance)

Process automation

- Use of digital technology to perform a business function
- Robotic process automation (RPA): use of software to perform high volume, rules-based, repetitive tasks

Robotic process automation

Benefits:
- Faster handling time
- Reduced errors
- Reduced costs
- Staff can focus on value-adding work

Artificial intelligence (AI)

- Ability of a machine to perform cognitive functions (perceiving; reasoning; learning; problem solving)
- AI depends on machine learning: Machines (algorithms) learn from data, identify patterns and make decisions without human instruction

Benefits and limitations of AI

Benefits:

- Fast, accurate, reliable processing of data (without need for human monitoring)
- Identify complex patterns in data
- Make consistent decisions

Limitations:

- Only as good as the data it receives
- Gaps or bias in 'training data'?
- Lack flexibility; task specific rather than multi-faceted

Mobile

- Laptops; tablets; smartphones
- Changes the way customers engage with organisations
- Facilitates 'on demand' consumption

3-D printing

Additive manufacturing: Create a physical object by printing additional layers of material

Benefits:

- Products can be easily customised
- Create complex products without complex equipment
- Reduce procurement and inventory costs ('print' as required)

Issues?

- Product control and regulation
- Impact on supply chain/logistics?
- Protecting intellectual property?

Data visualisation

- Present data in pictorial or graphical format
- Also, interactive visualisation: Drill down into charts and graphs for more detail

Benefits of data visualisation

- Understand data/ information quickly
- Identify trends
- Identify relationships

Blockchain

Key features:
- Shared ledger (distributed ledger)
- Single, agreed-upon version of the truth
- Records are permanent

Importance of security:
- Unique cryptographic signatures
- But still need to protect blockchain from cyber risk

Digital transformation and business models

Existing companies need to adapt their business models to succeed in digital era

Identifying new business models

Methodologies for identifying new business models:
- Scenario-based
- Epicentre-based
- Unorthodox
- Customer-centric
- Mirrored

Strategic choices for new, digital business models
- Build
- Buy (acquire a digital native)
- Partner
- Invest (in a digital start-up)
- Incubate / accelerate (a digital start-up)

Operating models

'Asset-light' operating models are outperforming capital intensive ones
- Greater flexibility
- Lower profit volatility
- Lower capital requirements

Digital operating models

Types of operating model:
- Customer centric
- Extra-frugal
- Data-powered
- Skynet
- Open and liquid

Digital capabilities
- Sense and interpret disruption
- Focus on customer problems
- Focus on user experience
- Understand and leverage data
- Build and maintain a digital team
- Partner and invest for non-core activities; make use of ecosystem partnerships
- Embed lean start-up principles

Key terms

Cloud computing: The delivery of on-demand computing resources – everything from applications to data centres – over the internet on a pay-for-use basis (*IBM, no date*).

Big data: 'High-volume, high-velocity and/or high-variety information assets that demand cost-effective, innovative forms of information processing that enable enhanced insight, decision making, and process automation' (*Gartner, 2018*).

Data analytics: The process of collecting and examining data in order to extract meaningful business insights, which can be used to inform decision making and improve performance.

Internet of things: Devices connected to each other, and to other applications, over the internet.

Process automation: The use of digital technology to perform a business process or function.

Robotic process automation (RPA): The use of software (a 'robot') that is programmed to perform high-volume, rules-based, repetitive tasks.

Artificial intelligence: 'The ability of a machine to perform cognitive functions we associate with human minds, such as perceiving, reasoning, learning and problem solving' and acting in a way that we would consider to be 'smart' (*McKinsey and Co, no date*).

Machine learning: Machine learning algorithms detect patterns and learn how to make predictions and recommendations, by processing data and experiences rather than by receiving explicit instructions. The algorithms also adapt in response to new data and experiences to improve their efficacy over time (*McKinsey and Co, no date*).

Mobile technology: Mobile technology is concerned with technology that is portable. Mobile technology devices include: laptops, tablet computers, smartphones, GPS technologies. Mobile devices enable users to communicate with one another in different ways, some of which may make use of the internet. Communicative features of mobile technologies include: Wi-Fi connectivity, Bluetooth and 4G technologies.

Data visualisation: 'The presentation of data in a pictorial or graphical format. It enables decision makers to see analytics presented visually, so they can grasp difficult concepts or identify new patterns' (*SAS, no date*).

Blockchain: 'A secure protocol where a network of computers collectively verifies a transaction before it can be recorded and approved' (*Schwab, 2016, p19*).

Digital transformation: The profound transformation of business and organisational activities, processes, competencies and models to fully leverage the changes and opportunities of a mix of digital technologies and their accelerating impact across society (*i-Scoop, no date*).

Activity answers

Activity 1: Big data analytics

The correct answer is:

(i) and (iii) only

Big data is collected from diverse sources, and much of the data is unstructured. For example, one potential source of big data can be the opinions and preferences that people express via social media – which is an example of unstructured data. Therefore Statement (ii) is incorrect.

Big data analytics enhances an organisation's ability to analyse and reveal insights from data which had previously been too difficult or costly to analyse, due to the volume and variability of the data involved. Statement (i) correctly identifies this point.

One of the key characteristics of big data is the speed with which data flows into an organisation (with much data being available in real time, or almost in real time). If an organisation can then also process and analyse this data quickly, this speed can improve the organisation's ability to respond effectively to customer requirements or market conditions. Statement (iii) correctly identifies this point.

Activity 2: Klarg Co

The correct answer is:

Partner

A partnering strategy enables established organisations to work with digital natives to learn about the markets they serve and the products and services they provide. This approach will be appropriate for Klarg because it will enable it to find out about the digital companies, without having to invest in them.

The other three strategies (buy, invest, incubate) will all involve some kind of investment (either in terms of capital, leadership or other capabilities), but Klarg's board have identified they do not want to make this kind of investment at the moment.

Test your learning

1 Gartner identified 3 'V' characteristics of big data, and a fourth 'V' has subsequently also been added to these.

Required
What are the 4 'V's of big data?

2 **Required**
What does the following describe?

'A machine's ability to perform cognitive functions we associate with human minds, such as perceiving, reasoning, learning and problem solving.'

3 **Required**
Which of the following statements are true?

A   Machine learning algorithms adapt in response to new data and experiences to improve their efficacy over time.

B   Predictive analytics provides recommendations for what to do in order to achieve goals or objectives.

4 Anspi Co is working to develop a new business model and is using the strengths and weaknesses of its existing business model as the basis for generating ideas for its future business model.

Required
Using the World Economic Forum (WEF) classifications, which methodology is Anspi Co using to develop its new business model?

A   Scenario-based

B   Customer-centric

C   Epicentre-based

D   Mirrored

5 **Required**
Using the World Economic Forum classifications, an organisation which makes intensive use of machines to increase productivity and flexibility in production, and which has an engineer-led culture dedicated to automation, has which type of operating model?

A   Data powered

B   Extra-frugal

C   Open and liquid

D   Skynet

Test your learning answers

Chapter 1

1   The correct answer is:

To achieve the organisation's objectives

Objectives must be identified first, then a suitable strategy can be developed to try to achieve them.

Understanding the organisation's environment and assessing its internal resources are important elements of strategic planning, but they are not the purpose of it. Controlling employee behaviour will also assist in achieving objectives but, again, is not the purpose of strategic planning.

2   The correct answer is:

(a) Analysis (or position)

(b) Choice

(c) Implementation

These are the three stages of strategy creation.

3   The correct answer is:

False

An emergent strategy develops out of the patterns of behaviour in an organisation, whereas a top-down strategy is imposed by senior management.

4   The correct answer is:

Position

PEST analysis is one of the tools which is used for analysing the external environment in the analysis stage of the planning process. The analysis stage can also be known as the position stage (ie understanding the organisation's current strategic position).

5   The correct answer is:

Emergent strategies are imposed on an organisation by senior management.

An emergent strategy develops out of patterns of behaviour in an organisation, rather than being imposed in advance by senior management.

6   The correct answer is:

- Review and control
- Corporate appraisal
- Mission and objectives

Although the model is used in strategic planning and strategic management, these are not specifically elements in the model. Similarly, change management may be required in strategic implementation, but change management itself is not one of the elements of the model.

Chapter 2

1   The correct answer is:

Mission

This is the definition of mission used by Johnson *et al* (2017).

A mission statement describes an organisation's current purpose, whereas a vision statement is more aspirational and forward looking, and a value statement focuses more on *why* an organisation does what it does, rather than its purpose.

2   The correct answer is:

True

Values help to establish **why** an organisation does what it does, and what it stands for. In this way, an organisation's values may help shape its mission statement – for example, the mission statement will need to be consistent with the organisation's values.

3   The correct answer is:

The directors come from a wide variety of backgrounds

This relates to 'diversity'. Diversity is important in helping the board generate different strategies, and to evaluate potential strategies from different perspectives. Therefore, diversity contributes to effective corporate governance, rather than being a feature of poor governance.

4 The correct answer is:

Corporate social responsibility is an organisation's obligation to maximise positive stakeholder benefits while minimising the negative effects of its actions.

There are many definitions of CSR, this answer is one of many acceptable responses.

5 The correct answer is:

Integrity

The FD appears to be deliberately presenting incomplete information in order to make the company's performance look better than it is (which is misleading to the shareholders).

Chapter 3

1 The correct answer is:

- Economic
- Political

The categories used to classify factors in PESTEL analysis are: Political, Economic, Social, Technological, Environmental (or Ecological), and Legal.

2 The correct answer is:

Threat of new entrants: **Low**

Bargaining power of suppliers: **Low**

The market share controlled by the 'Big Four' means they are likely to benefit from significant economies of scale, and to have a significant degree of control over the distribution network, making it difficult for new entrants to break into the industry. The barriers to entry into the industry are high; meaning the threat of new entrants is low.

The relative size of the supermarkets, compared to the suppliers, means that the bargaining power of the suppliers is low. Also, the fact that there are a number of different suppliers suggests it might be quite easy to switch between suppliers for different products. This ability to switch between suppliers will also reduce the bargaining power of suppliers.

3 The correct answer is:

Porter's Diamond

Porter's Diamond is a model for assessing national competitiveness, and so is the most appropriate model to use here.

PESTEL should be used for general analysis of the macro-environment. Porter's five forces assesses the factors that influence the level of profitability that can be sustained in an industry. SWOT analysis is used for assessing the strategic position of an organisation.

4 The correct answer is:

- Competitor analysis helps managers to understand their company's competitive advantages and disadvantages compared to its competitors.
- Competitor analysis helps to provide an informed basis to assist a company in developing its own competitive strategies.

Remember the definition of competitor analysis: the identification and quantification of the relative strengths and weaknesses (compared with competitors or potential competitors) which could be of significance in the development of a successful competitive strategy.

5 The correct answer is:

- Strengths
- Weaknesses

Strengths and weaknesses are internal factors; opportunities and threats relate to external factors in the environment.

Chapter 4

1 The correct answer is:

Geopolitics is the way that a country's geography, economics and politics affect its power and relationship with other countries.

This is one of a number of different definitions of geopolitics.

2 The correct answer is:

Social

The 'social' category in PESTEL looks at the way social and cultural factors affect customers' needs and requirements. Demographic changes and increasing customer empowerment will both influence customers' needs and requirements.

3 The correct answer is:

Experience provider.

Experience providers provide specialist competences in differentiated or unique functions.

4 The correct answer is:

Orchestration

Orchestration refers to the formal or informal co-ordination of interactions between participants in the ecosystem.

5 The correct answer is:

Rules

Rules (governing the environment) is one of the three components which can be used to define **interactions** in an ecosystem, not the participants.

6 The correct answer is:

The degree of enforceability and compliance in the ecosystem

This reflects the extent and formality of the orchestration of the ecosystem, not the complexity of the activities undertaken.

Chapter 5

1 The correct answer is:

Differentiation – focus

The company is making high-performance, luxury cars for a narrowly defined sector of the market.

2 The correct answer is:

Product development

Ansoff's matrix, a strategy of selling new products to an existing market represents product development.

3 The correct answer is:

Backward vertical integration

By acquiring one of its suppliers, the manufacturing is expanding backwards within its existing value network. Therefore, the acquisition represents backwards vertical integration

4 The correct answer is:

(i), (ii) and (iii)

A major disadvantage of joint ventures is that there can be conflicts of interest between the venture partners. These may arise over profit shares, amounts invested, management of the joint venture, or marketing strategy.

BPP
LEARNING
MEDIA

Profits from the venture have to be shared among the partners, reducing the amount each earns.

Partners can gain confidential information about each other, which one partner subsequently uses competitively against another.

5   The correct answer is:

Avoiding the problems of cultural change associated with organic growth

One of the major potential disadvantages of acquisitions are the problems of integrating the employees, systems and cultures of the company being acquired with those of the company making the acquisition. Therefore, instead of avoiding problems of cultural change, acquisitions would be expected to present greater problems in relation to cultural change than would be the case with organic growth.

Chapter 6

1   The correct answer is:

Option to make follow-on investments

Option to abandon a project

Option to wait

These are the types of options that can be valued when assessing a strategic project.

2   The correct answer is:

Game theory

The correct answer is: Game theory - this illustrates the way that strategic interactions between competitors produce outcomes that were not intended by any of the players.

3   The correct answer is:

Define the requirements of the project

The five stages are: Define the scope, identify the drivers for change, construct initial scenarios, identify the implications, and develop strategies.

4   The correct answer is:

Delphi method

The Delphi method (or Delphi technique) involves a number of experts being asked to independently and anonymously give their opinions and insights on a particular trend and how it may develop.

5   The correct answer is:

It allows management to forecast what is going to happen

Scenario planning is not designed to create a forecast or an accurate prediction of what is actually going to happen, but rather to create some insights into what **might** happen, and the uncertainties which an organisation might face in the future.

Chapter 7

1   The correct answer is:

An organisation's ability to renew and recreate its resources and capabilities to meet the needs of changing environments reflects its dynamic capabilities.

Firms need to possess dynamic capabilities (the ability to renew and recreate resources and capabilities) in order to maintain their competitive advantage in a changing environment.

2   The correct answer is:

Service

The primary activities (in sequence) in Porter's value chain are: inbound logistics, operations, outbound logistics, marketing and sales; service.

3   The correct answer is:

Introduction, Growth, Maturity, Decline.

These are the four main stages of the product (and also the industry) life cycles.

4   The correct answer is:

Cash cow

Although G&L's market share is only 11%, it is still the largest player in the market since its largest competitor only has a market share of 9.5%. G&L's relative market share is 1.16 (ie greater than 1) which constitutes a high relative market share.

Similarly, although G&L's revenue increased quite rapidly, the market is only growing slowly (1% in the last year). The BCG matrix measures market growth rates, rather than a company's growth.

G&L has a high relative market share in a market with low growth, meaning it should be classified as a cash cow.

5   The correct answer is:

(i) only

Competition is low in the introduction phase of the life cycle but increases thereafter.

Sales **volumes** are at their highest in the maturity phase, although the rate of sales **growth** is lower during the maturity phase than the growth phase.

Chapter 8

1   The correct answer is:

Feasibility

Feasibility is concerned with whether an organisation has the resources and capabilities to deliver a strategy.

2   The correct answer is:

Whether the strategy will help to generate or sustain a competitive advantage for the company

This relates to the strategic logic of the strategy, and therefore its suitability.

Whether the strategy will generate a high enough return to satisfy stakeholders, and the level of risk involved, relate to its acceptability.

Whether the company has enough resources to implement the strategy relates to its feasibility.

3   The correct answer is:

Mendelow's matrix

One of the considerations within 'acceptability' is how stakeholders will react to the proposed strategy. Using Mendelow's matrix would be a useful way of identifying relevant stakeholder groups, as well as their relative levels of power and interest.

The other tools mentioned would be more appropriate for assessing the suitability of a potential strategy, rather than its acceptability.

4   The correct answer is:

False

In order for a strategy to be feasible, an organisation either must already have the necessary people and skills to implement the strategy or **be able to obtain them**. Therefore, it is not necessary for an organisation to already have the necessary people or skills at the point the strategy is proposed – provided they can be obtained in time to implement the strategy.

5   The correct answer is:

No

The project has a negative NPV and therefore, based purely on the NPV, should be rejected.

	Year 0	Year 1	Year 2	Year 3	NPV
	$	$	$	$	$
Cash outflow	(125,000)				
Cash inflows		20,000	70,000	50,000	

	Year 0	Year 1	Year 2	Year 3	NPV
	$	$	$	$	$
DF at 8%	1.000	0.926	0.857	0.794	
Present Values	(125,000)	18,520	59,990	39,700	(6,790)

Chapter 9

1 The correct answer is:

Critical success factors

Critical success factors (CSFs) are the aspects of a product or service which a business must excel at in order to outperform its competitors. Key performance indicators (KPIs) are the measures which a business uses to assess how well it is performing its CSFs.

2 The correct answer is:

Using economies of scale to procure high-quality goods as cheaply as possible

Critical success factors (CSFs) identify what an organisation needs to do well in order to be successful and to achieve its objectives. An organisation can then use key performance indicators (KPIs) to measure whether or not it is achieving its CSFs.

Option 1 is an example of an objective, and Option 3 (the CSF) identifies one of the ways by which the organisation could achieve that objective. Options 2 and 4 are examples of KPIs.

3 The correct answer is:

(b) only

Option 1 is incorrect: Non-financial indicators which allow an organisation to assess how well it is performing against its critical success factors can often act as leading indicators, whereas most traditional financial performance indicators tend to be **lagging** indicators, reporting on past performance and past events.

4 The correct answer is:

(a) Financial

(b) Customer

(c) Internal business processes

(d) Learning and growth (or Innovation and learning)

There are four elements of the balanced scorecard, each being built around CSFs with resultant KPIs.

5 The correct answer is:

Flexibility

The four elements of the performance pyramid in the departments and work centres level (the lowest level) are: quality, delivery, cycle time (or process time) and waste. Flexibility is one of the measures of performance in the middle level (business operating systems).

6 The correct answer is:

(i) and (ii) only

In the 'building block' model, the four determinants of performance are: quality of service, flexibility, resource utilisation and innovation. Motivation relates to the rewards which encourage employees to work towards the standards set.

Chapter 10

1 The correct answer is:

Explaining the need for change

Retraining staff is part of the 'change' stage, while publicising success stories and creating new reward schemes are part of the 'refreezing' stage.

2   The correct answer is:

Adaptation

By definition, a change whose nature is incremental (as opposed to 'big bang') and whose extent (scope) is realignment is an adaptation in Balogun and Hope Hailey's classification.

3   The correct answer is:

Capability

The capability to manage and implement change is one of the contextual features highlighted by the change kaleidoscope, rather than one of the aspects of the cultural web.

The six manifestations of culture in the cultural web are: stories, symbols, routines and rituals, power structures, control systems and organisational structure; and collectively these manifestations underpin the organisation's paradigm.

4   The correct answer is:

(a)   Education and communication

(b)   Participation and involvement

(c)   Facilitation and support

(d)   Negotiation and agreement

(e)   Manipulation and co-optation

(f)   Coercion

These approaches describe a continuum of styles, with managers encouraged to be flexible eg to adopt the approach most suited to the circumstances in which they are managing.

5   The correct answer is:

Purpose

The leader has failed to communicate **why** the change is necessary.

6   The correct answer is:

A person, or group of people, who takes on the role of promoting strategic change within an organisation

A change agent is an individual, or group, that helps to bring about strategic change in an organisation. A change agent can be either internal or external to an organisation (meaning that they don't have to be a senior manager within the organisation). The change agent's role primarily relates to bringing about change, rather than identifying or recommending the need for change in an organisation.

Chapter 11

1   The correct answer is:

Agile business processes are a key feature which underpins successful digital enterprises.

Successful digital transformation requires a culture that promotes innovation and **encourages** risk taking ('failing fast') – not reducing the risks they are prepared to take.

Digital enterprises constantly strive to implement new, leaner operating models, underpinned by agile business processes.

2   The correct answer is:

Remove distortions in demand

Digital removes distortions in demand by allowing customers to have their own way: in this case, to watch programmes when they want to – rather than being restricted by a television schedule.

Unconstraining supply relates to digital's impact on reducing costs, meaning that firms can now provide services that were previously uneconomic to supply. However, the focus in our example of TV viewers is on consumer demand rather than producer supply.

3   The correct answer is:

(a)   Offering customers 'experiences' not simply 'products and services'

BPP
LEARNING
MEDIA

(b) Offering customers 'access' to products, instead of requiring customers to buy and 'own' them.

Hyper-personalisation involves (i) Giving customers control to customise their own product/experience and (ii) Providing more relevant interactions by analysing customer data and by harnessing the power of data analytics.

4 The correct answer is:

Engagement

Bounce rate and net promoter score are two of the indicators which can be used to measure 'engagement' – which effectively tracks customer satisfaction with a site.

Scale and active usage look more at quantitative elements – eg numbers of visitors and numbers of active users.

Churn rate is not one of the elements of digital traction metrics.

5 The correct answer is:

Failing fast

The notions of agility and 'failing fast' highlight the importance of speed of execution in rapidly changing business environments. There may be little benefit for an organisation in spending lots of time trying to develop a 'perfect' product if doing so means the product has almost become obsolete by the time it is launched (because the market has already moved on).

Chapter 12

1 The correct answer is:
   (a) Volume
   (b) Velocity
   (c) Variety
   (d) Veracity

These are the elements of Big Data per Gartner

2 The correct answer is:

Artificial intelligence. (Although artificial intelligence (AI) and machine learning (ML) are closely related, this is a definition of AI, not ML.)

This is one of many definitions of AI.

3 The correct answer is:

Machine learning algorithms adapt in response to new data and experiences to improve their efficacy over time.

One of the key features of machine learning is that it is iterative; models and algorithms adapt based on what they learn from new data.

Predictive analytics anticipates what will happen, based on data and patterns in the data. However, it is prescriptive (rather than predictive) analytics that provides recommendations for what to do in order to achieve goals or objectives. (So the second statement is false.)

4 The correct answer is:

Epicentre-based

In an epicentre-based approach, the company uses the strengths and weaknesses of its existing business model to generate ideas for its future business model.

Scenario-based approaches look to respond to the trends disrupting the industry, rather than the company's own (internal) strengths and weaknesses. Customer-centric approaches build a business model from the customer's perspective. Mirrored approaches look to imitate business models which have already been used by other companies in other industries.

5 The correct answer is:

Skynet

Making intensive use of machines and having an engineer-led culture dedicated to automation are key characteristics of a Skynet operating model.

Index

BPP
LEARNING
MEDIA

Bibliography

Aaker, D. and McLoughlin, D. (2010) *Strategic market management: global perspectives.* Wiley, Chichester

Accenture (5 April 2016) The rise of digital partnerships: fad or way forward, *The Telegraph* [Online] Available from: https://www.telegraph.co.uk/business/leaders-of-transformation/horizons/2016-digital-partnerships/ [Accessed 26 March 2019]

Adair, J. (1973) *Action-centred leadership.* London, McGraw-Hill

Alphabet (2017) *Code of Conduct,* [Online] Available from: https://abc.xyz/investor/other/code-of-conduct/ [Accessed 25 February 2019]

Ansoff, I. (1987) *Corporate strategy.* 2nd edition. London, Penguin

Balogun, J. and Hope Hailey, V. (2008) *Exploring strategic change.* 3rd edition. Harlow, Pearson Education

Balogun, J., Hope Hailey, V. and Gustafsson, S. (2016) *Exploring strategic change.* 4th edition. Harlow, Pearson Education

Beer, M. and Nohria, N. (2000) Cracking the code of change. Harvard Business Review, Vol78, May–June, pp133–141

Belbin, M. (1996) *Team roles at work,* Butterworth Heinemann, Oxford

Berger, L. (1994) Change management. *In:* Berger, L., Sikora, M. and Berger, D. (eds) *Change management handbook: a road map to corporate transformation.* Irwin, Burr Ridge

Bowman, C. and Faulkner, D. (1997) *Competitive and corporate strategy.* Irwin, London

Bridges, W. and Mitchell, S. (2000) Leading transition: a new model for change. *Leader to Leader,* Vol16(3), pp30–36

Cadbury Committee (1992) *Report of the committee on the financial aspects of corporate governance.* London, Gee

Carroll, A. (1979) A three-dimensional conceptual model of corporate performance. *The Academy of Management Review,* Vol4(4), pp497–505

Carroll, A. (1991) The pyramid of corporate social responsibility: towards the moral management of organizational stakeholders. *Business Horizons,* 34, pp39–48

Castro, D. and McQuinn (2015) Cross-border data flows enable growth in all industries. *Information Technology & Innovation Foundation,* February 2015, [Online] Available from: http://www2.itif.org/2015-cross-border-data-flows.pdf [Accessed 26 March 2019]

Chopra, S. and Meindl, P. (2016) *Supply chain management: strategy, planning and operation.* 6th edition. Harlow, Pearson. Christensen, C. (1997) *The innovator's dilemma.* Boston, Harvard Business Review Press

CIMA (2014) *Big data: readying business for the big data revolution.* London, CIMA

CIMA (2017) *CIMA Code of Ethics,* [Online] Available from: https://www.cimaglobal.com/Documents/Ethics/CIMA%20Code%20of%20Ethics%202017.pdf [Accessed 27 March 2019]

CIMA Code of Ethics, Section 100.5 (CIMA, 2017)

CIMA (2019) *Exam blueprints.* [Online]. Available from: www.cimaglobal.com/examblueprints. [Accessed May 2019].

Cyert, R. and March, J. (1992) *A behavioural theory of the firm.* Englewood Cliffs, NJ: Prentice Hall

Dahlstrom, P., Desmet, D. and Singer, M. (2017) *The seven decisions that matter in a digital transformation: a CEO's guide to reinvention.* McKinsey Quarterly, February 2017, [Online] Available from: https://www.mckinsey.com/business-functions/digital-mckinsey/our-insights/the-seven-decisions-that-matter-in-a-digital-transformation [Accessed 28 March 2019]

Datesh, J., Dietz, M. and Radnai, M. (2018) *Why banks are welcoming the disruptors*, McKinsey [Online] Available from: https://www.mckinsey.com/business-functions/digital-mckinsey/our-insights/learning-from-digital-threats?cid=podcast-eml-alt-mcq-mck&hlkid=f112b72fc6f244c89a0ca3e416c0f441&hctky=2702580&hdpid=335052c5-d04d-42a4-819e-c13e791d49b7 [Accessed 28 March 2018]

Davidson, S., Harmer, M. and Marshall, A. (2014) The new age of ecosystems: redefining partnering in an ecosystem environment, IBM Institute for Business Value [Online] Available from: https://www-01.ibm.com/common/ssi/cgi-bin/ssialias?htmlfid=GBE03617USEN [Accessed 29 November 2018]

Dawson, A., Hirt, M. and Scanlan, J. (2016) *The economic essentials of digital strategy*. McKinsey Quarterly, March 2016, [Online] Available from: https://www.mckinsey.com/business-functions/strategy-and-corporate-finance/our-insights/the-economic-essentials-of-digital-strategy [Accessed 28 March 2019]

Deloitte (2018) Our shared values, [Online] Available from: https://www2.deloitte.com/cy/en/pages/about-deloitte/articles/culture-beliefs.html [Accessed 24 February 2019]

Duffy Agency (2015) *Five ways digital is redefining growth strategy*, [Online] Available from: http://duffy.agency/blog/five-ways-digital-is-redefining-growth-strategy/ [Accessed 15 July 2019]

Elkington, J. (1997) Cannibals with forks: the triple bottom line of 21st century business. Chichester, Capstone

Encyclopedia Britannica (2019) *Enron – What happened?*, [Online] Available from: https://www.britannica.com/topic/Enron-What-Happened-1517868 [Accessed 24 February 2019]

Engelke, P. (2018) *Three ways the Fourth Industrial Revolution is shaping geopolitics:* World Economic Forum, [Online] Available from: https://www.weforum.org/agenda/2018/08/three-ways-the-fourth-industrial-revolution-is-shaping-geopolitics/ [Accessed 25 February 2019]

EY (2017) *EY infuses blockchain into enterprises and across industries with launch of EY Ops Chain*, [Online] Available from: https://www.ey.com/gl/en/newsroom/news-releases/news-ey-infuses-blockchain-into-enterprises-and-across-industries-with-launch-of-ey-ops-chain [Accessed 4 August 2018]

Financial Reporting Council (2018) UK Corporate Governance Code 2018. FRC, London

Finnegan, G. (19 February 2018) Your virtual doctor will see you now: AI app as accurate as doctors in 80% of primary care diseases, ScienceBusiness [Online] Available at: https://sciencebusiness.net/healthy-measures/news/your-virtual-doctor-will-see-you-now-ai-app-accurate-doctors-80-primary-care [Accessed 28 March 2019]

Fitzgerald, L. and Moon, P. (1996) *Performance measurement in service businesses: making it work*. London, CIMA

Gartner (2018) *IT glossary*, [Online] Available from: https://www.gartner.com/it-glossary/big-data/ [Accessed 18 December 2018]

GFI Software™ (no date) *On-premise vs cloud-based solutions*, [Online] Available from: https://www.gfi.com/whitepapers/Hybrid_Technology.pdf [Accessed 11 July 2017]

Giesen, E., Harmer, M. and Marshall A. (2017) In or out? Succeeding in the ecosystem economy? IBM Institute for Business Value, New York

Girzadas, J. (28 June 2018) Going from solo to ensemble: orchestrating an ecosystem for the future of business, Forbes [Online] Available from: https://www.forbes.com/sites/deloitte/2018/06/28/going-from-solo-to-ensemble-orchestrating-an-ecosystem-for-the-future-of-business/#4fb6498c749a [Accessed 26 March 2019]

Harvard Business Review (2018) *Using digital platforms and artificial intelligence to outpace rivals*, Harvard Business Review Analytics Services [Online] Available from: https://www.oracle.com/webfolder/s/delivery_production/docs/FY16h1/doc38/LPD100699002-White-Paper.pdf [Accessed 11 January 2019]

Herzberg, F. (2003) One more time: how do you motivate employees? *Harvard Business Review*, Vol81(1), pp87–96

IBM (2010) Meeting the demands of the smarter consumer, IBM Institute for Business Value [Online] Available from: https://www.ibm.com/downloads/cas/XQLQB7GL [Accessed 25 February 2019]

IBM (no date) *Cloud computing: a complete guide*, [Online] Available from: https://www.ibm.com/cloud/learn/cloud-computing [Accessed 28 January, 2019]

International Integrated Reporting Council (IIRC) (2013) *The international framework*, [Online] Available from: http://integratedreporting.org/wp-content/uploads/2013/12/13-12-08-THE-INTERNATIONAL-IR-FRAMEWORK-2-1.pdf [Accessed 22 September 2017]

i-Scoop (no date) Digital transformation: online guide to digital business transformation, [Online] Available from: https://www.i-scoop.eu/digital-transformation/ [Accessed 5 April 2019]

Johnson, G., Scholes, K. and Whittington, R. (2007) *Exploring corporate strategy*. 8th edition. Harlow, Pearson

Kanter, R. M. (1999) The enduring skills of change leaders. *Leader to Leader*, No13, Summer, pp15-2

Kaplan, R. and Norton, D. (1996b) Using the balanced scorecard as a strategic management system. *Harvard Business Review*, Vol74(1), pp75–85

Kaplan, R. S. and Norton, D. P. (1992) The balanced scorecard: measures that drive performance. *Harvard Business Review*, Vol70(1), 71–79, [Reprint available online] Available from: https://hbr.org/1992/01/the-balanced-scorecard-measures-that-drive-performance-2 [Accessed 22 September 2017]

Kaplan, R.S. and Norton, D.P., (1996a), *The Balanced Scorecard: Translating Strategy into Action*. Boston, Harvard Business School Press

Kelly, E. (2015) Business ecosystems come of age, Deloitte Insights [Online] Available from: https://www2.deloitte.com/insights/us/en/focus/business-trends/2015/business-ecosystems-come-of-age-business-trends.html [Accessed 26 March 2019]

Kerr, S. and Landauer, S. (2004) Using stretch goals to promote organisational effectiveness and personal growth: General Electric and Goldman Sachs. *The Academy of Management Executive*, Vol18(4), pp134–138

Kotter, J. (1996) Leading change: why transformation efforts fail. *Harvard Business Review*, March–April, [Reprint available online] Available from: https://hbr.org/1995/05/leading-change-why-transformation-efforts-fail-2 [Accessed 28 March 2019]

Kotter, J. and Schlesinger, L. (1979) Choosing strategies for change. *Harvard Business Review*, Vol 57, March–April, [Reprint available online] Available from: https://hbr.org/2008/07/choosing-strategies-for-change?cm_sp=Article-_-Links-_-Comment [Accessed 27 March 2019]

Laczkowski, K., Rehm, W. and Warner, B. (2018) *Seeing your way to better strategy*. McKinsey, [Online] Available from: https://www.mckinsey.com/business-functions/strategy-and-corporate-finance/our-insights/seeing-your-way-to-better-strategy?cid=other-eml-alt-mip-mck-oth-1812&hl kid=cd977298e8f04f4389f30349f66d4f85&hctky=2702580&hdpid=52b1936b-92c3-4d69-ae84-a210a877c6f3 [Accessed 27 March 2019]

LEGO (2018) Celebrating 10 years of crowdsourcing and co-creation with LEGO® fans, [Online] Available from: https://www.lego.com/en-sg/aboutus/news-room/2018/november/ideas-10th-anniversary/ [Accessed 25 February 2019]

Lewin, K. (1958) Group decision and social change. *In*: Newcomb, T. and Hartley, E. (eds) (1958) *Readings in social psychology*. 3rd edition. New York, Holt, Rinehart and Winston. pp197–211

Libert, B., Beck, M. and Wind, Y. (2016) The network imperative: how to survive and grow in the age of digital business models. Boston, Massachusetts, Harvard Business Review Press

Lynch, R. (2015) *Strategic management*. 7th edition. Pearson, Harlow

Lynch, R. L. and Cross, K. F. (1991) *Measure up! Yardsticks for continuous improvement*. Malden, MA, Blackwell

Marr, B. (2016) How to use analytics to identify trends in your market, *Forbes* [Online] Available from: https://www.forbes.com/sites/bernardmarr/2016/08/16/how-to-use-analytics-to-identify-trends-in-your-market/#6117d3ad2eff [Accessed 21 December 2018]

McKinsey and Co (no date) *An executive's guide to AI*, [Online] Available from: https://www.mckinsey.com/~/media/McKinsey/Business%20Functions/McKinsey%20Analytics/Our%20Insights/An%20executives%20guide%20to%20AI/An-executives-guide-to-AI.ashx [Accessed 28 March 2019]

McKinsey, (2019) *A winning operating model for digital strategy*. McKinsey Digital, January 2019, [Online] Available from: https://www.mckinsey.com/business-functions/digital-mckinsey/our-insights/a-winning-operating-model-for-digital-strategy?cid=other-eml-alt-mip-mck&hlkid=ecf2c371f8884c368d6adab66c5a6e9a&hctky=2702580&hdpid=824a0999-d3eb-418d-a973-8ff2463ceea3 [Accessed 5 April 2019]

Mendelow, A. (1991) *Proceedings of the 2nd International Conference on Information Systems.* Cambridge, MA, IEEE Computer Society.

Mintzberg, H. (1987) Crafting strategy. *Harvard Business Review*, July–August, pp66–75.

Neely, A. (1998) Measuring business performance. London, Economist books

Panetta, K. (2017) 8 Dimensions of business ecosystems, Gartner [Online] Available from: https://www.gartner.com/smarterwithgartner/8-dimensions-of-business-ecosystems/ [Accessed 26 March 2019]

Panmore Institute (2019) *Amazon.com Inc's Mission Statement & Vision Statement (An Analysis)*, [Online] Available from: http://panmore.com/amazon-com-inc-vision-statement-mission-statement-analysis [Accessed 24 February 2019]

Parker, G., Van Alstyne, M. and Choudary S. (2016) Platform revolution: how networked markets are transforming the economy – and how to make them work for you. Norton & Co, New York

Payne, C. (1997) Relationship marketing: The Six Markets Framework. Available from: https://dspace.lib.cranfield.ac.uk/bitstream/handle/1826/2910/SWP%2035-93.PDF?sequence=1 [Accessed 28 October 2019]

Pemberton, C. (2017) How to make ecosystems part of the business strategy, Gartner [Online] Available from: https://www.gartner.com/smarterwithgartner/how-to-make-ecosystems-part-of-the-business-strategy/ [Accessed 26 March 2019]

Peters, T. J. and Waterman, R. H. (1982) *In search of excellence.* New York, Harper and Row

Porter, M. (1980) Competitive strategy. New York, Free Press

Porter, M. (1985) Competitive advantage: creating and sustaining superior performance. New York, Free Press

Reardon, K. J., Reardon, K. J. K. and Rowe, A. J. (1998) Leadership styles for the five stages of radical change. *Acquisition Review Quarterly – Spring*, pp129–143

Reddy, N. (2018) How to harness the power of network effects, Forbes, [Online] Available from: https://www.forbes.com/sites/forbescoachescouncil/2018/01/02/how-to-harness-the-power-of-network-effects/#3781bb4562e8 [Accessed 26 March 2019]

Rockart, J. (1979) Chief executives define their own data needs. *Harvard Business Review*, Vol 57(2), pp81–93, [Reprint available online] Available from: https://hbr.org/1979/03/chief-executives-define-their-own-data-needs [Accessed 22 September 2017]

Sarrazin, H. and Willmott, P. (2016) *Adapting your board to the digital age*. McKinsey Quarterly, July 2016, [Online] Available from: https://www.mckinsey.com/business-functions/digital-mckinsey/our-insights/adapting-your-board-to-the-digital-age [Accessed 28 March 2019]

SAS (no date) *Data visualization – what it is and why it matters*, [Online] Available from: https://www.sas.com/en_us/insights/big-data/data-visualization.html [Accessed 5 April 2019]

Schwab, K. (2016) *The Fourth Industrial Revolution.* Geneva, World Economic Forum

Simon, H. A. (1982) *Models of bounded rationality*, Vol 1–3. Cambridge, Massachusetts: MIT Press

Stacey, R. (2007) *Strategic management and organisational dynamics: the challenge of complexity to ways of thinking about organisations.* Pearson, Harlow

Tagoe, N. (2016) Rethinking the business model, CGMA white paper, [Online] Available from: https://www.cimaglobal.com/Research—Insight/Rethinking-the-business-model1/ [Accessed 27 March 2019]

Teece, D. (2018) Business models and dynamic capabilities. *Long Range Planning*, Vol 51(1), February 2018, pp40-49

Teece, D. (2010) Business models, business strategy and innovation. Long Range Planning, Vol 43(2–3), April–June, pp172–194

Tesco (2018) Annual report 2018, [Online] Available from: https://www.tescoplc.com/investors/reports-results-and-presentations/annual-report-2018/ [Accessed 27 March 2019]

Tesla (2019) *About Tesla*, [Online] Available from: https://www.tesla.com/en_GB/about [Accessed 24 February 2019]

The Irish Times (22 September 2018) Inside Ryanair: Michael O'Leary's making of a 'nicer' airline, [Online] Available from: https://www.irishtimes.com/culture/books/inside-ryanair-michael-o-leary-s-making-of-a-nicer-airline-1.3634667 [Accessed 26 February 2019]

Tuckman, B. (1965) Developmental sequence in small groups. *Psychological Bulletin*, Vol 63(6), pp384-399

World Economic Forum (2016) *Digital transformation of industries – digital enterprise*, January 2016[Online] Available from: http://reports.weforum.org/digital-transformation/wp-content/blogs.dir/94/mp/files/pages/files/digital-enterprise-narrative-final-january-2016.pdf [Accessed 21 January 2019]

World Economic Forum (2016b) *What the sharing economy means for incumbents*, [Online] Available from: http://reports.weforum.org/digital-transformation/what-the-shift-from-ownership-to-access-means-for-industries/ [Accessed 28 March 2019]

World Economic Forum (2016c) *Why the only constant is change in mastering customer expectations*, [Online] Available from: http://reports.weforum.org/digital-transformation/outpacing-expectations-of-the-digital-customer/ [Accessed 28 March 2019]

World Economic Forum (2016d) *Fostering a digital workforce*, [Online] Available from: http://reports.weforum.org/digital-transformation/fostering-a-digital-workforce/ [Accessed 26 March 2019]

World Economic Forum (2017) Digital Transformation Initiative: unlocking B2B platform value, [Online] Available from: http://reports.weforum.org/digital-transformation/wp-content/blogs.dir/94/mp/files/pages/files/wef-platform-report-final-3-26-17.pdf [Accessed 26 March 2019]

World Economic Forum (2018) *Unlocking $100 trillion for business and society from digital transformation*, May 2018, [Online] Available from: http://reports.weforum.org/digital-transformation/wp-content/blogs.dir/94/mp/files/pages/files/dti-executive-summary-20180510.pdf [Accessed 5 April 2019]

Review form - CIMA E3 Strategic Management

How have you used this Course Book?

(Tick one box only)

☐ Self study

☐ On a course _____

☐ Other _____

Why did you decide to purchase this Course Book?

(Tick one box only)

☐ Have used BPP materials in the past

☐ Recommendation by friend/colleague

☐ Recommendation by a college lecturer

☐ Saw advertising

☐ Other _____

During the past six months do you recall seeing/ receiving either of the following?

(Tick as many boxes as are relevant)

☐ Our advertisement in Financial Management

☐ Our Publishing Catalogue

Which (if any) aspects of our advertising do you think are useful?

(Tick as many boxes as are relevant)

☐ Prices and publication dates of new editions

☐ Information on Course Book content

☐ Details of our free online offering

☐ None of the above

Your ratings, comments and suggestions would be appreciated on the following areas of this Course Book.

	Very useful	Useful	Not useful
Chapter overviews	☐	☐	☐
Introductory section	☐	☐	☐
Quality of explanations	☐	☐	☐
Illustrations	☐	☐	☐
Chapter activities	☐	☐	☐
Test your learning	☐	☐	☐
Keywords	☐	☐	☐

	Excellent	Good	Adequate	Poor
Overall opinion of this Course Book	☐	☐	☐	☐

	Yes	No
Do you intend to continue using BPP Products?	☐	☐

The BPP author of this edition can be e-mailed at: lmfeedback@bpp.com

Review form (continued)

Tell us what you think — please note any further comments and suggestions/errors below.